Cruisers, Cotton and Confederates

Liverpool Waterfront in the days of the Confederacy

2nd Edition

John Hussey

Acknowledgements

I would like to thank the staff at Liverpool Record Office and Maritime Museum for their infinite patience and courtesy.

Dorothy Davitt, a great teacher, who gave me the idea to write the book in the first place, and Sein Khan for his wizardry with my computer. If not for these two, I would still be dipping a quill pen in an inkpot. Thanks to Michael, who explained the significance of the Oba, in his home town of Lagos. Thanks also to Suzanne Lau whose creativity with layouts is a science in itself.

Special thanks must go to Bob Jones whose painstaking research on the life of James Dunwoody Bulloch is a ground-breaking addition to the history of the Confederacy in Liverpool. All the credit for Bulloch's genealogy in Waterloo and Liverpool belongs with Bob – I just wrote it down. Thanks also for putting me right on many other aspects of the story, too numerous to relate, and for being so generous with your time and advice. I hope I have done justice to your research.

Thanks to all the people who ever took the time and trouble to write a book or upload a website and share their knowledge with the world.

The final accolade goes to my wife for putting up with my eccentricities for so many years.

For
Leila and Gabriel
With love

First published 2008. Revised 2nd edition published 2009.

Published by Countyvise Limited, 14 Appin Road, Birkenhead, Wirral CH41 9HH.

British Library Cataloguing in Publication Data.
A catalogue record for this book is available from the British Library.

ISBN 978 1 906823 32 0

When the American Civil War broke out, England was in its Victorian heyday, the Empire was at its zenith and Liverpool was its second city - the largest port in the world and a maritime metropolis. The ten miles of waterfront was a seething ant-heap of humanity dedicated to a single cause, which was to serve, in some capacity, the ships which were the source of the wealth of the city.

Merchant princes lived in opulent mansions and the captains of ships and the captains of industry lived in Georgian opulence, cheek by jowl with overcrowded and insanitary courts where poverty was endemic and disease was rife. The story of Victorian Liverpool is chiselled on the tombstones of St. James' Cemetery with those telling of premature demise vying with others telling of tragedy at sea.

Drawn into this swirling maelstrom of activity by a need for ships, came Confederate agents from the deep south of America, followed by a squadron of northern spies. The War between the States had spilled over into England and the Liverpool docks became the background to a desperate struggle for control of the Southern seaboard.

The whole thing would be a footnote in the history books but for the voyage of a ship which was constructed on the Mersey, whose exploits across the oceans of the world captured the imagination of a worldwide audience, caused endless international incidents and brought Britain and America to the brink of war. The cruise of the *Alabama* is the focal point of Confederate operations in Liverpool from 1861 to1865 but must be set against the greater canvas to put it into context.

And the strangest thing of all is that none of it would have ever happened but for a mediocre plant of the mallow family - the ubiquitous cotton plant. King Cotton weaves its way throughout the story from beginning to end.

The days of the Confederacy in Liverpool are vanishing over the horizon with each passing day. The following pages are an attempt to recapture some of the fact and flavour of a unique era in the history of Liverpool.

"This cotton question will most certainly assume a serious character by the beginning of next year and if the American Civil war has not by that time come to an end, I suspect that we shall be obliged, either singly or conjointly with France, to tell the Northerners that we cannot allow millions of our people to perish to please the Northern states."

Lord Palmerston To Lord Russell

"The government of this country respect the law. They do not seize upon property to the loss and damage of its owners without proof that they are legally entitled to do so."

Lord John Russell to Charles Francis Adams

"The English government desires the separation of North America into two republics then England would have nothing to fear from either --- for she would dominate them."

Baron de Brunov
Russian ambassador

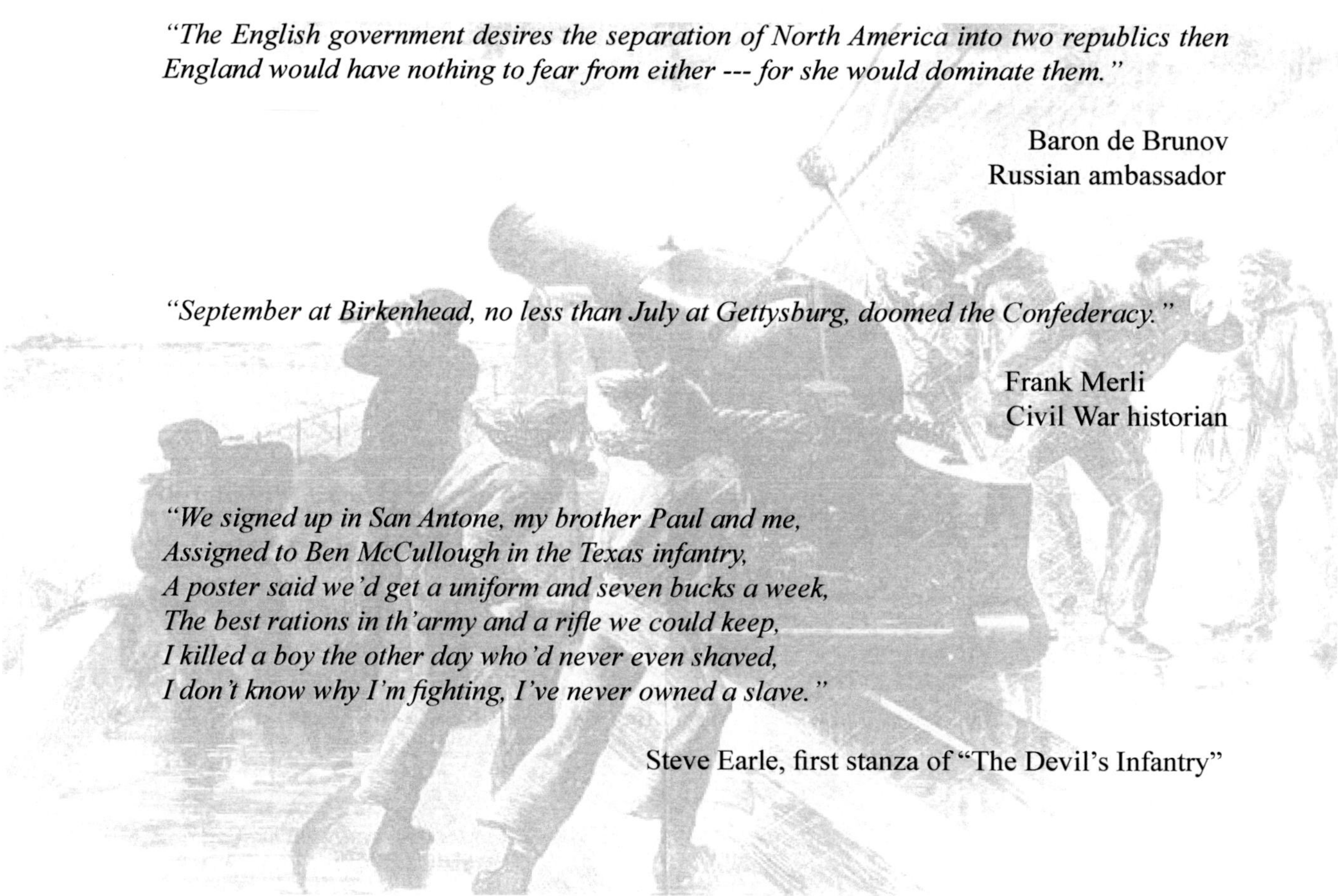

"September at Birkenhead, no less than July at Gettysburg, doomed the Confederacy."

Frank Merli
Civil War historian

"We signed up in San Antone, my brother Paul and me,
Assigned to Ben McCullough in the Texas infantry,
A poster said we'd get a uniform and seven bucks a week,
The best rations in th'army and a rifle we could keep,
I killed a boy the other day who'd never even shaved,
I don't know why I'm fighting, I've never owned a slave."

Steve Earle, first stanza of "The Devil's Infantry"

Contents

Page

A Confederate Agent 7
The beginnings of the Alabama 15
A Narrow Escape 27
Alabama - Two years before the mast 35
The Sinking of the Alabama 49
The Florida - The first cruise 61
The Florida - The second cruise 69
The Ironclads and the Shenandoah 77
James Dunwoody Bulloch 89
Pen Portraits 101
The Grand Southern Bazaar 117
The House in the Square 123
Portrait of a Lady - Mary Elizabeth Wright 131
The Tragedy of the Lelia 145
A Hazardous Occupation 163
The Liverpool Blockade-Runners 169
The Emily St Pierre 185
Douglas 193
Engines of War 195

"It is not generally known in America that our Civil War affected England and Liverpool to such a degree. This book adds to my own South Carolina family history and that of the historians who are researching the Southern efforts to obtain supplies by blockade runners."

Horry Frost Prioleau (descendant of Charles Kuhn Prioleau.)

"Liverpool's attention to the preservation of the histories of both our countries is exemplified by the restoration of the first American Embassy in England in Paradise Street in 2008, appropriately in Capital of Culture Year, 2008."

Diane Prioleau (descendant of James Maury, first American Ambassador to Liverpool and England, Paradise Street, 1790 to 1829.)

About the Author

Eyes Wide Shut

I was born in Smithdown General, more years ago than I care to remember; just 100 yards from the headstones of the Captain of the Marco Polo, Thomas Miller and several participants in the Charge of the Light Brigade. Martha Bulloch was still living in her ivory tower when I was a child. When I was small, we used to troop off to Sefton Park, where we played all day long on endless summer days which used to bubble the tar in the roads and we passed the house where James Dunwoody Bulloch lived, time after time. As kids we would enter the Sailor's Home just to listen to the exotic accents and I passed the home of John Low on the bus for years on the way to school. I went out into the Mersey many times, without knowing that we were sailing over the wrecks of two blockade-runners sunk 150 years ago. When I began work, I planted an Indian Cedar next to the American garden in Allerton =Hall, which is still there today, and I looked after the hothouses since fallen into dereliction. My grandparents are buried 10 yards away from the grave of a Confederate officer who observed the beginnings of the Trent Affair and I have passed the Liver Hotel many times, on the way to Southport. I remember the ruins of the Fawcett Foundry before it was demolished and never realised its significance. And Rodney Street, Abercromby Square, St. James's Gardens and so many other places have been commonplace for years. I know now that I never really knew any of them; I must have been sleepwalking for years.

John Hussey

A Confederate Agent

Josiah Wedgewood's famous motif. 'Am I not a Woman and a Sister.'

Chains

The social and political chains which have always bound England and America (two nations divided by a common language) have often been augmented by commercial links. In the years of America's Civil War they were stretched to breaking point. The Slave Trade had begun with English ships carrying African slaves to its Caribbean Colonies and when it extended to America the two countries became inextricably bound in a mutually beneficial industry in human trafficking. The English ships out of Bristol and Liverpool carried merchandise to the African coastal forts, picked up a cargo of slaves for America and carried cotton to England, in a trading triangle which was both ingenious and inhumane.

When the Abolition of the Slave Trade Act of 1807 was passed through Parliament (The Abolition of Slavery Act was passed in 1833) there was much weeping and wailing and beating of breasts from the ship-owners and merchants as they faced the loss of their lucrative trade but despite riots in Liverpool which were little more than vexed frustration on the parts of the merchants the Act passed through legislation more or less peacefully. The tears of the merchants soon dried up when they began to carry another cargo of lost souls escaping the Irish Potato Famine.

There is little doubt that England led the way in the abolition of slavery as an institution and as creditable as that may be it had taken many years of toil by William Wilberforce and his disciples, in the face of fierce opposition, to achieve that singular aim. William Roscoe's stand was particularly courageous in Liverpool, which was a hotbed of dissent by the ship owners. Thomas Clarkson had narrowly escaped with his life whilst preaching on the waterfront and John Newton preached against the slave trade in St. Georges Church (now Derby Square).

Their triumph must be tempered by the years in which millions of Africans were transported into bondage which amounted to well over a century but nevertheless it was the beginning of the end of slavery for Black Africans.

In historical terms, President Lincoln's avowed aim to abolish slavery in America followed hard on the heels of England's success and he was no doubt influenced to act from the moral stand-point set across the Atlantic. However, American Abolition turned out to be an infinitely more difficult task than in England and the threat of secession by the Southern States led directly to the American Civil War of 1861. The succeeding five years of traumatic and bloody strife were a pivotal part of American history and are stamped indelibly upon the American psyche. What the English achieved at the ballot-box, Americans were forced to achieve upon the battlefield and while America fought out a contest that would define the nation for all time the shock-waves travelled across the Atlantic and shuddered into the ships at anchor in Liverpool Bay, the commercial centres of Northern England and the cotton towns across the Pennines.

Gossypium
the cotton plant.

Tenuous Strands

The first cotton mill in England began operations in Manchester in the year 1640, which, within our terms of reference, makes cotton manufacture a venerable and ancient industry. But placed in the context of cotton being manufactured in India some 3,000 years ago the scenario takes on a different aspect and puts into perspective just how insular Europe had been for generations. The voyages of exploration in the 15th and 16th centuries changed all that and the opening up of The New World did exactly that - it opened up a whole new world of plants and animals previously undreamed of. Many of these plants and animals once so exotic and rare have become so commonplace that we have all but forgotten their origins but at the time of their presentation to an awed audience, plants such a tomatoes, potatoes, aubergines, tobacco and so many more were pure exotica. Following on behind the trail-blazers a whole host of plant-finders were commissioned by wealthy mansion houses all over Europe to seek out even more unknown species for the hot-houses of the well-heeled. Among the many species brought back was a plant native to Mexico which was not particularly outstanding when compared to beauties such as dahlias, zinnias, marigolds and so on but the cotton plant had unique qualities all of its own, far exceeding the ephemeral beauty of plants which were far more colourful.

Subsequently known by its Linnaean name of Gossypium, the cotton plant had been in use throughout tropical countries for centuries where quite independently each of the countries had discovered how to make cotton textile. India, Pakistan, China and others all made use of the cotton plant which had evolved slightly different forms in each part of the world. The Mexican cotton, Gossypium hirsutum, had been in use for thousands of years and the Aztecs

The Northern steamer George Griswold entering Liverpool with supplies for starving cotton workers.

and Mayans were accustomed to making colourful cotton textiles well before the custom spread into Mexico.

The original cotton plant grew to a height of 10 metres in the wild but as cultivation became more refined the plant was grown as a 2 metre high annual making the cotton bolls easier to harvest. The true value of the plant lay in the seed pods (bolls) which when ripe split open to reveal a downy covering protecting the seeds and the Mexican cotton had the longest thread of all the species.

It was quite out of the question to attempt to grow Gossypium in England, the cold climate would never sustain the heat-loving plant. But the damp climate was perfect for retaining the cotton fibre and keeping it supple and there was nowhere damper than Manchester which was and is renowned for its regular precipitations off the Pennines. Before long a thriving new industry grew in Manchester and gradually extended into the surrounding Lancashire towns where massive cotton mills burgeoned always by the side of a river or canal.

The Industrial Revolution saw the arrival of a whole host of inventions designed to make cotton processing more efficient - Hargreaves' spinning Jenny 1764, Arkwright's water frame 1767, Whitney's cotton gin 1793, and Jacquard's automatic loom 1805, took cotton manufacturing to even greater heights of production. By the middle of the 19th century, most of Manchester and its satellite towns were dependent on a chain of cotton mills which supported thousands of workers in the "dark, satanic mills"; a description which omitted the incessant noise which caused the mostly female workers to converse in a type of lip-reading they called mee-mawing and the constant rain of snowy cotton particles which at best caused chest infections and at worst ultimately killed. It was no coincidence that the long hours and the hard work caused the Manchester cotton mills to become hotbeds of the Suffrage Movement later in the century.

The Manchester Museum archives contain a 1777 deed for an Arkwright textile machine, textile sample books and a Trade Union letter protesting Manchester's initial support for the Confederacy.

Glad Tidings
another Northern ship bringing supplies to starving cotton workers.

The whole process was dependent on cotton grown in the Southern States of America and the Southern States in their turn were dependent on the African slaves who maintained and picked the cotton. When America determined that slavery was to be abolished and the threat of secession by the South came into the equation, the Civil War became an inevitability and when President Lincoln followed up with a blockade of the Southern ports then the whole of the cotton manufacturing infrastructure came crashing down.

The era between 1861 and 1865 came to be known as the Lancashire Cotton Famine and as the ships stood at anchor in the Mersey, the factories dependent on their cargo ground to a halt and the best part of a 500,000 work-force were thrown out of work. Things were even worse in a household which also contained a miner as the miners were subsequently made redundant as the demand for coal declined accordingly.

Rioting broke out as the spectre of poverty returned and there was a subsequent sympathy for the Southern States despite the fact that most workers were against slavery - it was a case of "needs must when the devil rides" and Confederate flags were commonly flown.

However, the Northern powers-that-be were not blind to the suffering of the cotton workers who were in today's parlance undergoing collateral damage due to the blockade. As a result, they sent out several ships such as the *George Griswold,* escorted by warships and laden with goods to relieve the starvation of the millworkers. The millworkers in their turn were not insensitive to the plight of the slaves and they identified with them as fellow workers condemned to a daily grind of crushing manual labour with the only difference being that the millworkers received a wage and had a freedom of sorts (it must be remembered that at that time Women's Suffrage was far in the future and many males were ineligible to vote - also working conditions were atrocious). Consequently, the initial condemnation of the North softened as workers recognized the justness of their cause and to their great credit, many Trade Unions advised their members to look beyond their own situation and sit it out.

It was particularly ironic that in reality the Cotton Famine was partially self-inflicted and quite how the millworkers (many of whom had resorted to begging) would have reacted to the knowledge that speculators were hoarding bales in order to make a killing is open to speculation. Apart from the obvious Slave and Master situation there were few issues in this struggle which were truly black and white and Jefferson Davis himself was known to have ordered an embargo on cotton-picking in the hope that it would induce England and France to intervene in the war.

In December of 1862, in the middle of a biting English winter and at a time when the Cotton Famine was hitting hard, Abraham Lincoln was moved to send a letter to the Manchester workers which was widely published in both countries. The letter was in response to a resolution of support by the labourers of Manchester which went to great pains to express their abhorrence of the institution of slavery. The Manchester letter was the first of many and Lincoln subsequently received a flood of letters of support from workers' meetings across England.

The Confederates were nothing if not resourceful and when the decision to provide blockade-runners and commerce raiders was made then it was to Liverpool and Birkenhead that they turned in their hour of need - and at the heart of the whole lengthy and tumultuous era of Slavery and Civil War was the ubiquitous cotton plant and very soon it would lead to the brink of war between England and America.

The Northern Blockade

Hostilities had no sooner opened in the spring of 1861 than President Lincoln ordered a blockade of Southern ports using the Northern fleet of warships. Their main mission was to prevent armaments and supplies reaching the Southern armies but at the same time they also prevented the movement of commercial shipping which had an effect on the movement of many goods but it was cotton in particular which was hit hardest with supplies down to a trickle.

Jefferson Davis was less upset by the lack of movement of cotton than he was of armaments and actually believed that cotton could be the saviour of the South, maintaining that England and France would never countenance the cessation of the long-stapled cotton vital to their economies. His theory was that the lack of cotton was causing so much unrest in both countries that sooner or later they would intervene and maintain the South as an independent nation.

At first glance, his views seem optimistic to the point of fantasy but the fact was that there were many politicians in the Palmerston government who tacitly supported the South. It wasn't too long before the subject was aired in open debate and there were many whose sympathies were strongly Southern and they began to speak out openly in favour of the Confederacy. In an infamous speech in Newcastle, no less a personage than William Gladstone (1809 - 1898) made his views known unequivocally that England should support Southern claims for separatism. Gladstones's stance was nothing short of sensational given that he was an acclaimed philanthropist and a Prime Minister in waiting. Not only that, he was a Liverpudlian born a short walk from the waterfront and in his youth could not have failed to see the multitude of slave ships in the docks. He would also have been acquainted with Roscoe who had fought so hard for Abolition and witnessed the riots against Abolition. A mere three decades previous to Gladstone's speech England's Parliament had courageously abolished slavery and here they were now supporting the thing that their predecessors had fought so long and hard to achieve by attempting to give active support to what was in the final analysis a slave-state.

There were several reasons put forward to explain England's stance - one was that the English identified strongly with Southerners because they were very similar in their customs, manners and chivalric *mores.* It was a case of the English gentry recognising Southern gentry as similar to their own which said more about Victorians than it did about Southerners. But this just disguised

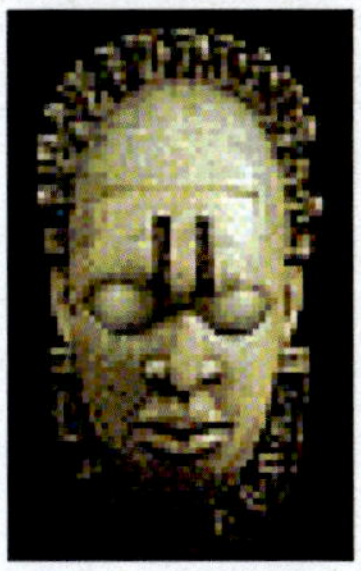

W E.Gladstone's attitude towards slavery becomes clearer in the knowledge that the four-times Prime Minister was brought up in a household which thrived on the profits made from the slave trade. Gladstone's father, Sir John Gladstone {1764 - 1851} made his fortune from tobacco and grain from America and owned several estates in the West Indies including the slaves, indispensable to their upkeep. W.E.Gladstone's maiden speech in the House of Commons was anti- emancipation and in effect, a vindication of his family business. Given his reputation for philanthropic works and given his superior education, it was surprising that Gladstone never once questioned his own ingrained acceptance of slavery as an essential part of the tobacco and cotton industries. Gladstone's attitude was a mirror image of the Southern, slave-owning culture on the other side of the Atlantic who were, in common with their British counterparts, very much an aristocratic minority.

The holds of the George Griswold being unloaded. One of the original barrels is on display in Rochdale Museum.

the real reason which was far less altruistic and was simply a matter of economics. Quite apart from the fact that many in the English government had a vested interest in maritime commerce, for every Northern ship out of action there were half a dozen English ones ready to take their place.

Although kept secret at the time it has subsequently come to light that the English government did succumb to the pressure put on them by Parliamentarians and actually discussed the logistics of sending a force in support of the South. It was only a fear of an invasion of Canada and a repeat of the 1812 war which prevented them acting.

In complete contrast to the politicians who ruled them, the millworkers who were being hit hardest had come to revise their support for the South mainly due to their revulsion with slave-labour and in part due to the relief ships, *George Griswold,* the *Hope* and *Achilles* sent by a Northern government to relieve their suffering. The millworkers had shown themselves to have far more integrity than their so-called superiors.

Jefferson Davis had proven to be more perceptive than at first thought but he was also aware that his hopes would never come to fruition and he was pragmatic enough to act on his own volition. The Northern blockade was hitting hard and a stock-take of the ships of the Southern navy was a swift and depressing affair consisting of several clapped-out slavers and a handful of varied small boats any of which would not last two minutes against even the smallest member of the Northern fleet. The reality was that there was no navy at all. Davis was painfully aware of the urgency to break the blockade and his first act was to create an infrastructure which could at least formulate a plan of action and at the head of that infrastructure he placed Stephen R. Mallory in the post of Secretary of the Navy. Mallory had the formidable task of being responsible for breaking the blockade. Mallory's background was as a politician and a lawyer which on the face of it hardly qualified him for such an arduous task but he had once been the Chairman of the Committee on Naval Affairs and had taken the trouble to learn all he could concerning modern ship design and armament which were fundamental when he came to discuss his policies. And if Jefferson Davis was fortunate in having Mallory in his camp then Mallory in his turn was even more fortunate to be introduced to a man who he could trust implicitly and could implement his plans.

James Dunwoody Bulloch portrait

James Dunwoody Bulloch was 38 years of age when the South seceded from the Union. He was the scion of a prominent Georgia family but had spent most of his life as an officer in the United States navy. In the latter years, he worked as a commercial sea captain out of New York where he had lived for many years. He resigned his commission on the day that he heard the news of the forthcoming war, gave it all up for an uncertain future and offered his services to what was laughingly called the Southern navy. Judah. P. Benjamin, the Confederate attorney general who was a mutual friend of Bulloch and Mallory, knew of Bulloch's credentials and immediately recommended Bulloch to Mallory.

Bulloch's initial interview was an immediate success and on his acceptance of service abroad Mallory and Bulloch spent days together formulating a policy which would provide ships to break the blockade. It was during these briefings that Bulloch and Mallory thrashed out the requirements of the Confederacy in terms of ships to break the blockade, the necessity for haste, various potential contacts and a secret code for communications between the two of them. Bulloch left on his mission with the title of Naval Procurement Agent and in order to avoid attention and at worst capture, headed inland and up to Detroit and into Canada where he sailed for Liverpool from Montreal on the steamer *North America.*

James Dunwoody Bulloch was not to know it but the curtain was about to rise upon a drama of epic proportions, spanning continents and including a cast of thousands of which he was about to take centre-stage as one of the leading players.

The Beginnings of the Alabama

Contacts

James Dunwoody Bulloch stepped off the Montreal ship and onto the Liverpool waterfront on the 3rd June 1861 and was confronted by a scene with which he would become familiar for the rest of his life - the ten miles of docks were a chaotic melée of horses, shipworkers, dockers, rope-makers and seamen, bustling around a waterfront full of sailing ships, unloading, loading, setting sail or arriving from some foreign port. It was the largest and busiest docks in the world with warehouses of monumental proportions stuffed with tobacco, cotton, and all manner of goods from all around the globe. There were pubs and grog shops on every corner and in Lime Street and Paradise Street they were never short of seamen from every port in the world - many of them returning to their ships wondering where their wages had gone. A measure of the size of Liverpool docks in those days was a scale model exhibited at the Great Exhibition of 1851 in the Crystal Palace which showed every dock with miniature ships at anchor comprising a total of 1500 ships.

Liverpool Landing Stage which was in existence until a gale blew it away in 2005 - note the telegraph office at right.

Bulloch's mission was daunting by any standards, requiring a man of many talents and carrying a responsibility which would weigh heavily on any man. Mallory's briefing had made it clear he would work alone and take decisions with which he would either stand or fall and Bulloch was well aware that he was to virtually create a Confederate navy from scratch - and time was of the essence. He quickly set about building a network of contacts which would form the backbone of the Confederate client agency in England. His primary contact was Charles Kuhn Prioleau, managing partner of the shipping and finance company Fraser, Trenholm and Company, whose offices were tucked away in a tiny, shady back-street to the rear of Princes dock - the Company was in actuality the English branch of John Fraser and Company who were based in Charleston, South Carolina. Prioleau was an

The offices of F.S.Hull in Rodney Street.

affable Southerner from South Carolina who had found it expedient to adopt British nationality but remained faithful to the Southern cause. It was explained that Fraser, Trenholm's role would be to receive money from the Confederacy into their safekeeping until such a time that Bulloch required it and then channel the funds into payments to the people he hoped to purchase his ships from. Bulloch quickly found that purchasing the ships he wanted would be more difficult than at first thought and gave up the idea in favour of commissioning his own ships from local ship-builders of which there was no shortage. It was at this point that Prioleau proved his loyalty - when Bulloch in his haste wished to begin building a ship immediately and the necessary funds had not yet arrived Prioleau told him to go ahead notwithstanding. Bulloch's next contact was to be far more important than either of them realized at their first meeting and he would prove to be an indispensable ally in Bulloch's managerial set-up. The purchase of any ship required the services of a solicitor and it was another fortunate chance which directed Bulloch to the offices of the worthy F.S. Hull, a lawyer as sagacious and cunning as any in the pages of a Dickens novel. There was little point in Bulloch trying to convince F.S.Hull that he was anything other than what he was (his accent was an immediate giveaway) and Bulloch explained his aims clearly and concisely and asked what would be any potential difficulties. The lawyer had no qualms about taking on such a client and his first task was to explain to Bulloch the meaning of the Foreign Enlistment Act (1819) which would, as he correctly forecast, be absolutely crucial to any purchase that had military connotations. Section 7 of the Act stated in no uncertain terms that in the case of warships:

"It was illegal for any British subject to sell any ship or vessel to a foreign belligerent if the said ship was to be used with the intent to cruise or commit hostilities against any foreign state with which Britain was at peace. Furthermore, British nationals who enlisted in the armed forces of a foreign government forfeited their rights as a British citizen".

On the face of it, the Act seemed to present an insurmountable hurdle to Bulloch's plans and the projected Confederate navy could have foundered there and then - but both Bulloch and Hull were far too tenacious to surrender

The old Custom House with Canning Dock in the foreground.

without a fight and the Act was the focal point of most of their discussions. The lawyer seemed to perceive the Act as a personal affront and from the moment that he was confronted with it he took a capricious delight in seeking out ways to confound everything that it stated. His use of semantics was nothing less than masterful and his basic premise was simple - that if a ship was not armed then it was not a warship which was akin to saying that if a gun wasn't loaded then it wasn't a weapon. The contention was of course ridiculous and everybody knew it but a government of Southern sympathisers was hardly likely to challenge it with much vigour. Hull's manipulations with the intricacies of English law had successfully paved the way for Bulloch to go ahead with his plans - the ramifications were far into the future when the Civil War was over. In his first month in Liverpool, Bulloch had built up what was in effect a management team devoted to building ships for the Confederacy - he had the backing of a prominent commercial firm with strong Southern affiliations, an excellent lawyer and Bulloch himself who provided the drive and initiative to make it all happen. The trio formed a formidable team. Furthermore, Bulloch was about to commission the building of what would be the first of the Confederate Commerce Raiders. It was a considerable achievement by any standards.

Contracts

Reassured by his lawyer's manipulations with the intricacies of the English legal system, Bulloch wasted no time in seeking out a ship-yard to build his first cruiser - he didn't have far to look in a vast area dedicated to maritime affairs; the ship-yard of William C. Miller and Sons was located just a short walk away from the offices of Fraser, Trenholm. Bulloch could not fail to pass the ancient Church of Our Lady and St Nicholas which remains the parish church of Liverpool and is also dedicated to mariners (St. Nicholas is the patron saint of sailors) and look out upon the panoramic view of the Mersey, 40 years before the trio of monumental Three Graces, the Cunard Building,

Port of Liverpool Authority and Liver Building obscured the view and created a shady canyon of the Strand. He would have undoubtedly passed No.22 Water Street where the officers of the United States Consulate were already spying upon his movements and he could not avoid the myriads of stubby colonnades and faux-medieval towers which made Jesse Hartley's Albert dock a unique example of dockside architecture. One of Hartley's follies was the entrance to the shipyard of William C. Miller and Sons which faced the steep slope of Upper Parliament Street with its grand houses built for a merchant aristocracy and the colossal warehouses housing their wealth.

Statue of John Laird in Birkenhead's Hamilton Square.

William Cowley Miller had served in the Royal Navy and already held blueprints which were suitable for Bulloch's conception of a Confederate blockade runner. She was to be a 700 ton steamer/sailing ship with 3 masts, 2 funnels and various other modifications which Bulloch insisted upon. The modifications and refinements were designed to keep the ship at sea for long periods and would change her appearance when opportunity demanded and Miller's began work on the ship which was to be called the *Oreto* ostensibly for a firm in Palermo. True to Hull's interpretation of the law, the *Oreto* would not be fitted with armament in a British port and to prying eyes would seemingly not be armed at all. However, the firm of Fawcett, Preston and Co. were secretly building the *Oreto's* engines to be fitted as a separate operation and they were also responsible for the armament which would also be fitted as a separate component. The Blakely cannons were cast here and proved to be a formidable weapon.

Bulloch's energy seemed boundless and late in the month of June with the construction of the *Oreto* underway, he took the ferry across the Mersey to Laird's shipyard. Lairds had opened its doors as the Birkenhead Iron Works under the firm hand of Scotsman John Laird and took its first order for a ship in 1828. In the following decade, Lairds had built 17 ships and continued to flourish for many years with the small hamlet of Birkenhead growing apace. There are several memorials to the Lairds in various places throughout the town including a marble bust in Williamson Art Gallery. The bust once stood at the entrance to Birkenhead General Hospital and was to commemorate John Laird M.P.'s generosity as principal benefactor to the hospital. Cynics have pointed out that the workers from Laird's shipbuilding yard were the main customers of the hospital which is a telling indictment on working practices of the day.

The Laird's technicians attempted to dissuade Bulloch that the ship should be made of wood - their contention was that wooden ships had over

Laird's shipyard, circa 1860.

centuries depleted England's oak forests to the extent that quality timber was at a premium and also the future of shipping was in iron ships. But Bulloch remained steadfast that the ship should be wooden simply because a traditional wooden ship could be repaired in any port in the world whereas iron was comparatively new and required specialist yards. Her coal bunkers were to be far in excess of the normal size which would enable the ship to remain at sea for months at a time. The ship would combine sail and steam so that when conditions were favourable her Captain could save on fuel. Laird's staff made no comment on the provision of a magazine below the waterline to protect its contents from shot and shell and they were similarly discreet at the provision of a retractable funnel and propellor. There was a further unique feature of the ship which was a condenser and cooler to provide fresh water - further enabling the ship to stay at sea longer.

Finally, the negotiations were completed and a contract drawn up in the presence of Bulloch, Prioleau and Hull and work began on the ship which was to be called the *290*. There's a strange prelude to the construction of the *Alabama* which could have led to major repercussions for all concerned; Macgregor Laird was the brother of John Laird and had travelled extensively throughout Africa - he was a committed abolitionist and had worked with Wilberforce on the anti-slavery bill. Macgregor died at the early age of 52 in January 1861, just a few months before Dunwoody Bulloch came calling.

St.Nicholas Church and the Strand, Circa 1860

Whether the *Alabama* would have gone ahead if Macgregor had been alive is a matter of conjecture.

During the cotton famine Liverpool merchants often formed a consortium to purchase a ship for the purpose of running the Northern blockade and bringing back cotton which would sell at inflated prices. It was a calculated risk but the outlay was spread and many merchants made their fortunes in a single voyage alone. The rumour began to circulate that the ship in Laird's dock was so-called because 290 merchants had banded together to commission another blockade runner but the truth was simply that the ship was Laird's 290th commission.

Atlantic Crossing

The summer of 1861 was possibly the most productive ever in the life of this most energetic of men and Bulloch's achievements thus far were remarkable to say the least. They were however, to become even more so when the Confederacy sent a dispatch to its agents in England that there was a shortage of supplies due to the massive numbers flocking to the colours. They were desperately in need of arms and supplies and the order was to gather as much as they could and transport it to the South - the logistics of the operation were down to the agents themselves. There was a hidden agenda in the order which was to attempt to prove to prospective suppliers that the blockade was not impregnable and could be breached. The company of Fraser, Trenholm and Co. were by this time fulfilling a far greater role than financial agents for the Confederacy and agents came and went constantly in civilian clothes using the offices as a base for their operations. Two of these agents were a Major Edward C. Anderson and a Major Caleb Huse who were employed as purchasing agents for the Confederacy and on this occasion they played a great part in securing equipment for the projected trip across the Atlantic (Anderson and Huse continued to secure arms for the South for much of the war and were instrumental in supplying the formidable Blakely cannon which was said to have played a great part in coastal defences. They shipped several cannon on the Fraser, Trenholm ship the *Gibraltar* in July 1863 for the defence of Charleston).

Sketch of the old Liverpool Tower

Bulloch's part in the operation was to purchase a ship sturdy enough to carry such a cargo and fast enough to run the blockade. He finally chose an 800 ton, iron-hulled steamer called the *Fingal* from a firm in Scotland and the contraband arms and supplies which had been gathered throughout the months of August and September were loaded onto the ship. The supplies were made up of 11,000 Enfield rifles, 4 cannon, 7 tons of shells, pistols, swords, sabres, medicine and clothing to the value of $250,000 on the open market but of inestimable value to the Southern war effort. Bulloch always had the knack of gathering people of resource and integrity around him and a certain John Low had helped him throughout the operation thus far and was now about to sail with Bulloch on the hazardous voyage across the Atlantic. John Low would have a distinguished career as an officer on the *Alabama* but he would never undertake such a desperate voyage as he did with Bulloch on the *Fingal* and the enormity of the task they faced could not be overestimated. The *Fingal* sailed from Greenock on 11 October, 1861, and right away the whole venture came close to disaster when it struck a coal ship off Holyhead. The *Fingal* proved to be the sturdier ship and the collision was violent enough to sink the unfortunate coal ship *Siccardi* - Fraser, Trenholm sorted out the whole incident and the *Fingal* sailed on.

The first stop on the Atlantic crossing was Terceira in the Azores where Bulloch chanced upon the isolated harbour which would later be useful when fitting out the *Alabama*. They reached Bermuda on November 2nd, taking on board the Savannah harbour pilot, Mr Macon, who had been transported there by the *CSS Nashville*, and nearing the final stage of their voyage, Bulloch spelled out to the crew the skill required to run the blockade. As luck would have it, a mist obscured the ship as they approached the harbour and after running aground on an oyster bank the *Fingal* sailed into Savannah on 14th November, 1861, with all flags flying, accompanied by the few small ships that the South could muster. There was an incident as they crept through the morning mist which was pure farce but could have been the undoing of the whole project; as the *Fingal* slowly sailed past the American ships there was an unearthly shriek which shattered everyone's nerves until it was found to be one of the cockerels caged on deck. One of the officers wrung its neck and all was quiet again until the same shriek unnerved them all again - the bird that had been executed earlier was innocent of all charges and it was its neighbour which was the guilty one.

A plaque fixed to the façade of Rumford Place.

The triumphant voyage of the *Fingal* had not only brought the largest single supply of arms to the South but had proved that the blockade could be beaten and a grateful Confederacy promoted Bulloch to the rank of Commander with John Low becoming a Master in the Confederate navy. The winter months were spent in conference with Mallory while the *Fingal* was loaded with cotton for the return trip, a task which proved to be slow due to the war effort. Bulloch was impatient to return to oversee the building of the two ships he had commissioned but the months of December, January and February went by until the *Fingal* was finally loaded and he could return. A measure of how fortunate the *Fingal* had been to beat the blockade was that once she got into port she couldn't get out and the months of preparation for the return journey were wasted when it was decided that the *Fingal* would be converted into an ironclad for combat against the blockading ships.

U.S. Coastguard during the Civil War.

An impatient Bulloch returned to England with Low at his side on a blockade runner called the *Annie Childs*, landing at Queenstown (now Cobh) in Ireland and arriving in Liverpool on 10th March 1862. The report that the *Annie Childs* dipped her colours three times while passing the *Oreto* in the Mersey sounds a little fanciful given that Bulloch wasn't on board at the time and was probably the overactive imagination of a Northern spy. After performing such a glorious feat as to cross the stormy Atlantic, run through the blockade and deliver an unprecedented load of arms to the Confederacy the *Fingal* was to come to a sad and undignified end stuck on a sandbank. In fact she became grounded on sandbanks as a matter of course in her short career as the ironclad, *CSS Atlanta* - it seems that her metal cladding had made the *Fingal* top-heavy and unwieldy to handle and rather than becoming a nemesis of the Northern navy she was in fact easy prey. In May 1863, she came to an ignominious end, grounded on a sandbank and blasted into surrender by the Northern monitor, *USS Weehawken* - an undeserving end to such an illustrious beginning.

Cloak and Dagger

Bulloch had set out on the *Fingal* having given Charles K. Prioleau carte blanche to ensure a smooth passage in the construction of the *Oreto* and the *290*, expecting to be gone no more than six weeks or so. In the event, his blockade-running adventure was to take almost six months in which time work on both ships slowed alarmingly. Bulloch had underestimated just how fundamental his presence was to the whole operation and while his subordinates were worthy people in their own right, none of them had the drive or initiative to take matters into their own hands. Worse still, Bulloch returned to find the shipyards and waterfront pubs infested with spies working for the North. Bulloch had barely departed on the *Fingal* when the man who was to become his Javert for years hence, set foot on the quayside.

Tenacious and single-minded, Thomas Haines Dudley would remain Bulloch's nemesis from the moment he took up his post as United States consul in Liverpool. A Quaker and Abolitionist, Dudley was as strongly committed to his own cause as Bulloch was to his, growing from early beginnings as a thorn in Bulloch's side to later impeding his movements considerably. Dudley was no stranger to the espionage game and early in his career he had once disguised himself as a slave trader in order to purchase back from their captors, slaves that had escaped to freedom but been kidnapped back. His influence was to become pervasive and his network of spies were to gather information which would not only hinder ships from leaving the Mersey but eventually prove to be a major factor in reparation claims after the war was over. For the time being, Dudley had set up office in a massive building on the waterfront, 22 Tower Buildings which replaced the ancient Liverpool Tower. The old Tower was all of 500 years old when it was demolished in 1819, its last inhabitants were Napoleonic prisoners of war. In its early days, the waters of the Mersey lapped at the base of the crenellated tower across a tiny beach but if Dudley needed a breath of sea air he was required to walk two minutes across the Strand to the Pierhead. It was a complete coincidence that the less salubrious but no less busy offices of Fraser, Trenholm were also two minutes away. Dudley quickly ascertained that there was a ship being constructed a mere 15 minutes walk along the docks looking suspiciously like a warship and he promptly hired the services of a detective to find out more. Matthew Maguire was an ex-policeman with extensive knowledge of the pubs and wharves throughout the waterfront and between himself and his agents they ferreted out a constant stream of information by any means they could - sometimes infiltrating the shipyards, other times listening to gossip and more often than not bribing employees. It was not difficult to obtain information about the *Oreto* but on this occasion Maguire reported to his employer the falsity that the ship was being built for an Italian mercantile firm and he also got the name wrong, calling the ship the *Orito*. Nevertheless, it was enough for the implacable Dudley who wasted no time in

US Consulate, circa 1860

Birkenhead landing stage, circa 1860.

approaching the Italian consulate who informed him that they knew nothing of any Italian ship. Dudley's suspicions were well founded and he began the first of many discourses with his superior Charles Francis Adams, a son of the illustrious John Quincey Adams, a previous American President, and the American Minister based in London. Adams was outraged that there was a Confederate ship being constructed in an English shipyard and appalled that a branch of the Civil War was being fought out on the Liverpool waterfront and was further dismayed by the diffident attitude of the British government. The Foreign Secretary, Lord John Russell under pressure from Adams ordered an investigation but seemed unworried by the implications. The investigation by customs officers was thorough, took note of the obvious martial elements of the ship and interviewed William Miller accordingly but concluded that although the ship was obviously built for war they could do nothing as there were no guns or arms aboard. Lord John Russell's subsequent letter to Adams informing him of the situation confirmed once and for all what he already knew - that the British government were tacitly complicit in the Confederate shipbuilding operations. F.S.Hull must have been hugging himself as his foresight and sagacity, not to mention mendacity, paid handsome dividends.

No matter how compliant the British government were, Bulloch knew that it was time for the *Oreto* to take to the sea and he put into motion his plans which retained to the last the illusion that the ship was neutral and kept within the dictates of the Foreign Enlistment Act, section 7 - as interpreted by Hull, anyway. The indefatigible Fraser, Trenholm as ever, efficiently cleared the documentation and obtaining a crew was not difficult in a city thronged with sailors but a captain was another thing altogether. Ship's captains were difficult to come by at the best of times but in this case the man chosen would need to be trustworthy and if not faithful to the Confederacy, at least malleable enough to work on its behalf - it was inconceivable and impractical that the captain would not be informed of the true nature of the operation. Once again, Bulloch's gift for attracting talented and committed worthies to his cause came to the rescue and a James Alexander Duguid stepped forward on the recommendation of his father-in-law, William C. Miller. Duguid was not only qualified as a ship captain but his relationship with Miller made him a perfect choice. His instructions were clear and simple - to sail the *Oreto* to Nassau where he would be met by Bulloch's associates and receive further instructions. Concurrent with the voyage of the *Oreto*, Bulloch had chartered a ship called the *Bahama* which would carry the armament to be fitted in Nassau, consisting in the main of four 7 inch rifled cannon along with gun carriages and shells. The final act in the theatrical pretence was a party of ladies who boarded the *Oreto* along with Bulloch on the understanding that they were to be part of a celebration of the ship's sea trials. The *Oreto* left Liverpool on the 22nd March, 1862, unloaded Bulloch and his ladies onto another chartered ship back to Liverpool in the Irish sea and sailed off to a chequered career as the *CSS Florida*.

Liverpool's Exchange flags, circa 1860. Around the statue of Nelson placed there in 1814, shipping agents and ship owners carried out their business, exchanging their cards and bills, hence the name of the site.

Et Tu Brute?

Liverpool Road is the busy main thoroughfare which runs for miles along the Liverpool waterfront and although it changes its name here and there, it is still the same main artery where not so long ago, shire horses clattered along to the Herculaneum dock, the Albert dock, Salthouse dock, Canning dock and on to the monolithic tobacco warehouses of Stanley dock. From there, the road meanders along to Seaforth and the massive container units and then enters a canyon of Victorian houses, leading to the Liver Hotel landmark. A little further on, there's a mansion set back from the road which is now a school but was once the home of an American cotton merchant. The only clue to the former owner's nationality are two American eagles on either side of the gate but very few people notice either the eagles or the house as they fly by at speeds which were unimaginable when it was first built.

When John de Costa first came to Liverpool as a shipping agent, his business thrived and on the proceeds he purchased the land on Liverpool road, and in 1861, he built the opulent mansion house called Claremont House. John de Costa had Southern affiliations and his business flourished to such an extent that Liverpool Corporation felt compelled to officially recognise his energy in promoting trade between the Confederacy and the port of Liverpool. The recognition took the form of a pair of ornamental gates fronting de Costa's mansion, with the American eagle insignia prominent on each gatepost.

Liverpool road was at that time a dusty track with horse-and-trap the usual traffic and there is little doubt that de Costa often made his way to the Liver Hotel which was known to have a clientele of Confederates and where he would have been welcomed with open arms. Seated among the varied customers, de Costa was no doubt privy to all manner of privileged information and would have been treated as a trusted friend.

Even before James Dunwoody Bulloch arrived in Liverpool, the American newspapers were reporting on his movements and he was soon surrounded by a host of spies with Matthew Maguire foremost among those employed by Thomas Haines Dudley. There were very few that Bulloch confided in but for the most part he believed that Confederate agents in England were trustworthy.

Bulloch may have known of the spies but he would never have seen the deluge of paperwork which was threatening to overwhelm the staff of Lord John Russell, consisting of petitions, affidavits, pleas for justice and veiled threats. All of these emanated from many sources, ranging from disgruntled sailors, Northern spies, captains claiming recompense for burnt ships and on to Charles Francis Adams, with his barrage of official letters to Lord John Russell. If Bulloch had by some mischance come into contact with this litany of injustice, somewhere in the voluminous files he would have come across a deposition which would have interested him greatly; the deposition gave evidence of the affairs of the Phantom, naming the captain as Tessier, a Mr Mann, as an official of Fawcett, Preston and W.C.Miller as the builder. The signature at the bottom would no doubt have startled Bulloch ---it was signed John de Costa.

If in this hypothetical scenario, Bulloch had delved deeper, he would also have come across another deposition signed by John de Costa; this time detailing the comings and goings of the Alexandra.

Evidently Bulloch never discovered de Costa's entry into the web of spies and spymasters and de Costa never seemed to benefit much from his deceit. If anything, his financial problems increased and in 1880, he found himself in the High Court, after which he lost his house, his land and his reputation. And also became lost to history.

A Narrow Escape

Sketch of the Alabama under sail

The metamorphosis of the 290 into the Alabama

Bulloch had only returned from America in March and in the same month had dispatched his first ship to the Confederate navy and now with the *Oreto* safely out to sea he was able to give his full attention to forwarding work on the *290*. Lairds were just as anxious as Bulloch to complete the job but refused to compromise on quality - already they had rejected two pieces of timber integral to the vital sternpost section and they were about to pay an inordinate amount of money for the required part. Bulloch was himself responsible in part for the delay as it was he who had stressed the need for quality throughout the ship and it was he who had ordered that the shipwrights stick rigidly to his written specification. The inflexibility of Bulloch's specification was for the time being a source of irritation for everyone concerned but would pay rich dividends in the long run.

The *Oreto* was a template for the construction and launch of the *290* and the Birkenhead ship followed closely the pattern of the *Oreto's* progress and the subsequent launch but every element of the *290*'s progress increased tenfold. The *290* was a far more prestigious ship than the *Oreto* and the Northern government having allowed one warship to slip through their fingers were not about to let another free. As a result, the *290* was subject to far more intense scrutiny than the *Oreto* and a constant stream of information from

Maguire's agents onto Dudley's desk became a veritable flood, with trivia interwoven with vital information being filtered into legible documents and forwarded onto Charles Francis Adams. Just as he did in the case of the *Oreto*, Adams subjected Lord Russell, as Foreign Secretary, to a constant barrage of harassment, with the object being to apply so much pressure that the Englishman would be forced to act and carry out Adams's ultimate aim to impound the ship. Adams underestimated Russell's diffidence in the matter and to Adams' frustration did exactly what he had done in the case of the *Oreto* which was to order a search by customs officers which once again came up with the same answer; - yes the ship had all the appearances of a warship but she was not armed and the impasse continued.

With the *290* near to completion and spies swarming everywhere an anxious Bulloch concentrated on putting some of the other pieces in place while he waited impatiently for Lairds completion date. The minutiae of getting the *290* to sea were extremely complex and timing was a major factor in every aspect of the operation. Bulloch spent much of his time in planning and organizing and the time to reflect on the overall scheme was a long way off but when he finally looked back onto his latest venture it could be described as nothing less than a masterclass in logistics. For the time being, Bulloch turned his attention to a 350 ton bark called the *Agrippina* which he purchased via his agents in London and ordered to be hidden in port off the Isle of Dogs in the Thames where it was least likely to be seen by prying eyes. A captain Alexander McQueen was appointed as master and the ship was duly loaded with uniforms, small arms, coal and most important of all the Blakely cannon. McQueen was an unknown quantity to Bulloch but once again his talent for finding suitable staff would pay dividends and as the *Agrippina* awaited orders another component in the great scheme was in place.

The Sailors Home was a recruiting centre for the crews of the Confederate ships. It was demolished in 1973 for no reason in particular.

The diplomatic in-fighting between Adams and the English Foreign Office was by this time reaching a frenzy and was exacerbated even further by the appearance of an official document called The Passmore Affidavit. Official documents have always carried more weight than verbal appeals and Lord Russell could hardly ignore the contents of a legal statement from Adams' law office. The Passmore Affidavit was a sworn statement by William Passmore of Birkenhead whose opening deposition stated: *"I am a seaman and have served as such on board Her Majesty's ship Terrible during the Crimean War."*

The document then went on to state at length that Passmore had been signed on the *290* as an Able Seaman and given a password which was "290". It was explained to him that his duties would be to sail and fight on behalf of the Confederate navy. He then went on to detail the parts of the ship which pertained to her being a warship, pointing out places for guns and all the paraphernalia of a warship. He then stated that James Dunwoody Bulloch was to be her captain and the ship would be called the *Florida*. Despite the misinformation at the end of the document, it was a written statement that the *290* was a Confederate warship and Lord Russell was becoming increasingly uncomfortable in his entrenched notion that he could not take action if the ship was not armed.

A frustrated Bulloch doggedly pursued a positive and active role in placing as many pieces as he could into place while he awaited news of the *290* and another detail was to instruct the ever-faithful John Low to lease the Mersey steam tug, *Hercules* to be ready for the day of the launch. In the meanwhile, Adams was making plans of his own. Tired of cajoling Russell, it had come home to him forcefully that most if not all of the British government were sympathetic to the South. Some members were of the opinion that the South had every right to be an independent nation and others retained a ridiculous affinity towards what they perceived to be a cultivated and civilized "little England" while yet another faction were plainly happy to cash-in on Northern misfortunes at sea. Even intellectuals and artists such as Huxley and Ruskin were Southern supporters which was more of a naïveté common to their calling than any other factor but there was one common thread which bound them all; they had all abandoned the precepts of anti-slavery which had been so hard fought for by their predecessors. From any perspective it was an incredible and shameless volte-face. Charles Francis Adams was not just a cipher - he was the representative of the President of the United States and in the absence of goodwill from the English he decided to invoke some

The old Sailor's Home, the ornate gates circa 1930.

of the swingeing powers invested in him, which is why Captain Thomas T. Craven of the American steam cruiser *Tuscarora* came to be sitting in Adams's office where the whole scenario of the impending launch of the *290* was explained to him. They came to the conclusion that although it would be easy (and tempting) to destroy the *290*, the political repercussions did not bear thinking about - the *290* was still legally a British ship. But there was nothing to prevent the *Tuscarora* from shadowing the *290* at all times so that if she dared to declare her true colours then the American ship could blow her out of the water with no fear for the consequences. The *Tuscarora* of necessity was to remain in Southampton until Adams's agents informed him of the launching date whereby Craven would immediately sail to Liverpool Bay. Given that the Queen's Proclamation of Neutrality stated that foreign ships at war could stay only 24 hours in port, Adams himself was not averse to bending the rules when it suited him.

One of the grandest parts in Bulloch's great scheme was the arrival of Raphael Semmes but since he had no control over Semmes's itinerary then Bulloch methodically carried on putting more pieces of his plan together. He had

The Alabama in pursuit

already recruited a captain for the *290* and true to form, Bulloch had chosen a conscientious and worthwhile man for the job. Captain Matthew J. Butcher, an ex-officer of the Cunard line, was to be the first master of the *290* when she finally left Laird's slipway, but for the time being he was charged with the responsibility of finding a number of crew members which was not difficult in a city like Liverpool. What was difficult was swearing them to silence which was not as successful as Butcher would have liked if William Passmore was to be believed. Passmore said in another of his written statements:

"Met the seamen, say thirty in number, on Saturday coming down Canning Street from the ship, playing "Dixie's Land" on a fife, concertina and a cornopean and they all took 4.30 Woodside boat for Liverpool. They still kept playing "Dixie's Land" on board the ferry boat. Went up to one of the men and asked him when he thought the ship would be going out. He told me that their bed clothes and bedding were on board and the boatswain had told those who were intended to go into her, to hold themselves in readiness for next week".

In May, 1862, Lairds were ready for the *290* to move out of the yard and onto the river in readiness for the final phase of the work which was to hoist her engines into place. The completion of the ship was a cause for celebration and Bulloch took a party of officials from Fraser, Trenholm, Captain Butcher and various officers across for the launch. The ship was finally to have a name and Bulloch's wife Harriot had been chosen for the honour of launching and naming the ship which was from that point onward called the *Enrica* - the Spanish version of Harriot. The engines were fitted in the middle of June and after trials the ship was to sail on Tuesday, 29th July - this was of course kept as quiet as possible.

The Passmore affidavit and the constant pressure from Adams had finally worn down Lord Russell's resolve and after a weekend of warnings from his own lawyers Russell gave the order to prevent the *Enrica* from sailing on the morning of Monday, 28th July to be implemented on the following day - Tuesday, 29th July.

Tuesday morning, 29th July 1862, dawned bright and clear and Bulloch and his wife Harriot were hosts to a party of officials and their guests accompanied by Captain Butcher, John Low and Clarence Yonge among others catching the ferry across to Seacombe dock where they were to join the *Enrica* in her final sea trials. Bulloch was keeping to the same charade he had played at the launch of the *Oreto* - who would think that a ship would be sailing with a host of crinolined ladies aboard? But his mind was as always elsewhere and in reality he was orchestrating the final overture in a complexity of operations designed to see the *Enrica* enter into the Confederate navy. Accompanied by the tug *Hercules*, the *Enrica* sailed out into Liverpool Bay and after a reasonable length of time Bulloch informed his party that the trials would continue throughout the night and it would be convenient if the *Hercules* returned them to Liverpool. Bulloch returned to Liverpool landing stage with his guests aboard the *Hercules* while the *Enrica* sailed on to Moelfre Bay off the coast of Anglesey where she was to await Bulloch's return. Tuesday morning, 29th July 1862, was also an auspicious day for Liverpool customs officers who had received a telegraph to detain the *Enrica* from sailing - by the time they had received the order and travelled across to Birkenhead the *Enrica* had gone.

The following day, Bulloch was once again at the quayside and on this occasion he was boarding quite a different party onto the deck of the *Hercules*. The 30 or so seamen were intended crewmen for the *Enrica* and they were bound for Moelfre Bay, a six hour sail away. Once there, Bulloch transferred his seamen to the *Enrica* and gave Captain Butcher specific instructions to avoid the usual exit from the Irish Sea and especially Queenstown and to sail to the Azores and the bay of Terceira which Bulloch had noted from his time aboard the *Fingal*. Bulloch watched the *Enrica* as she sailed out of Moelfre and headed for the northern tip of Ireland where she was to circumvent the coast and head into the Atlantic and south for the Azores. It was at Terceira that the whole complex scheme was to come together. The *Tuscarora* had been caught by surprise at the time of the *Enrica*'s sailing and missed her in Liverpool Bay. Captain Craven had followed her to Moelfre and missed her there and finally waited in vain in St. Georges Channel. The bird had flown and American officials were once again left wringing their hands. It was bordering on the supernatural, the way that Bulloch pre-empted every move that the Northerners made and it seemed fairly obvious that he was receiving information at the highest level. Bulloch has never divulged anything of that nature which is in keeping with his code of honour but speculation has been rife for years as to who was feeding him information. If the rumours are true then this man of many parts had outwitted not only the American Embassy but had shown himself to be even more adept at the spy game than even the esteemed Thomas Haines Dudley. With the *Enrica* on her way to Terceira and Captain McQueen ordered to join her there, Bulloch was forced to await the final piece of the puzzle; the Captain of the *Alabama* was of course an integral part of the whole scheme and Raphael Semmes had been chosen for the job. Semmes was Southern through and through with a similar naval background to Bulloch and when the pair finally became acquainted they immediately became firm friends with a mutual respect for each other's abilities. When Bulloch first arrived in Liverpool his family had remained in New York and it is probable that he lodged at the Liver Hotel in Waterloo which was a small suburb 5 miles outside the city with good transport links into his offices. It is also probable that he recommended the hotel to Semmes and folk memory persists that the two men spent several evenings there making their future plans. Semmes also met some of Bulloch's family who were living in 3 Wellington Street and spoke well of all of them. Several days after Semmes's arrival Bulloch chartered yet another steamer the *Bahama* and along with Semmes and another batch of crewmen for the *Enrica* set out on the 10 day cruise to the Azores. The tiny island of Terceira was the rendezvous point for the *Enrica*, the *Agrippina* and the *Bahama* but for Bulloch it was more than that - it was the culmination of a meticulously planned exercise which had occupied his thoughts for the whole time he had been in England. The *Enrica* was the first to arrive, with Captain Butcher sailing into Terceira on the 18th August 1862. It was a whole week before the *Agrippina* turned up having been delayed by bad weather. Although the week of waiting had been uneventful, Butcher had taken the precaution of calling the *Enrica* by yet another name, the *Barcelona*, hoping to confuse anyone who had heard the news of the flight of the *Enrica*. There was one incident which could have been disastrous when Clarence Yonge, the Paymaster, was drinking with the officers of another ship and let slip that the *Barcelona* was a Confederate ship - fortunately there were no repercussions but his indiscretion had been noted and was just one of a number which were to occur later with Semmes eventually being forced to take action. The arrival of the *Agrippina* marked a flurry of activity with the two ships lashed together while the stores and armament were transferred onto the *Barcelona*. This was no little job and was still going on the next day when Bulloch and Semmes arrived on the *Bahama*. This was the first time that Semmes had seen his command and he was overwhelmed at her excellence and commented favourably upon all the additional features while praising Bulloch for his zeal and energy in producing such a gem. On 24th August, 1862, with the ship fully fitted out with cannon and stores and gleaming from top to bottom, Raphael Semmes in full dress uniform formally addressed the crew. He read the details of his commission from Jefferson Davis and Stephen Mallory and gave the crew a rousing speech, at the end of which a cannon was fired, the Stars and Bars replaced the Union Jack and the band played Dixie. But most importantly, the ship known as the 290, the *Enrica* and the *Barcelona* shed all its various guises and for the first time proclaimed its allegiance to the Confederacy and sailed off under its true name - the *Alabama*. As the magnificent cruiser sailed away, there is no doubt that it was an emotional moment for Bulloch. He had been the very heart and soul of every aspect of the *Alabama's* conception and construction, he had outwitted the agents and politicians at every turn and he had directed a logistical operation which was pure theatre in its dramatic conclusion. But what made the moment even more poignant was that Stephen Mallory had previously promised that Bulloch would be the man to captain the *Alabama*. It was little consolation to know that the reason he had been replaced by Semmes was that his skills as a procurer of Confederate ships were indispensable and his very brilliance had held him back.

Confederate Screw Steamer, 'Alabama'
"Feby.25th, 1863.

"Dear Cousin, - I am in the vessel mentioned above and like her pretty well; only I wish I was out of her and my prize money in my pocket. I should then be coming towards home. We have taken about 35 vessels including, including the California steamer, bound from New York for Aspinwall. She had about 140 marines on board, and we thought we should have to fight; but we fired a shot from the gun I was at, and it nearly knocked her foremast down. A man-of-war steamer, which we had to take by force, we sunk in seventeen minutes. We were going to the coast at Galveston to pick out some odd craft to fight us. There were in this place, a good many vessels, but by Providence we escaped with one man wounded in the mouth: he is now all right. We are now out at sea, and there is one man leaving the ship, and I thought I would send you this bit of a note to let you know where I am. I must now conclude as there is a full-rigged brig in sight. We can't say what she is, but if she be a Yankee she will be on fire directly.

– I am &c."

The above letter was published in a Rochdale local paper in 1863, with the introduction: *"The following letter will be read with considerable interest as the writer is a youth who not long ago left our town, and as it appears, embarked in an undertaking of no little peril. The letter is in pencil and had been hurriedly written:-"*

The "California steamer" referred to is almost definitely the *Ariel* which was captured on the 7th December, 1862, with 150 marines aboard, and the "man-of-war" is obviously the *Hatteras*, sunk in January, 1863.

For some reason, the newspaper neglected to give the writer's name, but it is thought to be a youth named Bell who was obviously well educated, in an age when illiteracy was the norm. Despite being in the epicentre of the cotton famine, the Rochdale Observer was a staunch supporter of the Northern cause but published several similar letters from Rochdale seamen, ignoring the fact that they were aboard Southern ships.

THE ALABAMA

TWO YEARS BEFORE THE MAST

The Alabama
by Samuel Walters

The Rebel Cruisers

The *Alabama* was one of a dozen ships commissioned by the Confederate government to counter the blockade of Southern ports by the union navy. Her remit was to lure Union ships away from their posts along the Southern coastline and to destroy Union shipping wherever she found it - whether it be commercial or naval. The *Alabama* carried out her orders to the letter and created such havoc among Union ships that after the war it took years to restore American merchant shipping to anything like it had been before the war. A further measure of her success was that in 1872, at a court of arbitration in Geneva the court decreed that Great Britain should pay the United States $15.5 million dollars reparation for ships and cargo destroyed during the *Alabama's* two year rampage. From the first day of her commissioning, the *Alabama* had ranged across the Atlantic from the Eastern seaboard and as far as Ireland like a fox in a henhouse scattering Union ships into panicked flight until the Atlantic became an empty ocean and the *Alabama* was compelled to seek her prey in more exotic ports. The total shipping sunk or burned by the *Alabama* was an incredible 53 in number and a further 11 were taken as prizes or sold.

No matter how hard the *Alabama* and others like her fought their war at sea there was no doubt that the war between the States would ultimately be settled by the great set-piece battles on the mainland but the *Alabama* was no mere sideshow to the main event and as time went by her value began to be more and more an exemplar of Confederate defiance. Her expertise at destroying merchant ships was becoming legendary but as a symbol of Southern pride she was priceless.

Just as priceless was the Southerner who captained the *Alabama*, Captain Raphael Semmes. The *Alabama* was an undoubtedly fine ship but it was Captain Semmes's energy, imagination and daring which was the driving force behind what was to become a Confederate legend.

Raphael Semmes

Raphael Semmes was born in Maryland in 1809 and but for the the deaths of both his parents while he was still a child Raphael would probably have followed his father into tobacco farming. As it was, his upbringing became the responsibility of his two uncles who ensured he received a private school education in Georgetown from where he entered Charlotte Hall Military Academy. In 1826, Semmes became a midshipman and in 1832 graduated first in his class. His first posting after graduation was at Norfolk Naval Base where he was assigned the maintenance of the chronometers - a task which fascinated the young Semmes and would later lead to an unusual occupation while aboard the *Alabama*. In 1837, he married a New Jersey girl named Anne Elizabeth Spencer and served aboard a ship called the *Somers*. The *Somers* was never a happy ship and a mutiny ended with the three ringleaders hanged. It was hardly an auspicious start for Semmes but the experience was later to be invaluable when the time came to deal with another mutiny. The *Somers* later capsized - to nobody's great regret. Semmes's career in the U.S. Navy then led onto service in the Mexican War from where he became Lighthouse Inspector for the Gulf of Mexico and further promotion saw him take up a post as Secretary of the Lighthouse Board in Washington D.C.

His service with the U.S. Navy ended in 1861 when *Alabama* joined the other Southern states and seceded from the Union. - Semmes resigned immediately and began a new career in the Confederate Navy under the Confederate

President Jefferson Davis. In what could have been a dress rehearsal for service on the *Alabama*, Semmes's first duty was to refit a ship called the *Habana* which was duly re-named the *CSS Sumter* and took to sea under the now Captain Raphael Semmes who had the dubious honour of being Captain of the sole ship in the Confederate Navy. Semmes was undismayed by such trivialities and went on to burn the Union ship, the *Golden Rocket* as a prelude to a six month spell of sea-going action which concluded with the capture of 18 prizes. The glorious career of the *CSS Sumter* ended at Gibraltar where Semmes was forced to abandon the ship when the engines began to fail. Although Semmes was unaware of it at the time, his adventures aboard the *Sumter* were merely a rehearsal for the greater trials that lay in his immediate future.

The Alabama's retractable funnel.

Paradoxically it was the burning of the Norfolk Navy Yard which led to the South having no means of providing ships for its Navy and led on to purchasing ships from yards in Great Britain and was the reason why Semmes found his next assignment to take command of one of those ships. When Semmes sailed from Liverpool accompanied by James Dunwoody Bulloch, the ship's officers (many of whom had served with him on the *Sumter* including Irvine Bulloch, James's half-brother, the ship's surgeon Galt and the rock-solid Kell) and a crew recruited on the Liverpool waterfront, he travelled on the steamer *Bahama* reaching Terceira in the Azores on August 20th, 1862, to rendezvous with a ship called *Enrica*. A Captain Butcher was in the process of transferring the ship's armament from his own ship, *Agrippina* onto the *Enrica*. The siting of the armament and the commissioning of the ship was the final act in a byzantine and clandestine operation which Bulloch had implemented throughout and he overlooked operations with pride as the commissioning ceremony took place and the Confederate flag was unfurled and the *Enrica* made its final metamorphosis into the *CSS Alabama*. Few people knew that Bulloch had been promised the captaincy of the *Alabama* which was why he had lavished so much care and attention on her construction but it was his very conscientiousness which made him indispensable as an agent and he had reluctantly been persuaded to give way to Semmes.

And it was as Captain of the *Alabama* that Semmes took charge of a sleek and gleaming, brand new, custom-built Confederate Commerce Raider. Semmes was delighted with his new charge and especially pleased with the innovations and the quality. He was not slow to praise James Dunwoody Bulloch for all the work that he had put in on the ship and he was probably aware that Bulloch was keenly disappointed not to be the man taking her out to sea. The *Alabama* was built in an age when steam was superceding sail but the

The retractable propellor

Alabama combined both and thereby got the best of both worlds - she could steam for 12 days at a time and supplement her power by sail whenever the situation called for it. The *Alabama* was built upon an oak frame housing iron coal-bunkers and boasting a condensation apparatus which provided fresh water at all times and she displaced 1040 tons. She was 220 foot long with wire rigging, long lower masts and the bottom was sheathed in copper. Nothing had been omitted and a retractable propellor reduced drag when speed was required while the funnel dropped into a well, performing the same function and also changing the appearance of the ship - combined with false colours the *Alabama* was effectively camouflaged. The armament fitted at the Azores was also cutting-edge technology for the era consisting of six 32 pound broadside cannon, a 68 pound smoothbore cannon and a formidable 100 pound, rifled Blakely gun. Carved into the steering wheel was the legend *Aide Toi et Dieu T'Aidera* (God helps those who help themselves) and there was nothing more appropriate. The Georgian-born executive officer and faithful Lieutenant to Semmes, Lt. John Mcintosh Kell wrote: *"I think she was the most beautiful ship that ever touched the sea".* The greater part of of the crew were recruited from the Liverpool wharves and later supplemented by Dutch, French, Canadian, Spanish and Malayan seamen with a crew of 120 seamen being the ideal number aboard. Kell initially called the Liverpool seamen "Incorrigible young rascals" but both he and Semmes were forced to alter their opinion and they came to have a healthy respect not only for their abilities but for their intelligence. Many of them were talented in various ways and surprisingly well-read, factors which may have influenced Semmes's reaction when faced with the second mutiny of his career. As time went by, the crew developed a patriotism for a place they had never seen and most evenings would end with renditions of "Dixie" or "The Bonny Blue Flag" to a background of guitar and fiddle after backgammon or chess sessions but the favourite pastime was counting their prize-money - of which they received very little in the long run. They called Semmes "Old Beeswax" after his habit of curling his moustaches. The excellence of the crew was a major factor in the success story of the *Alabama* and the idiosyncracies of the various crew members were a source of never-ending wonder to Arthur Sinclair. He told a story of "a Liverpool hard case named Egan" who hid the ship's cat for a prank, upsetting the crew to such a degree that the Captain was forced to take a hand. Lashed to the sail, Egan confessed he had stuffed the cat down a gun-barrel and pushed the tampion back - the tampion was removed and the cat found safe and a relieved crew returned to work.

The Odyssey of the Alabama

The *Alabama* wasted no time in carrying out her duties and throughout the remainder of 1862 in her travels throughout the Atlantic, she destroyed a total of 27 ships. Among her first victims were *Ocmulgee, Starlight, Ocean Rover, Alert, Weathergauge, Altamaha, Virginia* and *Elisha Dunbar.* Semmes had immediately gone for the United States whaling fleet which was operating off the Azores and he followed up by causing havoc in a second whaling fleet working the Grand Banks off Newfoundland (Kipling's Captain's Courageous gives a graphic description of the harsh life of a whaling crew at this time.) In a very short time the crew of the *Alabama* quickly learned a modus operandi which was used as a template for most succeeding encounters and would become a trademark for the following two years; flying false colours was unethical but effective and enabled the *Alabama* to board a ship, evacuate the crew, strip any valuables and then burn her. *Alabama's* remit was never about killing and the crew of a stricken ship would invariably be dropped off at the nearest landfall apart from one or two who fancied life as a Confederate raider.

Very quickly the *Alabama* became the scourge of merchant shipping and the sight of her sail on the horizon sent shivers through Union ships. They were never speedy enough to escape the *Alabama* and resorted to sailing under false colours themselves. It was a ploy which was to little avail as the *Alabama* unerringly sought out her prey and identified Union shipping quite easily. Semmes was unstinting in his praise of the master's mate, James Evans, formerly of the *Savannah,* who could detect the nationality of a ship from miles away and in Semmes's words "Had a peculiar talent in this respect".

Alabama leaving the Tonawanda

October, 1862, proved to be an exceptionally bountiful month for Confederate raiders and in mid-Atlantic Semmes found himself with an embarrassment of riches. Having captured a ship called the *Wave Crest* followed closely by the *Dunkirk*, Semmes sighted the *Tonawanda* sailing into an already bulging net. Semmes could never resist a prize and the *Tonawanda* carried a singularly excellent cargo. She also carried a number of women and children passengers for which the *Alabama* had no provision aboard ship. Reluctant to relinquish his prize, Semmes put a crew aboard and kept the *Tonawanda* in tow. Several days later, yet another another merchantman was spotted making the crossing and despite the encumbrance of his captures Semmes approached alongside, as always flying false colours, closed to the ship and sent "my card of invitation, being a blank cartridge and a change of flags".

The ship was the *Manchester* bound from New York to Liverpool and soon joined the growing flotilla of captured ships which were fast becoming an embarrassment and an encumbrance. In his usual pragmatic way, Semmes solved the problem by transferring the crews of the *Wave Crest*, *Dunkirk* and *Manchester* aboard the *Tonawanda* (after stripping her cargo) and allowed her to sail on; no doubt her Captain looked back at the flames from the burning ships which could so easily have included her.

October 1862 was an eventful month in another more unwelcome way when Semmes described the Alabama being caught in a cyclone. He was quite dispassionate about the cyclone, looking upon it as a curious force of nature which the Alabama managed to cope with extremely well. It was left to Arthur Sinclair to describe events more fully.

Part of the original United States Constitution had included the keeping of slaves and although slavery was practised for the most part in the Southern states, it was still legal throughout the North prior to the Civil War. Although it was fairly minimal, slaves were retained without censure and one of the prizes taken from the *Tonawanda* was a 17 year old Negro slave named David White who was the property of a Delaware citizen. Adding insult to injury, slaves were also subject to the Federal draft and David White was escaping to Europe to escape both incursions on his freedom.

Raphael Semmes found the situation both ironic and amusing and he signed David on as a wardroom steward with the same pay and rights as every other member of the crew. The young seaman took a liking to Doctor Galt and in between his duties, David could always be found in Galt's company.

David had many opportunities to escape during shore leaves and was approached by U.S. consuls on several occasions but chose to stay on board the *Alabama* and carried out his duties up to and including the bitter end.

Semmes was always fond of White and Bartelli and was genuinely distressed when he found that they had both drowned when the *Alabama* went down and was at a loss to know why neither man had told anyone that they couldn't swim.

The young David's death was particularly poignant; it seemed that whichever way he twisted and turned he could never escape bondage of one sort or another.

The War of Words

Raphael Semmes

Is the voyage of the of the Alabama relevant today ? Certainly not to the average Liverpudlian, struggling to come to terms with the new Industrial Revolution of computer technology and the lack of oil, which is the new global currency. Over the years, for the very few who are familiar with the name, the Alabama has become just a vague folk memory, refracted into what we would have liked it to be and turned into a glorious mélange of corsairs and swashbuckling scousers roaming the seven seas in a ceaseless search for treasure. The perverse pride in the notoriety of the Alabama will always take precedence over its true significance.

The truth, as always, is rather more prosaic; the Alabama was custom-built as a commerce raider and her wholesale destruction of Federal merchant ships was translated into lurid tales of a succession of desperate sea-battles in which the Alabama always came off best. On her voyage across the sea-lanes, the Alabama had become famous across the globe. Newspaper headlines were written in lurid terms and crowds flocked to see the Alabama wherever she landed. The fondness of the newspapers for a penny-dreadful standard of reporting (which sold newspapers) dwelled on emotive expressions such as "ghost-ship", "rebel raider" and "sea-wolf" which captured the imaginations of its readers but obscured the real issues. The enduring fables on the streets of Liverpool today are a testament to the power of the press to propagate myths.

North and South were of course sharply divided as to the reputation of the Alabama and the ship was as reviled in the North as it was revered in the South, just as its captain was demonised and lionised in equal measure. For those who claimed it was no more than a pirate ship burning its helpless prey there were others who countered that the Alabama was merely doing at sea what the Federal forces were doing on land.

As an exercise in seamanship, guile and a dogged devotion to the work in hand, Raphael Semmes's epic voyage set the benchmark for the art of commerce raiding. So much so, that half a century later, First World War U-boat captains were exhorted to adopt the Alabama's methods for their own use. Raphael Semmes's war was one of attrition rather than the traditional broadside battles of another age but he did have one thing in common with Stephen Decatur - they were both at one with the credo: "My country right or wrong". And there has been an unbroken line of Alabama's in the United States Navy ever since.

As for the buccaneering crew, few of them had any affiliation to the South and as far as the fifty or so Liverpool crew members were concerned, most would have been hard-pressed to point it out on a map.

They may have sworn allegiance to the South and sang rebel songs each evening but if the truth be told, they retired to bed dreaming dreams of riches beyond measure in Northern prizes and any booty they could find.

As compelling as the odyssey of the Alabama can be, the real interest of the ship is as the focal point of a four year period in Liverpool's maritime history which has strangely faded from public consciousness. The impact of the Alabama can only be placed into context according to the background of the time when two incongruous cultures, Confederate and Victorian, came together to form a curious alliance, in a city where fabulous wealth and grinding poverty existed cheek by jowl.

Many of the docks and buildings where the events took place are still recognisable today while others have sadly vanished for one reason or another. The Custom House was destroyed in the May blitz, the old St John's Market was a victim of the 1960s architectural pogroms, the Sailor's Home is now recognised as municipal vandalism, and so it goes on. But with a little imagination, the docks can still be visualised as they were in Victorian times and one inspired architect has incorporated a stone frieze commemorating the shipyards which were located to the rear of the new arena.

After the Civil War, the Liverpool shipyards closed down one by one with Potters not even reaching into the 1900s. W C Miller's yard was never the same after the death of Thomas Miller and Quiggin's yards managed to hang on until they closed in the late 1950s. In complete contrast, Lairds went on to become one of the finest shipyards in the world and its historic ships are legendary throughout the world.

On the other side of the Atlantic, although slavery and secession were well documented reasons for the Civil War, there were several concomitant matters which were of concern to the North and one of them was the very real fear that the South would expand into the Western territories. The Indian nations had a short reprieve during the war but Western expansion did take place afterwards and the now United States went on to its own Manifest Destiny crushing the indigenous tribes as they went. The much criticised British Imperialism appeared quite bland in comparison and the praiseworthy North American humanitarianism shown over the slavery issue was never extended to the native Americans.

The British government paid a high price for allowing the Florida to slip away in March, 1862, followed by the Alabama in July, 1862. Their avowed neutrality in the American Civil war was not only seen to be false but they had let loose the deadliest pair of raiders that British shipyards could produce. The effects upon Northern shipping were devastating as both ships sank over a hundred American merchantmen between them. The Northern reaction to this monumental blunder by the British government was fortunately restrained at the time and restricted to official complaints but America never forgave the Alabama, and in 1872, the price for Lord Russell's complicity was paid in full. At the Hotel de Ville, in Geneva, in a room called Alabama Hall, a plaque written in French, defines the ruling which instructed Britain to pay the United States $15.5 million dollars in reparation for damage caused by the commerce raiders.

Although it was not discernible at the time, the ruling was not just a major embarrassment but the first crack in the previously indestructible armour of the British Empire. It also defined in no uncertain terms the determination of the newly United States to determine her own destiny and never be overawed by the Old World Empires.

To all intents and purposes the matter ended there in Geneva. In retrospect, Britain had gotten off lightly and the world moved on but it is a disturbing thought that things could have been so much worse and if in some alternative universe, the South had prevailed, how would history have judged us then?

If 1862 was a bumper year for a harvest of whalers and merchantmen - with *Lamplighter, Lauretta, Crenshaw, Baron de Castine, Levi Starbuck, T.B.Wales, Emily Farnum* and the *Lafayette* (the captain of the *Brilliant* complained bitterly that Semmes burned his ship and then lay in wait for any rescuers who came along) all falling into the hands of Semmes and his ever-more efficient crew, then January 1863 was to provide an even more unique experience for the *Alabama* - a battle with a Union warship and fought at night. Cruising off the Gulf of Mexico, Semmes was on the lookout for a flotilla of Union warships which were eventually sighted outside Galveston. Sighting an unidentified ship out at sea, the Union Commander ordered the sidewheel warship *Hatteras* to investigate and nearing the ship Captain Blake shouted "What ship ?" with the response that it was the British Naval vessel *Petrel* (Blake must have misheard because in his report he quoted it as *Vixen*).

Hatteras was both curious and careless enough to sail closer until the *Alabama* sprung the trap, unfurled her colours and declared her name and intention. The two ships cleared for action but within 13 minutes the broadsides from the *Alabama* had shot to pieces the Union ship which began to sink fast. Semmes wasted no time in picking up the crew who were all in the water and immediately sailed off for South America, dropping his guests off at Jamaica on the way.

The sinking of the *Hatteras* was a humiliating defeat for Captain Blake and in his report he attempted to ameliorate the loss by stating that the *Alabama* was "underhanded in her tactics" and " a pirate ship" and the *Hatteras* was outclassed in every way. Nevertheless, he was severely reprimanded by his superiors and spent the remainder of the war trying to regain his former reputation - he paid a high price for his boldness in confronting the *Alabama*. There were no questions asked as to why only one ship had been ordered to investigate the unidentified ship when another four were standing to, doing nothing in particular.

As for Semmes, he wrote an indignant letter making it clear that Blake's report of a great disparity in firepower made the fight unequal was untrue and two ships of equal firepower and manpower had fought an equal battle in which the only superiority was *Alabama's* boldness and morale.

It wasn't only the members of the Hatteras who were left high and dry in Jamaica. John Low had first detected and reported Clarence Randolph Yonge's indiscretions in the bars of Terceira but Yonge had been shooting his mouth off in Liverpool pubs even before that. Originally, Bulloch's clerk, it was thought he might be safer at sea and found himself as assistant paymaster aboard the Alabama. Yonge was nothing if not consistent in his loose-lipped talk and it was in a bar in Jamaica that he was found spilling the secrets of the Alabama to a wide-eyed audience which included officers from the U.S. Consul's office. Semmes was not slow to deal with the matter and left Yonge on the quayside in Jamaica to find his own way out of his difficulties. True to his devious nature, the ever slippery Yonge took up with an impressionable mulatto girl and ignoring the fact that he had a wife in America married her in Kingston and took her to Liverpool along with her mother where he left them to fend for themselves in a country and climate totally alien to their experience - after swindling them of the little they had. Semmes was both scathing and scornful of Yonge in his Memoirs of Service Afloat written in 1869 although he would not mention him by name in deference to Bulloch's feelings. He detailed with disgust the man's treacherous behaviour to the ship and to the Jamaican girl but reserved his worse insults for Yonge's subsequent behaviour in serving as a spy for Charles Francis Adams calling him one of "Adams's hangers on" which was just about the worst thing anyone could be in Semmes's eyes - a Northern sympathiser.

Constantly crisscrossing shipping lanes, the *Alabama* had all but cleared the mid-Atlantic of commercial shipping and it was a brave ship indeed that attempted the crossing without some trepidation. Following the euphoria of sinking the *Hatteras* the *Alabama* sailed haphazardly down the coast of South America where in March 1863, near to the equator, the *Morning Star* was unlucky enough to be captured in the by now familiar manner. Having a neutral cargo, she was allowed to sail on to her destination, London, under the proviso of a $60,000 dollar bond. Pickings were becoming thinner now and it was May 1863 before the *Alabama* caught the clipper *Talisman* out of New York and bound for Shanghai - she was duly burnt and the passengers transferred to a passing British ship. One month later, June 1863, off the coast of Brazil, the *Conrad* bound for Buenos Aires was stopped and Semmes made the unusual decision to commission her into the Confederate Navy and rename her the *Tuscaloosa* with the indefatigable John Low in charge accompanied by midshipman George T. Sinclair. The *Tuscaloosa's* orders were to proceed to Brazil and report on Confederate shipping, capture and burn where she could and rendezvous with the *Alabama* at the Cape of Good Hope. Semmes's plan was nothing new - it was in effect to use the captured ship as a tender and a look-out but the plan was only mildly successful due to the differential in sailing speeds and the lack of any means of long-range communication.

Captain Winslow and the officers on the Kearsage.

The sinking of the Hatteras.

As the depredations continued and the threat of the *Alabama* became feared even further afield, Semmes was compelled to seek out his prey in evermore distant waters to fulfil his relentless obsession with the destruction of Union shipping. The *Alabama*'s fame had spread far and wide and when Semmes sailed her across the South Atlantic and into Capetown thousands were lining the shore to see the infamous *Alabama.* They were rewarded with an impromptu performance of the *Alabama's* capabilities which was as unexpected as it was theatrical. As the *Alabama* was entering port a ship called the *Sea Bride* was departing and Semmes promptly took her as a prize before sailing regally into harbour.

Semmes and his crew were feted as celebrities while the *Alabama* was refitted but they would not have been so carefree if they had been aware that the Union warship *Vanderbilt* was prowling out at sea. There was an ominous foretaste of what was to come as the *Vanderbilt* waited for the *Alabama* to emerge and it was just good fortune that a battle was averted. As the *Alabama* sailed out of harbour a sea-mist came down and she sailed past the waiting warship all unknowing - the final battle delayed for some time in the future. Her destination was Singapore via the Indian Ocean which soon yielded a new crop of commercial shipping to plunder, with the *Winged Racer, Amanda* and the *Contest* all falling prey to the *Alabama* during November and December of 1863. The *Contest* was a fast tea-clipper and as an ex-winner of racing tournaments she would have been expected to be capable of out-running the *Alabama* but on this occasion her luck ran out and with the wind against her she went the way of so many others and was captured, plundered and burnt.

It's difficult to imagine at this distance in time the thoughts of the many captains and crew who were forced to watch their ships burnt and sunk. They were after all magnificent vessels and manned for the most part by dedicated seamen. But the humiliation and helplessness must have been devastating particularly in view of the fact that they were not equipped as warships.
As for the Alabama, it is glaringly obvious that she was a particularly ruthless predator and no ship was safe from her attentions. While it was to Semmes's credit that his exploits rarely cost lives, his treatment of captured ships was merciless and he showed no remorse at the destruction of the many fine ships that he destroyed.

Sailing into Singapore harbour, Semmes broke out into a fever of Orientalism when he saw the multi-coloured garments of the various nations gathered at the quayside. He went on to describe in glowing terms "the Malay, the Japanese, the Hindoo, the Persian, the New Zealander, the Sumatran" and he even spotted several "Wild Tartars" - but it was the "Chinaman" who excited him into the most passionate admiration.

As the days went by, Semmes was puzzled as to why the crowd increased daily and wondered "what had excited all this curiosity among those simple inhabitants of the isles and continents". It eventually emerged that a vague knowledge of the Civil War and a foggy notion of slavery and Negroes had coalesced into the firm belief that the hold of the *Alabama* held a race of giant Negroes in chains ready to be unleashed by Semmes in time of war:

"They waited patiently for hours under their paper umbrellas hoping to catch a sight of these monsters".

It was the Malays who first coined the name "ghost ship" in relation to the *Alabama* due to its habit of seeming to appear out of nowhere. The crew of course enjoyed the delights of life ashore and in time-honoured fashion wasted no time in doing what sailors do when in port - and for the first time ever, the officers of the *Alabama* were confronted with a mutiny. The altercation arose from a minor disagreement between officers and men which turned ugly. When fuelled by drink some of the crew drew sheath-knives and belaying-pins with a bloody clash seeming inevitable. Semmes broke the stand-off by snatching the drunken mutineers one by one, tying their hands behind their backs and pouring buckets of salt-water over them until they were sober. The sight of a row of matelots soaked to the skin with buckets on their heads caused widespread mirth and the whole incident ended in laughter. One of the potential mutineers was heard to say:

"Old Beeswax was hell upon watering a fellow's grog"----- and life went on as before.

Semmes was never slow in handing out praise and gave full credit to Kell and Dr Galt for their energy in refitting the ship. He also praised the P&O Steamship Co. for their excellent wharf arrangements as the *Alabama* once again set forth to wreak havoc among Union shipping. It was only a matter of a few hours before the *Alabama* encountered "an American looking ship" in the Straits of Malacca and despite the Union Jack flying from her top-mast Semmes was not convinced and sent across Master's Mate Fullam to examine her papers. The papers stated that she was the English ship *Martaban* but Semmes was still suspicious and for the first time ever he personally boarded a captured ship. Semmes was scathing in his identification of many signs of the ship being American not least at the accents which were unmistakably American and Captain Pike was finally forced to admit the ship was in reality the *Texan Star*. The bluff had failed and the ship's fate was sealed and she joined so many others by being sent to the bottom in flames.

Semmes' route back was via the southern tip of India, down the east coast of Africa to Capetown and back into the cold waters of the South Atlantic. In April 1864, she was once again off the coast of South America and heading north on her customary meandering course. The *Alabama* and her crew were in a sorry state - the ship was in dire need of a major overhaul and the crew and officers were worn out physically and mentally. Semmes himself confessed to being tired of the unrelenting strain of command and he planned to get his ship into dry dock and for all of them to have a long break from the sea. Nevertheless, the sight of the *Rockingham* bound for Cork once again galvanized him into action and he carried out his usual procedure of looting, taking prisoners and burning his victim. During the same month of April, the *Tycoon* had the dubious honour of being the 64th and final ship taken by the *Alabama* and her crew joined those of the *Rockingham* in shackles. They were soon to find themselves standing on Cherbourg harbour wondering how to make their way home as so many had done before them.

Passing the Azores, the *Alabama* seemed to be retracing her course and heading straight back to where she had originated. In the month of June 1864, she entered the English Channel and made for harbour in Cherbourg and the end of a two year odyssey which had made her both famous and infamous across three oceans.

Semmes and Kell on deck

Ships taken by the Alabama

9/9/1862	Alert	3/2/1863	Palmetto	5/8/1863	Sea Bride
9/9/1862	Weathergauge	21/2/1863	Olive Jane	6/11/1863	Amanda
13/9/1862	Altamaha	21/2/1863	Golden Eagle	10/11/1863	Winged Racer
14/9/1862	Benjamin Tucker	27/2/1863	Washington	11/11/1863	Contest
16/9/1862	Courser	1/3/1863	Bethian Thayer	24/12/1863	Martaban
17/9/1862	Virginia	2/3/1863	John A. Parks	26/12/1863	Highlander
18/9/1862	Elisha Dunbar	15/3/1863	Punjaub	26/12/1863	Sonora
3/10/1862	Brilliant	23/3/1863	Morning Star		
3/10/1862	Emily Farnum	23/3/1863	Kingfisher		
7/10/1862	Dunkirk	25/3/1863	Charles Hill	14/1/1864	Emma Jane
7/10/1862	Wave Crest	25/3/1863	Nora	23/4/1864	Rockingham
9/10/1862	Tonawanda	4/4/1863	Louisa Hatch	27/4/1864	Tycoon
11/10/1862	Manchester	15/4/1863	Kate Cory		
19/10/1862	Lamplighter	15/4/1863	Lafayette 2		
23/10/1862	Lafayette 1	24/4/1863	Nye		
26/10/1862	Crenshaw	26/4/1863	Dorcas Prince		
28/10/1862	Lauretta	3/5/1863	Sea Lark		
29/10/1862	Baron de Castine	3/5/1863	Union Jack		
2/11/1862	Levi Starbuck	25/5/1863	S.Gilderslieve		
8/11/1862	Thomas. B. Wales	25/5/1863	Justina		
30/11/1862	Parker Cooke	29/5/1863	Jabez Snow		
5/12/1862	Union	2/6/1863	Amazonian		
7/12/1862	Ariel	5/6/1863	Talisman		

The Sinking of the Alabama

Durand-Brager painting of the fight between the Alabama and the Kearsage

The Alabama's Last Fight - Preliminaries

The *Alabama* that limped wearily into the English Channel and slipped quietly into Cherbourg harbour on the 11th June 1864 was a far cry from the fearsome raider that had splashed down Laird's slipway nearly two years previously and a lifetime ago. The unremitting pursuit of every Union ship that came into sight had taken its toll upon the pride of the Confederacy and she was literally coming apart at the seams. Previous repairs at Capetown and other ports had been little more than running repairs and now the *Alabama* could put off a major overhaul no longer with the copper bottom coming away from the wooden hull and the boilers leaking at every joint just two of the problems. It was not just the ship which was looking the worst for wear, the officers and crew were tired of the incessant chase and Cherbourg was meant to provide a safe and long-lasting break for the crew while the ship was in dry dock. Cherbourg was a National French port and foreign ships required permission to remain from no less a personage than the Emperor Napoleon the Third himself. Whilst awaiting that permission, it was no small surprise to Captain Semmes

Painting of the crowd gathering to watch the duel off Cherbourg.

to see the Union warship *Kearsage* sail into the same harbour and demand the surrender of the prisoners taken from the *Alabama's* last two prizes. Semmes invoked some of his early training in law and refused on the grounds that the *Kearsage* was adding to her crew in a neutral port - the *Kearsage* never stayed long enough to drop anchor and immediately sailed back out to sea. In the short time that the *Kearsage* was in harbour she had stayed a fair distance away from the *Alabama* - a small detail which was not noticeably strange at the time but would become painfully clear in the days ahead. Immediately after the departure of the *Kearsage*, Kell's report stated that he was called to the Captain's cabin and asked *"I am going out to fight the Kearsage, what do you think of it?"* There then followed a discussion as to the relative merits of the two ships in which it was concluded that the *Alabama* was the faster ship but the *Kearsage* was *"built for war."* Semmes never realized just how well she had been *"built for war"* until it was too late. The *Alabama* was speedy and handled well while the *Kearsage* was far superior at close range with her 11 inch guns a fearsome and formidable armoury.

Sketch of duel between the Kearsage and Alabama

Captain John Ancrum Winslow was a very different personality to Semmes and both men were acquainted from their service during the Mexican War. Winslow was a strict Episcopalian, anti-slavery, played it by the book and took few chances - the complete antithesis of the impulsive Semmes. It was a measure of Winslow's devotion to duty that when ordered to command the *Kearsage* he arose from his sick bed immediately to take up his command. His sickness was not one that could be taken lightly as it was probably malaria which was debilitating enough but he also had a severe eye infection. His doctor warned him that if he went to sea he would almost certainly lose the sight in one eye and that's exactly what happened. In a perverse way, Winslow's stubbornness worked in his favour as all his crew knew what he had done and respected him all the more.

It was unfortunate for everyone aboard the *Alabama* that Winslow's nature also included meticulous planning and for his encounter with the *Alabama*, Winslow had outdone himself by copying a ploy used successfully by Farragut two years previously. The *Kearsage* had been fitted with a heavy chain curtain which covered both sides of the ship from the rail to the waterline and not content with this, Winslow had ordered the chain to be concealed beneath wooden planking which followed the contours of the ship so as to be completely invisible unless inspected from close up. The *Kearsage* had in effect been converted into an Ironclad and it was this that was to prove the downfall of Captain Semmes. It is said that Semmes would never have fought the *Kearsage* had he known of "the cheat" as he later called it but he was warned of the chain curtain days before the fight by French officials. The reasons Semmes went ahead with the fight were two-fold; by the time he knew of the chains it was too late to withdraw without accusations of cowardice and more pragmatically, Semmes realized that he needed to beat the *Kearsage* and be on his way before the inevitable squadron of Northern warships turned up and sealed the fate of the *Alabama*. He really had no choice in the matter.

There was then a sense of inevitability when on the Sunday of the 19th of June 1864, escorted by the French Ironclad *Couronne*, the *Alabama* sailed out into the Channel to take part in a sea-battle to be fought in the old-style - a duel of cannonades between two equally matched opponents (or so Semmes thought), a scenario which would not have been unfamiliar to Drake or Raleigh. Lining the shore were hundreds of expectant sightseers from miles around - some from as far away as Paris. Out at sea were a number of curious boats including French pilot boats and the English steam yacht the *Deerhound*. The *Deerhound* was privately owned by a Mr John Lancaster who had only decided to take to sea at the last minute after a heated family discussion concerning the propriety of watching a battle on the Sabbath as opposed to attending church. Lancaster's sons won the day and it turned out to be quite fortuitous for the crew of the *Alabama*. The *Kearsage* stood 6 or 7 miles out to sea and in the three quarters of an hour it took to reach his opponent Captain Semmes gave his instructions for the forthcoming fight. The orders were detailed and complex but the crew of the *Alabama* knew them well and carried them out efficiently; the yards slung in chains, stoppers prepared for the rigging, magazine and shell rooms opened, decks sanded, water tubs filled and so on in a well-drilled operation that was routine for the sailors. What was not routine was the speech that Captain Semmes was about to give for the first time since the ship's commissioning and standing on a gun carriage Semmes addressed the crew in a rousing speech which glorified their past achievements and roused them to new glories. The address was given in utter silence and ended in rousing cheers.

The Sea Battle

The first shots fired were solid shot from the *Alabama* at one mile distance, swiftly returned by the *Kearsage* as the two ships circled around a common centre. The deadly dance was in order to maintain respective broadsides and the *Alabama* was deftly handled to fire shot after shot into the *Kearsage*. Captain Semmes expertly positioned the ship and his gunners responded accordingly with accurate fire into the sides of the *Kearsage* - each one of which failed to explode and fell into the sea. After 15 minutes in which the impotence of the *Alabama* was only too apparent, Semmes ordered a change to shell fire with very little difference and the *Alabama* began to suffer damage from the seemingly impervious *Kearsage*. Semmes' report stated:

"The firing now became very hot and the enemy's shot and shell soon began to tell upon our hull, knocking down, killing and disabling a number of men at the same time in different parts of the ship."

Xanthus Smith (1839-1929) painting of the duel.

In desperation, Semmes ordered a return to solid shot and from then on the *Alabama*'s gunners fired a continuous cannonade alternating between shot and shell.

Broadside after broadside struck the *Kearsage* with nothing to show but complete frustration among the *Alabama's* gunners and as the two ships circled closer, the 11 inch guns of the *Kearsage* caused more carnage on the deck of the *Alabama*. Kell later painted a graphic picture of the death and destruction among the crew, relating the coolness under fire of the young Midshipman, the heroism of a seaman who threw a spinning shell overboard and the steadfastness of Surgeon Llewellyn.

At one point they were forced to heave "the mangled trunks of the dead overboard in order to man the pivot gun." As the uneven contest continued, the circle grew ever closer giving the guns of the *Kearsage* even more of an advantage and after 1 hour and 10 minutes Kell went below to see the extent of the damage and immediately reported that the ship was sinking fast. Semmes reluctantly ordered a cease fire and the youngest officer aboard, the 22 year old Irvine Bulloch fired the final shots before the *Alabama's* colours were struck.

Rescue

With no guns firing and the colours struck and the ship listing badly all hands required no further encouragement to abandon ship. They had fought a good fight but were forced to bow to the inevitable. All but the dead on deck made it into the sea and as they clung to wreckage and cartridge boxes they saw the *Alabama* settle stern foremost and enter into her watery grave. Even in mid-summer the Channel is freezing cold and many died as they awaited rescue - Kell's words were: "Many poor fellows died of lack of timely aid." After twenty minutes or so, the French pilot boats began to pull men from the water and soon after the *Deerhound* steamed up and managed to rescue 40 or so men, including Semmes and Kell. Two boats from the *Kearsage* turned up belatedly. Kell was distressed to watch the deaths of several men he knew well, in particular Surgeon Llewellyn who died in the sea "so near to home" while Semmes's faithful servant Bartelli drowned, telling nobody that he was unable to swim, until it was too late. David White was another casualty unable to swim. John Lancaster finally gave Captain Semmes the news that everyone had been picked up and asked where he could take them. Semmes was exhausted from his ordeal but he was lucid enough to realize that he was "under English colours" and asked to be taken to Southampton (as a neutral, Lancaster was not obliged to hand over any of his rescued.)

Postscript

Semmes was feted in the drawing rooms of England and one female admirer presented him with a massive silken Confederate flag. He was also presented with a gold-mounted sword by officers of the Royal Navy to replace the one he had thrown into the Channel in order that it was not taken as a trophy.

Both Semmes and Kell were forced to revise their opinions of the Liverpool crew they had taken aboard two years previously and report after report has nothing but praise for their courage and proficiency.

Semmes lamented the loss of the fine painting of the Alabama which had been hung on the wall of his quarters. He had taken the precaution before the fight of leaving his collection of 75 chronometers in safekeeping - they were trophies from every ship that the Alabama had taken along with others from Semmes's days aboard the CSS Sumter. The chronometers were later taken to Liverpool aboard the Hornet and sold. Sometime afterwards, the officers of the Alabama received sealed envelopes each with a share of the money received in the sale - it was the only prize-money ever paid from the Alabama.

There were fifteen black crew members aboard the Kearsage during the battle. One of them was the gunner of the Dahlgren 11 inch cannon which did so much damage and he was awarded the Naval Medal of Honor for his courage that day.

Aftermath

Both Semmes and Kell wrote detailed reports of the action from beginning to end and although they differ in style, they are identical in content. They both begin by accurately reporting the loss of 9 crew members killed, 20 wounded and 12 drowned but Semmes's account then somewhat understandably becomes bitter, cynical and sarcastic in turns as he describes each event. His greatest complaint is the hidden chain each side of the *Kearsage* and he is scathing at what he calls *"the cheat"* perpetrated on his ship; it was, as he pointed out an unfair fight which he would never have engaged in had he known and would have won easily if the chains had not been in place. He returns to this theme several times stating that over 30 shells hit the *Kearsage* to no avail. He is particularly bitter of one shell in particular which was taken as a trophy by the *Kearsage* and has since become famous - a rifled percussion shell was one of the very few which hit an unprotected part of the ship and struck the *Kearsage*'s stern post where the cap failed to explode. Semmes's statement on the subject says it all; *"If the cap had performed its duty and exploded the shell I should have been called upon to save Captain Winslow's crew from drowning instead of his being called on to save mine. On so slight an incident - the defect of a percussion cap - did the battle hinge. The enemy were very proud of this shell - IT WAS THE ONLY TROPHY THEY EVER GOT OFF THE Alabama!"*. His bitterness echoes down the years.

The unexploded shell in Annapolis Naval Academy

The shell was found stuck in the woodwork of the *Kearsage* and later presented to President Lincoln and was then housed in the Naval Academy at Annapolis. Semmes's rage was not confined to the Gods of War and defective percussion caps - he reserved a withering condemnation of Captain Winslow's tardiness in sending ships to the rescue and accused him of firing upon the *Alabama* 5 times after she had struck her colours in which he went into great detail concerning the timing of the final shot and the lowering of the flag.

Kell's report was a more balanced and philosophical account of the events but even so it did state exactly the same things. Kell praised the accuracy and proficiency of the gunnery of the *Kearsage* thus damning them even more when he also said that they fired 5 times after the *Alabama* struck. Kell was also scornful of the rescue boats sent by the *Kearsage* and stated unequivocally that if it had not been for the French pilot boats and the *Deerhound* then many more men would have drowned.

John Lancaster was of the same opinion and in a letter to the London Daily News his words were: *"Not one half of the crew of the Alabama would have been saved if their safety depended upon Captain Winslow".*

But no matter how many recriminations were levelled Captain Winslow's way, the fact remained that the odyssey of the *Alabama* was over. It had been a fine run while it lasted and as the adventure was ending the legend was just beginning.

Casualties

At the conclusion of the battle between the *Alabama* and the *Kearsage* the casualties were summarised as:

9 men killed - most of them manning the gun.
20 men wounded including Captain Semmes.
12 men drowned.

Kell

Kell was universally acknowledged as the finest Lieutenant that Semmes could ever have had and in their time on the cruise of the *Alabama* had exhibited wisdom and seamanship and fidelity of the highest order. Semmes owed a great deal to Kell but never so much as in the final hours of the *Alabama*. Semmes was wounded in the arm and exhausted as they awaited rescue in the freezing waters of the Channel and it was to Kell that Semmes owed his life, keeping him afloat until they were pulled into the *Deerhound's* boat. It was not just his life that he owed to Kell but also his liberty when Kell suggested to his Captain that he lay concealed in the bottom of the boat as the boats of the *Kearsage* looked for him; Kell pretended to be a *Deerhound* crew member and shouted that Semmes had drowned.

Surgeon David Herbert Llewellyn was one of the most popular men aboard ship and it was a great tragedy when he sank below the surface as a boat was pulling to his rescue. He was much lamented not only by his ship-mates but also his colleagues in London. They later erected a bust in his memory which stood for many years in the courtyard of the old Charing Cross Hospital until the building was demolished, circa 1965, and the memorial was lost.

The South Will Rise Again

At the end of his report, Lt Kell had drawn a map of the battle, tracing the course of the *Alabama* from when she left harbour at Cherbourg to the final conclusion. There is a dotted line showing the *Alabama* sailing out to meet the *Kearsage*, clearly marked as 7 miles out, then follows a line of 7 circles showing the course of the battle which work out to a distance of 4 miles and then a tiny drawing of the *Alabama* illustrates where she went down "in 45 fathoms". Another tiny boat approaching the *Alabama* is the *Deerhound*. The map has a freshness about it and is reminiscent of something a schoolboy might have produced using compass and ruler.

Kell's map was an almost stylised version of the battle but nevertheless it gave a good idea of what took place and where and an approximation of the *Alabama's* final resting place. By present standards it was nowhere near detailed enough to pinpoint the exact location and for well over a century the wreck lay 200 feet down, battered and torn by the turbulent waters of the Channel. There were never any serious attempts to locate the wreck and it may never have been found but for the French navy's custom of using the site as a training ground and after decades of trawling the area in which ships must have passed over the ship many times, in 1984, the French minesweeper *Circe* stumbled on the wreck of the *Alabama*. It was 7 miles off shore - just where Kell's map said it was.

There was great excitement when the news that the *Alabama* had been found was proclaimed to the world and the prospect of raising her from the depths was the main subject in the press - after all the *Mary Rose* had been resurrected and she was 300 years older. The *Liverpool Echo* confidently predicted that the *Alabama* would be raised from her watery grave and stimulated reader's imaginations with extravagant visions of an immaculately restored *Alabama* as the pride of the newly restored Albert Dock. The Americans were not without some claim to the ship - it was of course American owned - while the French had not only re-discovered the ship but it was also within French territorial waters. The people of Cherbourg also held a sentimental affinity to the *Alabama* as it was its last port of call. The whole affair threatened to become a diplomatic tug-of-war until it died down as quickly as it had arisen when it was found to be out of the question to raise the *Alabama*. For a start, after 120 years of buffeting by the Channel tides, there was very little left of the wooden structure and what remained was mainly metal artefacts scattered about the ocean bed. The location of these artefacts changed on a daily basis according to the whims of the currents. Furthermore, such were the hazards of the cold and treacherous Channel tides that the window of opportunity for diving was a paltry three weeks in early summer and even then dives of a very short duration. Nevertheless, the Joint French and American Scientific Committee for the *CSS Alabama* was formed comprising a dedicated team of divers, archaeologists and historians who worked on the difficult task for the following four years. The results were a harvest of valuable artefacts to be shared between America and France where they would be restored and retained. There were oil-lamps, cutlery, thimbles, coins, decorative flush-toilets and so many other artefacts telling of life aboard any ship of the era but perhaps the most poignant of all of them was the gun.

The three-ton Blakely cannon was the largest of all the items to be raised and it was found to be still loaded and ready to fire - still proclaiming Southern defiance to the world after all these years. The cannon can be found in Cherbourg museum and in the Cherbourg cemetery there is a monument to the dead of the *Alabama* and several graves of those who lost their lives.

Postscript

Edouard Manet travelled from Paris to see the fight between the Alabama and the Kearsage. The forthcoming battle had been an open secret for weeks throughout northern France and people travelled for miles around to see it. Thousands flocked to the seafront at Cherbourg which was indicative of just how famous the Alabama had become. In the event, the battle took place six miles out in the Channel which must have left those without telescopes seeing very little at all. Manet was reputed to have taken out a small boat in order to get a better view.

The painting is a colourful and striking interpretation which is unusual in that unlike many other pictures of the event, it places the battle secondary to the small boat racing to the rescue in the foreground. The painting was the first historical event that Manet ever painted and he only worked on very few after that, notably The Execution of the Emperor Maximilian.

Liverpool Maritime Museum contains a painting of the *Alabama* and a small model of the ship in a glass case. Within the case is a signet ring which belonged to Robert Hobbs, quartermaster on the *Alabama* since she was first commissioned. Liverpool born, Hobbs was wounded in the final battle between the *Alabama* and the *Kearsage*.

The ring has the inscription; *Hobbs R. Enrica. Laird xx 111 Lx11.* It was purchased by the Museum in 1995 and the vendor's father won the ring in a card game in the 1920s.

As romantic as this story is, there is another version which is a little more prosaic but has more than a ring of truth to it (no pun intended). It appears that the R.Hobbs in question is a different person altogether from the Liverpool Hobbs and refers to Russell Baker Hobbs of Delaware. R.B. Hobbs signed on the *Alabama* in South Africa and absconded when the ship was in port at Singapore. He was found by crew members of the *Alabama* who dragged him to face a vengeful Raphael Semmes who reduced him to the ranks. Hobbs had regained his former position by the time the *Alabama* faced the *Kearsage* and he was subsequently captured and brought aboard the *Kearsage* where he was paroled by Captain Winslow.

Hobb's brass ring

All of the crew of the *Alabama* lost their possessions when the ship went down and Hobbs was no exception which meant that he must cross the Channel to reach Southampton first of all, possibly working his passage or possibly via a sympathetic ship's captain. Once in Southampton, he needed to get to Liverpool and the offices of Fraser, Trenholm in order to receive his pay and it is probable that it is at this juncture that he sold his ring. Given the publicity attached to the sinking of the *Alabama*, Hobbs would have received a reasonable sum although the ring was only brass and it was this money that enabled him to travel to Liverpool where Fraser, Trenholm maintained their impeccable reputation and paid his back-pay. The Gothic lines of the Sailor's Home would have no doubt sheltered Hobbs for several nights until he booked passage for New York and his first purchase was a local newspaper detailing the dead and wounded of the *Alabama*. From New York, he boarded a train for Delaware and would have been excused for thinking he was home and dry. But Hobbs was never a man to accompany on any clandestine affair, and at Dover station Hobbs once again found himself in the custody of those he least wished to see. On this occasion, the members of the Provost Marshal's office had caught up with him and despite his document signed by Captain Winslow detailing his allegiance to the North, his newspaper with his name on the *Alabama's* list damned him. Hobbs was sentenced to one year and one day in jail and on his release he took work as a painter and decorator. Hobbs was unfortunate in being one of only a very few who were punished for his alleged crimes and it was even more ironic in that he was never a Confederate loyalist and had never been to the South - his service aboard the *Alabama* was simply as a mercenary with no affiliation to anything but his own cause.

Russell Baker Hobbs died in 1906. As for the ring, it seems reasonable to assume that it could have been lost in a card game - but by the person who purchased it from Hobbs.

There is also a tiny anchor made from a brass fitting from the engine room of the *Alabama*. It was made by a Mr A. H. Smith of Patterson, New Jersey in 1881. He sent it to a relative, Mrs Elizabeth Smith of Fenwick Street, Liverpool who was a "painter of gas and lamp globes and shades."

The first photographic record of any conflict is the Crimean War just a few years before the American Civil War.

There are several photographs of ships during the Civil War but by far the best record are the numerous sketches and drawings by American and British artists. Many of the sketches of ships in the Mersey are contemporary engravings by William Woods of Everton whose main patron was The *Illustrated London News.*

The sketch below illustrates the great Dahlgren cannon which damaged the *Alabama* to such a degree.

Although the sketches are drawn from imagination based on accounts from survivors, many of them are works of art in their own right and they portray events better than photographs in many instances.

The sketch is not as colourful as the Manet interpretation but it is certainly more evocative of the battle.

Alabama sinking

THE FLORIDA

THE CSS FLORIDA - 1ST CRUISE

"Instead of the cross an albatross about my neck was hung....."

The trials and tribulations of the first Confederate raider

As idle as a painted ship upon a painted ocean...

Despite having an almost identical beginning to her career, the *Florida* never achieved the famous (or infamous, depending on where you stand) victories or enjoyed the same cachet as her sister ship, the *Alabama*. The *Florida* was dogged by bad luck, misfortune and tragedy right from the outset and just when she was thought to have overcome them all, she was struck down one last time by the heavy hand of fate. Given the amount of difficulties the *Florida* was forced to surmount, her achievements were quite remarkable. Some of her misfortune can be attributed to her construction and size which never allowed her the firepower or the sailing stamina of an *Alabama*. Bulloch had tried to apply his own specification to the ship but the original model was to the design of a British naval warship much smaller than the *Alabama* and no matter what modifications were applied they were never enough. The armament was not big enough and the coal bunkers, although relatively large were too small to keep her at sea for more than three weeks at a time which meant that she left a trail of ports she had entered and was easily traced by Northern shipping.

Much of the success of the *Alabama* was down to an ability to roam the seas for months on end and pop up unexpectedly and disappear just as quickly. Although it is an axiom that "you make your own luck" in the case of the *Florida* there is no doubt that in the main her problems were brought about by sheer bad luck. Although it would be easy to lay the blame at the captain's door as Mallory soon did, the fact is that Captain Maffitt was nothing less than an extremely conscientious, courageous and efficient officer.

John Newland Maffitt, a native of North Carolina and the son of an Irish Methodist minister appropriately entered the world aboard ship in mid-Atlantic in the year 1818, as his parents were emigrating to North America. His naval background was very much the same as Bulloch's and Semmes's in that he served his time as a midshipman and built a reputation for being an audacious and imaginative officer. His knowledge of the North American coastline was encyclopaedic and his credentials for captaining a blockade-runner were impeccable.

The *Florida*'s difficulties began even as she was being built in Miller's shipyard as the *Oreto* and Dudley's agents were swarming all over the waterfront. The pressure from the American Embassy became so insistent that the ship was forced to leave hastily for fear of being impounded and Captain James A. Duguid sailed for Nassau on the 22nd March, 1862 with a crew of 52 seamen recruited from the Liverpool waterfront. The ever trusty John Low was aboard carrying instructions from Bulloch for her new Captain, John Newland Maffitt. On the other side of the country, the *Bahama* received a telegram to sail from Hartlepool at the same time, loaded up with armament and supplies to be transferred to the *Oreto* in Nassau.

The *Oreto* arrived in Nassau on April 28th 1862 and Maffitt took command on the 13th of May - a date which the notoriously superstitious sailors might have considered ominous. The pressure from the United States Embassy followed the *Oreto* to Nassau and the transfer of materials was halted by U.S. Consulate officials who demanded the ship's seizure by British officials. Just to add to her woes, the officers of the *Oreto* had neglected to inform the crew that they would be serving the Confederacy and many of the seamen objected to the deceitful manner in which they had been recruited. As a result of the consulate's strenuous complaints, the British officials were forced to take action and at last impounded the ship, releasing her two days later because she was not armed. The weeks were slipping by, and it was in the latter part of the month of June before the decision was taken to transfer the guns and stores to a ship called the *Prince Alfred* which then sailed to a deserted island 60 miles off Nassau. The stores and guns were finally off-loaded from the *Prince Alfred* and the *Oreto* was finally fitted out and commissioned as the *CSS Florida*; another month had slipped by and it was now 17th August, 1862. It was hardly an auspicious beginning but things were about to get worse.

At length did cross an albatross....

At a time when Maffitt might have justifiably felt that his troubles were now behind him and the *Florida* could begin her work as a Confederate raider, just five days after Nassau, the dreaded Yellowfever swept through the ship like wildfire. Yellowfever was endemic throughout the Indies and South America; a viral disease spread by mosquitos which killed within five days or at best left the victim drained for months with a sickly pallor which gave the disease its name. There was no known cure in those days. Maffit's steward was struck down and died almost immediately and one by one the remainder of the crew went down like skittles, most dying and odd ones here and there surviving by luck alone. Maffitt made the decision to make for Cardenas in Cuba to seek whatever medical aid was available, completely ignorant of an epidemic of the same disease that was sweeping the country. By the time they reached Cardenas, the ship was being crewed by five fit men.

Laurens Read was one of the crew to lose his life. Laurens was the 16 year old step-son of Maffitt.

Another possibly even more poignant tragedy was that of Lieutenant J.M. Stribling who had accompanied the arms and stores from England aboard the *Bahama*. Stribling was due to return home to his young and beautiful wife when he made the fateful decision to volunteer for service with Maffitt aboard the *Florida*. Stribling had sailed with Semmes in his days aboard the *CSS Sumter* and came extremely highly regarded - it was his sense of duty that led him to disaster as he also succumbed to the fatal fever. Lt Stribling fought hard to survive the illness but sadly died on 12th September. Maffitt, perhaps mercifully, was in no condition to know these things as he also was struck down. Unable to leave his cabin for days on end, he was near to death's door when he opened his eyes and proclaimed courageously; *"I have no time to die, there is too much to do."* Between August 17th and August 31st the crew of the *Florida* were scythed down by an unrelenting grim reaper until the deadly disease finally passed over leaving a stunned and silent ship at anchor.

The ship drove fast, loud roared the blast, the southward aye we fled....

It wasn't until September 1st that Maffit had recovered enough to stagger from his sick bed and climb on deck once again. It is a matter of conjecture how he felt when he surveyed his shattered realm with just a few surviving seamen going about their work like wraiths and the miasma of death lingering throughout the planking but he must have been heartsick, to say the least. It is a measure of the man's courage that he made plans to begin once again where many a man would have given up there and then. Maffit decided that his first priority was to refit his ship and obtain replacements for his depleted crew and to this end he made for Mobile - but fate hadn't finished with the *Florida* just yet and more hammer blows awaited the doom-laden ship.

On September 4th, 1862, the *Florida* approached Fort Morgan and true to form, she was faced with not one Northern warship but three between her and the coast. Hosting English colours, the *Florida* boldly sailed straight for her objective only to be ordered to stop by the *USS Oneida.* Ignoring the imperative, the *Florida* hoisted the Stars and Bars and throwing caution to the wind headed straight onward. She was immediately attacked by the *Oneida*, the *Winona* and the *Seaman*, all three firing round after round at the fleeing ship, some of them broadsides from as near as several yards away. Maffitt was unable to fire back as he hadn't enough crew to sail the ship and man the guns at the same time and so for a hazardous two hours the *Florida* was subjected to withering blasts from all sides, any of which had the capacity to cripple her. One shot went straight through the ship, beheading a seamen as it passed and emerging on the other side without exploding. Eventually, the trial by fire was ended and the *Florida* limped into harbour with several men dead, others wounded and her masts shot to pieces.

After running the gauntlet of Northern guns and the *Florida* safely at anchor, bloodied but unbowed, there was a strange sequel to the *Florida*'s miraculous escape; the captain of the *Oneida*, Commander Preble, was dismissed for allowing his prey to escape, only to be reinstated shortly afterwards. Preble was one of Maffitt's oldest friends and the incident is another reminder that the Civil War set brother against brother. But there was more to come when Maffitt himself was dismissed by an irritable Steven R. Mallory who, ignoring the fact that she had just humiliated three Northern warships, was understandably impatient to hear some good luck attached to the *Florida*. Maffit's dismissal was taken a step further than Preble's when a new captain of the *Florida*, Lt. Joseph N. Barney, was appointed but stood down when the order was rescinded at the last minute. There were narrow escapes to be found in all quarters that autumn.

The ship was cheered, the harbour cleared....

Repairs to the *Florida* began in October, 1862, and took longer than normal due to the wartime conditions prevailing and it was not until January, 1863 that the ship was once again ready to go to sea. A crew had been recruited and Maffit knowing many of them previously, was scathing of some and complimentary of others. Nevertheless, the *Florida* sailed out of Mobile on January, 10th 1863 with flags flying and hopes high only to run aground on a sandbank straight out of port. Having unloaded her guns to lighten ship she was towed free and the guns laboriously hoisted back on deck. Maffitt must have thought the *Florida* would never get to sea when to his embarrassment the ship ran aground again and the whole process had to be repeated. The squadron of Northern warships prowling outside the harbour must have been a daunting prospect for Maffitt, recalling the pounding his ship had taken just a few months earlier but for the first time in her career, the *Florida* came out of a situation unscathed and sailed off into the Atlantic having eluded a total of twelve Northern ships in a boisterous chase which lasted well into the night.

Painting of the Florida

The *Florida* had left the Mersey on March 22nd, 1862, and it was January 10th, 1863, when she left Mobile. There was little wonder that Mallory was fretting, as the intervening 10 months had been little but a catalogue of disasters and it was to Maffits's credit that he was still at the helm, defiantly proceeding to salvage some of the *Florida*'s pride after a series of blows which would have finished a lesser man. But the *Florida* was under full sail and it was time to show her mettle at last.

On January 12th, the *Florida* captured her first ship, the brig *Arabella* and on surrendering to her guns, the yankee ship was promptly burnt and the crew taken on board the *Florida*. On January 19th, the *Estelle* was taken and at the same time Maffitt was forced to seek a port for refilling her depleted coal bunkers after just seven days at sea. This was a problem that the *Alabama* was never subject to and it would be a constant thorn in the side to the captain of the *Florida*. On this occasion, Maffitt made for Havana where the local U.S. consul tried to detain the ship and Maffitt sailed as quickly as he could but he had left a trail. Worse still, he found that the coal was of such poor quality that it needed to be replaced and Maffitt was forced to sail for Nassau. But the *Florida* was at last running into some good fortune and just four miles outside Havana he captured the *Windward*, allowing the crew to row to shore while the ship was burnt. The same afternoon, the *Corris Ann* was taken and both captains complained that they had been deceived by the *Florida*'s English colours. Once in Nassau, 26 crew members deserted which would have been unfortunate if Maffitt had not had the luck to find six new recruits who he said were worth all of the others put together.

Once more at sea, on February 1st, Maffitt came across what he believed to be the sidewheel war steamer, *Santiago de Cuba* which was too well armed for the *Florida* to attack with any confidence. Maffitt took two days to escape his pursuer and was later full of chagrin when he discovered that his opponent was the *Sonoma* which he was certain to have beaten in battle. But the *Florida*'s luck was holding when just four days later, the formidable federal cruiser *Vanderbilt* made an appearance, circled the *Florida* several times and sailed away. The *Vanderbilt* had been searching for the *Florida* and it was an occasion when Bulloch's foresight had saved the day as the two hinged funnels he had insisted on came into use and altered the *Florida*'s appearance enough to fool the Federal warship.

The following nine months were an unqualified success for the *Florida* as she criss-crossed the Atlantic sea-lanes capturing on average one ship per week. Nearly every ship complained that the *Florida* had fooled them by flying the

English flag and nearly all of them were taken aboard the *Florida* while their ships burned. Several of the captured seamen signed on the *Florida* and those who did not remained in chains until a passing ship agreed to take them on board. Most of the ships who took the stranded crews were British adding fuel to the rumours that the British were complicit in the Confederate larceny on the high seas.

On the 12th February 1863, the *Florida* captured her greatest ever prize when the *Jacob Bell* surrendered and was promptly plundered and burned. Her cargo alone which was tea and firecrackers from China to New York was worth $1.5 million dollars.

On March 6th, the clipper ship *Star of Peace* was captured, on March 12th it was the *Aldebaran* and on March 28th, the *Lapwing* was captured with Maffitt delighted to find her bunkers full of coal which he transferred to the *Florida.* On this occasion, Maffitt decided that the *Lapwing* would be more useful as a tender and he put Lt. Averett aboard with 15 men with orders to harass enemy shipping and keep the *Florida* supplied with coal. The plan sounded good in theory but the *Lapwing* was too slow to cause enemy shipping a problem and she could never keep up with the *Florida*, regularly missing rendezvous points. Her ineffectiveness sealed her fate when she was burnt at Barbados and the crew made their way to Brest to meet up with the *Florida.*

The *Florida* continued adding to her tally of captured ships throughout the summer months of 1863 with cruises along known shipping lanes interspersed with trips to re-coal. Every ship captured went some way to restoring the *Florida*'s credibility and the political repercussions and newspaper headlines must have been quite edifying for Captain Maffitt. The *Oneida* was captured in April, the *Crown Point* in May, the *Benjamin F. Hoxie* in June and in another attempt to solve his problem of having to seek ports where he could fill his coal bunkers Maffitt captured two other ships which he converted into tenders cum cruisers, the *Tacony* and the *Clarence*. Both ships were reasonably successful, managing to capture 22 ships between them. The *Clarence* was the first tender to be captured and finding the *Tacony* more

Sketch of the burning Jacob Bell

suited to his purpose, Maffitt summarily burnt the *Clarence* and transferred her crew and armament to the *Tacony*. On June the 25th, 1863, the *Archer* was taken which meant the end for the *Tacony* and the *Archer* went on to more destruction. Lieutenant C.W. Read made a name for himself aboard the *Archer* with a daring raid on the harbour at Portland, quietly sailing in and coolly destroying the United States revenue cutter, *Caleb Cushing*. Flushed with success, Read made plans to do the same in New York harbour but was unable to locate a River Pilot to guide him through Hell's Gate. And so it went on until late August when Maffitt decided that the *Florida* required a total refit and made the decision to head for Brest harbour where he could lay up for repairs. Two days out of Brest harbour, the *Florida* encountered the *Anglo Saxon*, out of New York and burned her in the English Channel before proceeding onto Brest. Maffitt had also taken the decision that as far as the *Florida* was concerned, his sailing days were over. The stresses of the last eighteen months had taken their toll on Maffitt and the attack of yellow fever had exacerbated an existing heart condition causing him to write to Commander M.F. Maury in Paris to ask to be relieved of his command. Maury sent him a complimentary letter and accepted Maffit's resignation. The final six months of the *Florida*'s chequered career had gone a long way to making up for her previous misfortune with a total of forty seven prizes taken by the *Florida* and her satellite ships; Maffitt finally stood down with his reputation intact and the *Florida* redeemed. John Newland Maffitt eventually travelled to Liverpool where he sat his examinations for commercial shipping master in British waters. He eventually captained several blockade-runners. Like Dunwoody Bulloch, he was afraid that he would be brought to trial if he returned to the United States.

THE FLORIDA

THE CSS FLORIDA - 2ND CRUISE

"At length did cross an Albatross, through the fog it came...."

The continuing trials and tribulations of the first Confederate raider

Captain Charles Manigault Morris

As idle as a painted ship......

Nothing ever came easy where the *Florida* was concerned and so it proved with her refit in Brest harbour which was estimated to take four to five weeks. As things turned out, she entered Brest on August 23rd, 1863 and did not emerge until February, 1864 - nearly six months inactivity once again. The delays all hinged upon the ship having been built in a British shipyard and spare parts of necessity were required to be sent from England with all the time and money that entailed. Not only were the parts required to be English, it was found that the engineers also needed to be from England also, as the French fitters were unfamiliar with the machinery. The difficulties sent the cost of the refit spiralling and one of Maffitt's last orders before he stood down was to discharge fifty-nine crew members in an attempt to cut costs. On the face of it, the order seemed perfectly logical as the men were standing idle for months on end and still being paid but the ramifications of the decision became more far reaching than anyone could have imagined. He was not to know it, but Maffitt had inadvertently left the incumbent Captain of the *Florida* with a major headache instead of the smooth transition he might have expected.

Maffitt was ordered to hand over his command to none other than Commander Joseph. N. Barney who had come close to taking over on a previous occasion. Commander Barney was fated never to take the *Florida* to sea and after taking over the ship in September, 1863 and supervising most of the repairs he fell ill with chronic dyspepsia occasioned by life aboard ship and the poor diet which puts into perspective just how tenacious her previous Captain had been. On January 9th, 1864, the unfortunate Barney was forced to relinquish his post and Lieutenant Charles Manigault Morris took charge of the *Florida*. Morris was a native of South Carolina and like Bulloch had resigned his commission in the United States navy on the outbreak of war. He had been designated as a Captain on one of the ill-fated Laird Rams and was fortunate to be on hand at just the right time.

Captain Morris's first task was to find a crew to replace those who had been dismissed six months previously which proved to be far more difficult than recruiting in a British port and he ended up with a mixed bag of Europeans with little experience and virtually unskilled. This later led to conflicts with the existing crew who resented having to pass their expertise on to nationalities with no loyalty to the Confederate cause and were perceived to be little more than mercenaries.

There was another unexpected sequel to Maffitt's final order; understandably piqued at their seemingly off-hand dismissal the fifty-nine crew members were even more incensed when they had difficulty obtaining their pay. Maffitt had given each man a promissory note to be presented to James Dunwoody Bulloch in Liverpool which would result in their wages being paid. Unfortunately, Bulloch was out of the city when the sailors came calling and their simmering resentment promptly turned into an aggrieved anger which saw them marching straight to the United States Consulate and into the welcoming arms of Thomas Haines Dudley.

CSS Florida

The wily Dudley while paying lip-service to these poor stranded mariners was secretly delighted and requested a signed grievance which he would do his very best to deal with. The sailors, once so loyal to the Confederate cause, then wrote an account of their grievance and each one undersigned the document. As soon as the men had left his office Dudley contacted Charles F. Adams to pass onto him the names of a substantial number of the crew of the *Florida*, many of whom were the original crewmen from Liverpool. Adams of course was not slow to approach Lord Russell with indisputable proof that British seamen were fighting for the Confederacy and the incident turned out to be a major embarrassment for the British government. Some of the crewmen may have been just a little chastened when Bulloch returned and paid them their money as agreed without demur.

Destruction of *Jacob Bell.*

The helmsman steered, the ship moved on.....

In a situation prescient of the forthcoming duel with the *Alabama* (June 1864) Captain Winslow's *Kearsage* hovered around Brest awaiting the departure of the *Florida*. The *Kearsage* was forced to keep cruising up and down the coast as there were three channels leading out of Brest harbour and the *Florida* could have taken any one of them. Captain Winslow was as frustrated as Captain Morris at the *Florida*'s inactivity and at one point he challenged the *Florida* to come out and fight. These were exactly the same tactics he would use against the *Alabama* but unlike Raphael Semmes, Captain Morris refused to take the bait and stayed in port which was probably a wise decision in regard to the subsequent fate of the *Alabama* which was a much larger ship. The news-sheets made much of Southern honour being maligned and so forth but there's little doubt that the *Florida* would have stood no chance against the *Kearsage* especially with a Captain who had never yet sailed his ship. For months on end the *Kearsage* stood outside Brest until on February 10th she was ordered to Cadiz and the *Florida* left Brest and headed out to sea while the opportunity was there.

Morris wisely used the first few weeks to get used to his ship and train his crew. As Captain Maffitt had found before him, the *Florida* required frequent re-coaling and the *Florida* was out at sea only three weeks before she called into port to re-coal. It was March 29th, 1864 before the *Florida* captured her first prize, the *Avon*, which was subsequently looted and then used as target practice. On May 18th the *George Latimer* was captured followed by the *W.C.Clark* and on July 8th, the *Golconda*. As the *Florida* cruised into regularly used shipping lanes her prizes increased accordingly and on July 9th the *Margaret Y Davis* and *Greenland* were caught on the same day while the following day was even more bountiful when four ships were caught on the same day - on July 10th, at 3 a.m, the *General Barry* was captured, followed quickly by the *Zelinda* and then the *Howard* which was bonded - all the ships were captured before 10.am proving a good morning's work in the waters outside Maryland. The 10th July turned out to one the finest days in the *Florida*'s history when Captain Morris captured a fourth ship in the afternoon; the *Electric Spark* was a brand new propeller steamer and Morris made plans to convert her into another Confederate cruiser. Unfortunately for Morris and the Confederacy he changed his plans when his First Engineer complained that one of his engineers had broken an ankle depleting an already short-staffed engine room. Morris was never the flexible and energetic Captain that Maffitt was or he would have sought ways and means to circumvent the problem and given the quality of the *Electric Spark* it should never have been burned but that is the order that was given and carried out.

The *Florida*'s resident Albatross made a fleeting appearance when Midshipman William B. Sinclair lost his life directing operations to transfer the money safe from the prize to the *Florida* - the longboat overturned and while his crew clung onto the boat awaiting rescue Sinclair bravely but unwisely decided to swim for the ship and was never seen again. There were rumours that a shark had been circling, but whatever the reason, a young and efficient officer had been lost, souring what had up till then been a day for celebration.

The *Florida* continued her cruise throughout August and September but there were never any more spectacular prizes and Morris was efficient without being inspirational. Late in August he decided to make for a neutral port in Brazil for repairs and re-coaling.

When Dunwoody Bulloch had commissioned his ships, he always tried to make provision for his cruisers to remain at sea for long periods of time hence his insistence upon a combination of steam and sail. A ship at sea for months at a time left no trail for Northern warships to follow neither did it allow for sightings in ports which attracted attention. The *Alabama's* ability to remain at sea for months at a time and appear unexpectedly earned her the name of "Ghost Ship" and was a contributory factor in her success but although Bulloch had specified large coal bunkers on the *Florida* also, in relative terms they were far smaller than the *Alabama's* capacity and in the final analysis, it was this that brought about her downfall.

The Albatross did follow.....

On October 4th, 1864, the *Florida* sailed into Bahia harbour on the Brazilian coast and straight under the scrutiny of the United States warship, *Wachusett*, commanded by Commander Napoleon Collins. Whether Captain Morris should have sailed right out again or whether he should never have trusted that the United States ship would observe Brazilian neutrality is open to debate but the fact remains that he anchored alongside an enemy warship and made little provision to defend his ship. Collins was naturally suspicious

The Florida pursuing the Star of Peace. (Century Magazine)

and sent across a small boat pretending to be from the British ship *Curlew* and ascertained that the ship was the *Florida*. Little happened in the next three days but the Americans, Confederates and the Brazilian authorities were aware of the potentially explosive situation and the Brazilian provincial President, da Silva Gomez approached both Morris and Collins seeking assurances that Brazilian neutrality would not be violated. As a further precaution, Gomez ordered the *Florida* moved so that the ships of the Brazilian navy were between the two protagonists

The following morning, on October 5th, the United States consul, Thomas F. Wilson, drew up alongside the *Florida* in person in a small boat to deliver a letter to Captain Morris. The letter did not acknowledge his proper title and as a result, Morris refused to open it. The following morning, the 6th October, Mr L deVideky came alongside as an emissary of Consul Wilson bringing another letter which was improperly addressed, referring to the sloop *Florida*, and Morris again refused to open the letter. Mr deVideky then told Captain Morris the contents of the letter which was quite simply a challenge to leave port and fight the *Wachusett* in open combat. Morris's reply was as follows;

"I would neither seek nor avoid a contest with the Wachusett but should I encounter her outside of Brazilian waters I would use my utmost endeavours to destroy her."

Consul Wilson was beside himself in his efforts to force a fight between the opposing ships and on receipt of Captain Morris's rather ambiguous reply, in conference with Napoleon Collins they both agreed that the *Florida* was faster and the only way to capture her was in port. However, Collins was adamant that he would take no part in violating Brazilian neutrality leaving Wilson to seek other methods of capturing the *Florida*. Wilson appeared to be obsessed with destroying the Confederate ship and he had no compunction in exceeding his remit when he employed the *Wachusett*'s paymaster and and the 1st Lieutenant in a venture all of his own making - how Napoleon Collins felt about the situation is not recorded. Wilson's idea was simple enough - to hire a tug and ram the *Florida* at anchor. The plan might well have worked but for the first tug being too small to be effective and the second broke down with machinery failure. Wilson was far from finished and after haranguing Collins once again, Collins was persuaded to convene all his officers to vote upon whether or not they should break International rules and attack the *Florida* in a neutral port. Every officer but one agreed to the plan and Collins reluctantly made plans to destroy his enemy. How he felt about having democratic elections upon vital and illegal plans aboard his own United States warship is open to question but there is little doubt that Collins was being railroaded into carrying out Consul Wilson's plans and not his own. At 3 a.m on the morning of the 7th October, the *Wachusett* quietly left her anchorage and slipped around to where the *Florida* stood at anchor. Steaming at full power, the warship headed straight for the *Florida* and rammed her at speed cutting down her bulwarks and main and mizzen masts. The damage was severe and the *Wachusett* backed off as pistol shots were exchanged, firing two broadsides as she went and giving the *Florida* an ultimatum of "Surrender or be blown out of the water!".

Captain Morris was ashore leaving Lieutenant T.K.Porter with the unenviable task of dealing with the unprecedented situation. His guns were not loaded and there was not enough men aboard to man them anyway leaving Porter no alternative but to surrender his sword, the ensign and the ship. Collins was far from happy with the result of his ship's action - he was confident that ramming the *Florida* at full speed would have sunk her leaving him to escape unencumbered - but the *Wachusett*'s anchor was still dragging as she aimed at the *Florida*. Collins blamed a Lieutenant Beardslee for the anchor and the broadsides but the matter was never taken any further. A hawser was attached to the crippled ship and she was being towed out to sea when an enraged Brazilian city (which was generally sympathetic to the Confederate cause) came to life like a horde of angry bees; the United States Consulate was attacked and the flag dragged through the town, the forts opened fire on the *Wachusett* and two ships of the Brazilian navy gave chase, later being out-distanced. Consul Wilson had taken the precaution of sailing away on the *Wachusett*, never to return. The *Wachusett* and *Florida* sailed side by side for a further twenty-three days, landing at St. Bartholemew in the West Indies. Lieutenant Beardslee was either incredibly incompetent or used as a scapegoat by Collins but as well as his previous reprimands he was also blamed for the *Florida* drifting twenty miles off her anchorage.

On November, 24th, 1864, the *Florida* had been escorted to the Northern shipping base of Virginia where she lay at anchor under the guns of the ironclad, *Atlanta*. The engineers had been dealing with a leak which became the focus of the subsequent investigation when the *Florida* suddenly sank in nine fathoms of water in the Hampton Roads. The investigation concluded that the *Florida* sank due to a leak and a failure of the pumps to deal with it. There were several factors which made this explanation both simplistic and suspicious; the leak was small and manageable until for no reason it suddenly increased, the pumps inexplicably failed just as the leak got worse and despite the area being awash with tugs none was available to help. And in circumstances which beggar belief, the cutter which could have towed her to safety was short of oars.

The political fallout from the attack in a neutral port and the "accidental" sinking of the *Florida* earned the north worldwide condemnation. European governments were scornful of the United States hypocrisy in light of her previous condemnation of the infractions of other countries, the Confederacy were of course outraged and the Brazilians were still raging that the deceit should have been carried out in Bahia. The Northern government rode out the storm, appeasing the Brazilians, making conciliatory gestures to the Europeans and dismissing Wilson who was the prime mover behind the whole affair. Commander Napoleon Collins (who must have wished he had never heard of Wilson) was brought before a court martial and subsequently found guilty and ordered to be dismissed. Gideon Welles, Secretary of the navy refused to accept the verdict and the punishment was never carried out.

Mr L deVideky who had delivered the ultimatum to Captain Morris was genuinely contrite about the way things had turned out and wrote to Morris to express his disgust for Consul Wilson and the manner in which he had been deceived.

An embarrassed Captain Morris complained in his report that when the *Wachusett* had rammed the *Florida* fifteen men jumped overboard to swim for safety and nine of them were shot down in the water as they swam.

Regardless of how many words were penned about the "hypocrisy", "deceit", "lawlessness" and so on and no matter how many diplomatic complaints were dispatched, the fact remained that the *Florida* had sunk and her career had come to an ignominious end. The United States government never stated it but their attitude could be summed up simply as " all's fair in love and war" and that's how the matter remained.

CSS Florida

Ships Captured by the Florida

First Cruise 1863	Capt, Maffit	Second Cruise 1864	Capt Morris	Clarence and Tacony
Date	Ship	Date	Ship	Ship
Jan 19	Estelle	Mar 29	Avon	*Clarence*
Jan 22	Windward	May 18	G. Latimer	Kate Dyer
Jan 22	Corris Ann	June 17	W.C.Clarke	Kate Stuart
Feb 12	Jacob Bell	July 1	Harriet Stevens	Mary Alvina
Mar 6	Star of Peace	July 8	Golconda	Mary Schindler
Mar 12	Aldabaran	July 9	M. Y Davis	Whistling Wind
Mar 28	Lapwing	July 9	Greenland	*Tacony*
Mar 30	M. J. Colcord	July 10	General Barry	Arabella
Apr 17	Commonwealth	July 10	Zelinda	Ada
Apr 23	Henrietta	July 10	Howard	Byzantian
Apr 25	Oneida	July 10	Electric Spark	Elizabeth Ann
May 6	Clarence	Aug 22	S'thern Rights	Goodspeed
May 14	Crown Point	Sept 26	Mandamis	L.A.Macomber
June 6	Southern Cross			Marengo
June 14	Red Gauntlet			Ripple
June 16	Ben. J. Hoxie			Rufus Choate
June 27	V.H. Hill			Umpire
July 7	Sunrise			*Archer*
July 8	W.B.Nash			Caleb Cushing
July 8	Rienzi			
Aug 6	F. B. Cutting			
Aug 6	Southern Rights			
Aug 21	Anglo Saxon			

N/B The *Clarence* transferred to *Tacony* which transferred to *Archer*.
The ships left behind were burnt.

The Ironclads and The Shenandoah

The continuing career of James Dunwoody Bulloch

One of the Laird Rams in harbour.

The Laird Rams

James Dunwoody Bulloch's demonstration of how to beat the Northern blockade while aboard the *Fingal*, not only delivered a cornucopia of military riches into the welcoming arms of the Southern armies but also sowed the seeds of the future direction in which naval operations would be heading. In a series of meetings with Stephen Mallory while waiting to return to Liverpool, it was impressed upon Bulloch the necessity for the South to take on the United States navy on its own terms and Mallory saw Ironclads as the answer. It was his firm belief that two Ironclads of superior design would not only shatter the supremacy of the U.S. ships but swing the balance of the war in favour of the Confederacy. It was clear that Mallory was a strategist of the highest order and he translated his plans concisely and emphatically to Bulloch while he had the chance - despatches and letters were no substitute for man to man talks. As Mallory saw it, the *Florida* and the *Alabama* would soon be wreaking havoc among the commercial shipping of the North, there were numerous blockade-runners already in place and dodging Northern ships on a regular basis and it was now time to attack the Yankee fleet itself. Mallory was well aware that the patrolling U.S. ships were not only carrying out blockade duties but far more importantly were supporting their troops on land with supplies and guns and when the opportunity arose with covering fire. Mallory could not stress enough that the Ironclads were *"of paramount importance"* - words which must have rung in Bulloch's ears all the way back to Liverpool. A measure of Mallory's impatience for his Ironclads was the fact that Lieutenant James H. North was already in Britain on a similar mission. His search for a shipyard to build an Ironclad had taken him to Glasgow where the so-called "Scottish Monster" was taking shape on the banks of the Clyde.

Bulloch returned to Liverpool in March, 1862, and found the spies and politics surrounding the construction of the *Florida* and the *Alabama* increasingly worse than when he had left and in anticipation of even more of the same he was moved to draft a letter to Mallory which was completely absent of any self-pity but proposed an alternative. Bulloch's letter proposed that the wooden sections of the Ironclads be constructed in a Southern port and the metal sections, numbered and shaped, along with the arms, be transported across the Atlantic and completed in the South. The scheme was innovative to say the least and Mallory declined to take up the proposal but in the light of future events he may have reflected that it had its merits and was achievable. Bulloch's first duty was to get the *Florida* and the *Alabama* out to sea but in between he approached Lairds about the Ironclads. Laird's shipyard saw every commission as a challenge - just as they would throughout the next 150 years - and after months of planning they contracted to build the ships in July 1862. Ironclads were at that time, the cutting-edge of naval warships. They were grim and forbidding floating fortresses, impervious to shot and shell and quite capable of destroying any ship afloat and the Laird Rams were to be superior examples of the type.

Numbered No. 294 and 295 respectively, the Rams would be 235 ft in length with a 42ft beam weighing 1896 tons. The metal casing consisted of 4 inches of armour plate fitted to a 12 inch thick teak backing and a further skin of 1 inch iron plate on the inside. The two revolving turrets were the main firepower, each containing the finest 9 inch, rifled cannon, with each cannon weighing an incredible 12 ton and firing a shell of 220 lbs and each turret further reinforced by an extra inch of metal all around. Any further argument would be settled by an enormous underwater ram projecting from the prow - a perfect copy of the weapon utilised by the Roman trireme, 2,000 years ago. The finished product would be a formidable, Wellsian fighting machine.

If Bulloch thought that the political fall-out over the construction of the *Alabama* and the *Florida* was heavy he soon came to realise that it was nothing compared to the overwhelming interest generated by the Laird Rams. Spies were everywhere and information ranging from the correct to the wildly speculative landed on Dudley's desk by the day. These were forwarded in dispatches to Charles Francis Adams who used them as the basis of his interminable struggle with the seemingly immoveable, Foreign Secretary, Lord Russell. The heartily despised Clarence Randolph Yonge was as ever spreading Chinese whispers throughout the corridors of power but the bedrock of Adams's argument harked back to the disgruntled sailors dismissed from the *Florida* in the Autumn of 1863. John Newland Maffits's dismissal of the sailors at Brest had already had repercussions for the new captain of the *Florida* but Maffit's actions were now to go far beyond any reasonable expectations. Charles Francis Adams claimed that the crewmen had not been dismissed at all but sent to Liverpool to await the launch of the Ironclads and take them by force if the situation arose. Also, a letter given to the seamen from Maffitt to Bulloch never reached its destination and ended up in the hands of Adams's lawyers who used it as proof of Confederate plotting. In spite of Adams's constant barrage of objections Lord Russell stood firm that the Ironclads would not be impounded.

As the Ironclads began to take shape throughout the summer months of 1863 and were seen to be on their way to becoming the formidable fighting ships that Mallory had envisaged, the clamour for their seizure became proportionately louder. Bulloch was confident that the ships would be allowed to sail and in messages to Mallory kept him informed of their progress but always flexible and endlessly resilient he also decided to insure against any setbacks and approached the French counting house of Messrs Bravay. The Bravays agreed to a transfer of purchase in their name, on the pretext that they were acting on behalf of the Khedive of Egypt, going so far as to name the Ironclads, *El Tousson* and *El Munassir*. Once the ships had left the Mersey, they would then revert back to Confederate ownership with nothing to stop them but an exchange of cash and a surfeit of paper-work.

By the time the Rams were nearing completion (one was one the river in July, 1863) Charles Francis Adams was frantic in his efforts to prevent them sailing as he envisaged the two warships disappearing out of the Mersey as the *Florida* and *Alabama* had done. Despairing and desperate despatches to Lord Russell were met with a wall of silence and he seemed to be oblivious to the gravity of the situation. Lord Russell might have reconsidered had he known that the Lincoln administration had seriously discussed the possibility of sending several warships of the Yankee fleet down the Mersey to destroy the Ironclads at anchor an action which would have made war inevitable. Adams had all but given in when he penned a last desperate plea to Russell which ended:

The Majestic overseeing the Rams

"It would be superfluous in me to point out to your Lordship that this is war." Russell always denied that it was this phrase that finally galvanized him into action but despite the wording being ambiguous, the fact remains that within the week the order went out to stop the Ironclads from sailing. To reinforce the order, a body of marines was placed aboard the two ships and the *HMS Majestic* stationed in the Mersey. The Ironclads were formally detained on October, 27th, 1863 and remained so until February, 1864.

It was a bitter pill to swallow for Bulloch, who had the unenviable task of reporting to the Secretary of the Confederate Navy, Stephen Mallory, that the long-sought-after warships had been detained when their ambitions were so close to reaching a satisfactory conclusion. Letters were sent to and fro and a British delegation travelled to Egypt to ask Ismail Pasha if he had indeed ordered the two ships (to which he replied in the negative) and the Confederacy petitioned Napoleon IIIrd to intervene on their behalf (he also said no) but it was all to no avail. To Bulloch's great chagrin, the ships never reached the Confederacy and eventually ended up as additions to the Royal navy.

CSS Stonewall

The positive attitude of the Messrs Bravay had appealed to Bulloch and he decided to spread his search for Ironclads even further when he approached French shipyards even as the Laird Rams were still on the ramps. The Confederate Commissioner in France, John Slidell, smoothed the way with the Emperor Napoleon III and arrangements were made with the Arman shipyard in Bordeaux to build two Ironclads and two corvettes (*Yeddo* and *Ocassa*) on behalf of the Confederacy, with a further two corvettes (unnamed) to be built at Nantes. The contracts were signed in July, 1863, just as the Birkenhead Rams were due to sail. Bulloch had been handling millions of dollars on behalf of the Confederacy but for the first time in all of his dealings, money for the new ships was not readily available until Mallory made it available via the Erlangar Loan. The Loan was a measure of the desire that Mallory had for Ironclads and at the same time a clear illustration of the trust he placed in Bulloch's judgement. The Ironclads were named the *Cheops* and the *Sphinx* and all was going well until the Emperor was persuaded by his ministers to alter his open-handed policy and the two ships were forbidden to be handed over to the South. The Emperor's change of heart coincided with whispers to his Foreign Minister, Drouyn de Lhuys by Northern agents and came at a time when the Confederacy was suffering setbacks on the battlefield - both things

Portrait of Napoleon III

which influenced his volte-face. The Confederacy not only lost another two Ironclads to the cause but a great deal of money which was never recuperated.

The fate of the Ironclads was for one to be sold to Prussia and the other to Denmark. As tenacious as ever, Bulloch followed the Danish ship's progress and an offer to buy the Danish Ram was subsequently agreed to. Bulloch never publicized the actions of one of his intermediaries, a soldier of fortune, named Henri de Rivière who opened one of the bilgecocks on the ship's trial run, making the ship sluggish and an unattractive proposition for the Danes.

One of the Laird Rams

Despite his embarrassment at the deception, Bulloch had finally obtained an Ironclad which sailed from Copenhagen in January, 1865. By the time the ship was fitted out in the usual clandestine manner and a crew recruited, the *CSS Stonewall* sailed to Lisbon and then onto Havana where Captain Page was informed that the war was over - he was later accused of being tardy. The crew were paid off in Cuba and the ship formally surrendered to the United States of America in July 1865.

Bulloch had finally obtained his Ironclad and although it was to little effect, he had the satisfaction of knowing he had carried out his orders right until the bitter end.

CSS Shenandoah

Although the sinking of the *Alabama* was a hammer blow to the Southern cause, the celebrations by the Northern administration were taken as a measure of her success and a back-handed compliment to her efficacy as a commerce-raider. As a result, Stephen Mallory sent a despatch marked *Urgent!* to Bulloch to provide a successor to the most feared raider the Confederates ever had. Bulloch responded in his usual energetic manner and acquired a ship far sooner than Mallory could have ever envisaged. On a visit to the Clyde in the autumn of 1863, Bulloch had noted a handsome ship in the harbour loading for its first voyage outward bound to Bombay and tucked the information away in his mental filing system marked 'pending'. Bulloch was always appreciative of fine ships and on many occasions soliloquized over the design and lines of ships he came across - the ship on the Clyde was one that he had rhapsodised about and when Mallory's orders arrived the *Sea King* was the ship that Bulloch chose. From experience, Bulloch had learned to be ultra-cautious in his dealings and made a point of never setting foot aboard his new purchase, although it must have grieved him to have to stay away. All the purchasing and other details were carried out by a third party in London where the ship was moored.

In the meantime, Bulloch did make a point of going aboard an iron-screw steamer called the *Laurel* working between Liverpool and Ireland which he declared perfect as a tender for his new ship and later as a blockade-runner. The *Laurel* was placed in the care of a shipping agent advertising her for a trip to Havana - the true freight was already designated as stores, arms and crew for the *Alabama's* successor. Bulloch had taken precautions to a higher level when he ordered that the agents acting on his behalf should issue bills of lading, print tickets and write down passage money paid so that any curious shipping clerks would have no reason to be suspicious.

Bulloch's mysterious ship sailed from the Thames on the 5th October, 1864, and as soon as her departure was reported by telegraph the *Laurel* was made ready to sail. Bulloch went to extraordinary lengths to allay suspicions and the "passengers" of the *Laurel* assembled at Princes Landing Stage where they boarded a tug to take her out into the river to the waiting ship. Several of the crew were old hands from the *Alabama* and the remainder were made up of seamen from the Liverpool waterfront - the Sailors Home which was sadly demolished in 1973 was a favourite recruiting centre. Bulloch took the precaution of waiting two weeks before he wrote to Mallory to tell him that both ships were on their way to Madeira and for the first time he felt safe to divulge the name of the ship - the *Sea King*.

Despite all his precautions, the *Sea King* had sailed past the warships *Niagara* and the *Sacramento* as they came out of the mouth of the Thames. Whether they would have engaged in British waters is debatable.

Bulloch's detailed orders to the officers aboard the *Sea King* were a first-class lesson in communications, ensuring a smooth passage of arms and stores and crew to Funchal where they picked up Lt Commanding James I. Waddell accompanied by his staff officers who also received sealed envelopes. Amongst the welter of fine detail, Bulloch, almost as an afterthought, casually instructed that the *Sea King* be christened *CSS Shenandoah* and then continued with his written litany of minutiae. Nobody who ever worked for Bulloch, in any capacity, was at any

The Shenandoah among the whalers.

time ever in any doubt as to their instructions. Lt Commander, Waddell's orders were simple and clear - he was to sail to Sydney, Australia where he would ensure a full stock of coal and stores and from there into the North Pacific where the whaling fleets were to be his prey.

Right from the beginning of his ship-buying career, it had always been Bulloch's policy to keep potential crew members in ignorance of their voyage and their allegiance to the Confederacy until they were aboard ship. The reasons were obvious and most of the crews had never objected but on this occasion, the ploy backfired badly when of the 80 men carried out to Madeira a miserly 23 consented to sign on with the remainder demanding to go home. The reasons were not hard to divine - the sinking of the *Alabama* and the *Florida* gave food for thought and at the same time the war was going badly for the South - nothing succeeds like success. Waddell was undaunted and began his command of the 220 ft long, 35 ft beam, sail and steam cruiser with only 42 crew. Of these, Irvine S. Bulloch was master, W.B.Smith paymaster and Matthew O'Brien chief engineer, all old hands on the *Alabama* - the remainder were made up of recruits fresh from the Naval Academy who made up in enthusiasm what they lacked in experience. The adage "one volunteer is worth ten pressed men" was never so true.

The *Shenandoah* left Madeira on October 20th, 1864 and on January 25th, 1865 was in Melbourne, having burnt 8 United States ships en-route. Bulloch followed her passage by the orders he had given and on the 21st May, 1865 the ship was becoming jammed in ice in the Sea of Okhotsk where Waddell wisely retreated and headed for the Arctic Sea. It was in this area that whalers were captured and burnt at a prodigious rate - between the 22nd June and 28th June the *Shenandoah* captured 24 ships, 10 of those were caught in one day, on the 28th June. If anybody ever questioned the morality of burning civilian whaling ships going about their legitimate business, Waddell could always point to General Philip Sheridan's destruction of the Shenandoah Valley, the previous August. The "Breadbasket of the Confederacy" had been razed to the ground and the farmers left to starve. Dunwoody Bulloch and General Sheridan were both pragmatic enough to know that wars were not just won by glorious cavalry charges and set-piece battles. In the meantime, Bulloch was frantically trying to find a method of

The Shenandoah in the Arctic.

communicating with Waddell to inform him that the Civil War had effectively ended when the Confederate armies had collapsed in April, 1865. Bulloch felt *"a grave responsibility"* to somehow get word to Waddell and not without good reason as the *Shenandoah* was gleefully and illegally burning United States whalers in blissful ignorance of the changed situation.

Unsurprisingly finding whalers in short supply, Waddell headed further south and beyond the Aleutians came across a British barque called the *Barracouta* which gave him the news that Jefferson Davis had been taken prisoner and the Confederate government had ceased to exist. Waddell was in a difficult position as a ship of war still in operation, and reluctant to take his chances with the Northern administration he decided to head for Liverpool where he hoped to receive a fair hearing given that he had illegally sunk a great number of American whalers. He dismounted the guns, closed the ports and whitewashed the funnels, returning the ship to the appearance of a mercantile screw-steamer and arrived on November 6th at Birkenhead where she dropped anchor a cable-length behind *HMS Donegal* and surrendered to Captain Paynter. It was the final act of submission by the Confederacy.

After the usual diplomatic exchanges, the *Shenandoah* was ceded to the American government and sailed to New York, eventually being sold to the Sultan of Zanzibar to be fitted out as a luxury yacht. In 1879, after 14 years of service the *Shenandoah* ended her days wrecked on a coral reef. Bulloch always appreciated fine ships and often went into raptures over their *"graceful lines"* and *"curved bows"* and he waxed lyrical when he wrote of the fate of the *Shenandoah; "The teak planks were torn from her bottom by a rough scrape on a coral reef and her iron ribs were left to rust and crumble on a melancholy island in the Indian Ocean".*

The *Laurel* sailed on to Charleston when she had finished as a tender and carried valuable supplies for the Confederacy, returning to Liverpool re-named as the *Confederate States*. She went on to run the blockade several times until she became lost to history.

The Blockade-Runners

Although the long-distance and well-armed commerce raiders and the futuristic Ironclads occupied the greater part of Bulloch's procurement work, he also involved himself in obtaining blockade-runners, ships which were of necessity fast and maneuverable and low in the water to avoid detection. The number of blockade-runners coming out of Liverpool from the beginning of the Civil war was exceptionally high and kept the shipyards on each bank of the Mersey busy throughout the conflict. When General McRae of the Confederate Treasury persuaded the government at Richmond that cotton needed to be exported from the South as a means of re-filling the war chest, it was Bulloch who picked up the baton and went about his work in his usual energetic manner. It is known that Bulloch purchased the *Coquette* on the Clyde but Bulloch also ordered another ten to be constructed in Liverpool yards (John Newland Maffitt recovered from illness, commanded the *Owl* along with E.M.Anderson of the *Alabama*). He made a point of being as secretive as possible over their purchases and stipulated that they must always be in the name of private purchasers making it difficult to know just how much involvement Bulloch had in each of the ships - it's almost certain that he was involved in all of them in some capacity, even if it was merely being kept informed. Blockade-runners were comparatively cheap and fast to build and several trips often recouped any outlay they sustained but the history of each ship reveals a remarkable difference in their successes and failures, ranging from ships which ran the blockade at will to others captured almost immediately.

Bulloch always denied any involvement with the *Phantom.*

The *Colonel Lamb*, one of the fastest ships on the Mersey, ran the blockade twice but was later sold to a Greek group and re-named the *Bouboulina.* She sank in the Mersey off Rock Ferry in November, 1867 after a boiler exploded killing 12 men.

After the humiliation of capture on her first outing, the *Bat* had the distinction of being used as Admiral David Dixon Porter's flagship - Lincoln sailed on her several times and so did General Sherman in March, 1865. The *Lelia* was the most unfortunate of all the blockade-runners and in a poignant incident she was overcome by a storm on her maiden voyage (January, 14th 1865) before she had reached the mouth of the Mersey. Commander Arthur Sinclair perished, along with Thomas Miller the scion of the ship-building company, 8 passengers, 37 crew and 2 pilots - 49 in all.

The CSS Shenandoah in the Bering Sea

James Dunwoody Bulloch arrived in Liverpool as a stranger in a strange land and immediately set out on his mission with unprecedented energy and ingenuity. He loved the sea and he loved ships and Liverpool was at that time a mercantile Mecca where he felt at home right from the start. He had a seemingly limitless capacity for fine detail and involved himself as Procurement Agent despite his longing to return to sea.

In his brief to procure ships for the Confederacy he went far beyond what was expected and it is no exaggeration to say that he was the driving force behind what went to make up the Confederate navy: the *Alabama* and the *Florida* were the flagships of the Confederate navy and as commerce raiders, they were unequalled. Most of the blockade-runners built in Liverpool were at the instigation of Bulloch and the *Shenandoah* was his brain-child. The Laird Rams were a departure from the usual ships that Bulloch commissioned in that they were warships as opposed to commercial runners and raiders. The Rams were the cutting edge of naval warfare in Victorian times and Mallory was convinced that they would have scythed through the Northern warships and altered the course of the Civil war at one fell stroke. He was probably being optimistic to the point of fantasy but there's no doubt whatsoever that the Rams would have given a different dimension to the war and challenged the Northern command of the Eastern seaboard.

In the final analysis, all Bulloch's efforts were doomed to failure just as the fight for Southern independence was doomed and although his energies were applied on behalf of the Confederacy, he was motivated solely by an ingrained patriotism and not for any affiliation to slavery - Bulloch's whole life was devoted to his career as a seaman.

Bulloch never returned to live in his homeland and remained in Liverpool as a nationalised British citizen, where he turned his considerable energies into stemming the tide of abject poverty endemic throughout the city. His particular charitable work was in the numerous Orphanages which could be found in every district.

He made his living as a cotton merchant in a building near to Rumford Place where in his old offices the cotton plant had once been the basis for decisions far more vital than mere costs and bales.

Bulloch's two volume memoirs also took up much of his time and they are written with a clarity and conciseness and diplomacy which defined James Dunwoody Bulloch's whole career.

Bulloch's son Stuart joined the British army and fought in the Dardanelles.

Despite James Dunwoody Bulloch's prodigious efforts to provide ships which would break the Northern blockade, the blockade remained in place throughout the Civil War and eventually formed a stranglehold which effectively choked Southern supply lines altogether. Blockade-runners steamed out of the Mersey, the Clyde and the Thames and Southern consortiums acquired ships from sources of their own but they were never enough, and in the latter days of the war, the South became so desperate for supplies that they offered a bounty for every Northern ship sunk.

During the death throes of the Nazi regime in the 2nd World War, they increasingly turned to scientists to provide the Secret Weapons which would miraculously turn the war in their favour. There was nothing new about the situation and similar instances throughout history can be quoted ad infinitum, so it was nothing revelatory when the Confederacy also began clutching at straws and turned to Secret Weapons of their own in a desperate bid to break the grip of the Northern blockade. And into the breech stepped an inventor named Horace Lawson Hunley, with what was a primitive forerunner of the submarine that he called the *Hunley.*

The omens for the *Hunley* were less than encouraging when a prototype named the *American Diver* lived up to its name and sank in a storm off Mobile in January, 1863. Nevertheless, in February of 1864, the *Hunley* travelled by rail from Mobile to Charleston where it was greeted with great excitement as the saviour of the South. The commander of Charleston's defences was a little more sceptical and called it "the fish, torpedo boat" which was a fair description. The *Hunley* may well have been cutting-edge technology at the time, but in an age when even sophisticated machines such as the *Kursk* are capable of disaster, then the *Hunley* takes on a distinctly Heath Robinson appearance. The submarine was 40ft long and 4ft high, had 10 portholes and a snorkel which allowed air into the vessel using a hand-pumped bellows. Hunley had experimented with steam and discarded it in favour of a propellor shaft, hand-cranked by no less than 7 operatives and the ship was steered from the front, using a joystick. It was clear even then that it would take a brave man to go underwater in Hunley's Secret Weapon.

But underwater the *Hunley* did go and promptly sank, killing 5 crew members. On a second test-run, the ship sank again, killing Hunley himself and all of the crew.

A measure of the South's desperate straits was that a few days later, the Charleston authorities raised the *Hunley* from its watery grave and prepared her for sea once again. Commanded by Lt George Dixon, on 17th February, 1864, the submarine headed out of Charleston harbour straight for the Union warship, the *Housatonic*, lying five miles out at sea. At 9pm in the evening the lookouts spotted the strange underwater vessel heading towards them but it was too late to manoeuvre out of harm's way and the *Hunley's* primitive torpedo blew the *Housatonic* to pieces. It was the first sinking of a ship by a submarine. The *Hunley* had little time to enjoy her success and sank for the last time shortly afterwards.

In 1879, a Manchester clergyman named George Garrett followed on where Hunley left off and patented a 45ft long, steam-driven submarine called the *Resurgam.* Built in Birkenhead by Cochrane and Co. the submarine came to an ignominious end off Rhyl when the ship towing her developed engine trouble in a gale, resulting in the loss of the submarine before she had begun her career.

There's a scale model of the *Resurgam* in Birkenhead museum, looking very similar to the *Hunley* in every way.

James Dunwoody Bulloch (1823 - 1901)

An American by Birth, An Englishman by Choice

The Early Years

Even a cursory observation of James Dunwoody's life prior to his enlistment into the Confederate navy reveals an upbringing which was an ideal preparation for what was to come. A Southern background, a distinguished ancestry and a naval career with its rich melding of intellectual discipline married to hands-on seamanship was so perfect that a casual observer could be forgiven for believing that it was pre-ordained. The Confederate government were fortunate to have had the services of such a man in their hour of need and he was probably unique in combining every element required to carry out his mission.

James Dunwoody Bullochs' origins and family background are extremely complicated but never less than fascinating.

James Dunwoody Bulloch's ancestry is derived from his Scottish antecedents who settled in America in unusual circumstances. In 1699, Archibald Stobo and his bride, accompanied by others of their faith, sailed from Edinburgh to Panama on an expedition financed by the Presbyterian church to set up outposts of Christianity in the New World. Unfortunately, Panama was the worst place they could have chosen. They found the previous settlement burnt to the ground, the place was rife with disease and the Spanish were hostile to their faith. The site they had chosen was untenable and after the loss of many lives, the expedition was forced to return to England on a ship called the *Rising Sun*. On the return journey, the ship stopped at Charleston, South Carolina and Archibald, as a renowned preacher was asked to give a sermon to the local congregation. While Archibald and his wife were ashore, a violent storm broke and a bolt of lightning struck the *Rising Sun*, killing everyone aboard and sinking the ship. Archibald took this as a sign that they were meant to remain in the New World and that's where they remained.

The original Pioneers

The beautiful "Mittie"

One year later the Stobo's had a child named Jean who grew up to marry a local man, James Bulloch - their union was the beginning of a dynasty spanning centuries and traceable right up to the present day.

Jean and James left Charleston to take advantage of a land grant and moved to Georgia where their son, Archibald Bulloch served as speaker in the Georgia Royal Assembly and was later president of the Provincial Congress of 1775. He was also reputed to have fought against the British in the Revolutionary Wars.

The Bulloch family had made their home in Savannah and by 1790 were firmly established in growing cotton for the lucrative cotton trade employing slave labour in the traditional manner.

The original James Bulloch's great-grandson also called James Bulloch was reputed to be dashing and handsome and had been courting a Southern Belle, called Martha Stewart since they were both very young. Martha Stewart was the daughter of a cotton shipper and to all intents and purposes, her attachment to the scion of a cotton-grower was a match made in heaven and although the lovers did eventually get together, it was not before a lengthy and byzantine interval which saw them both go in different directions. The story goes that Martha was not short of admirers and James was not long on indulgence and the couple argued and separated. At this point, the story of the star-crossed lovers enters into the realms of romantic fiction and could easily be the template for any number of steamy Southern novels.

One of Martha's most ardent suitors was the widowed John Elliott who happened to be twice her age. Opposed to that, Elliott was not short of money and was headed for the U.S. Senate. Still Martha dallied perhaps hoping that James would re-enter her life. As it happened, James came back into her life in a most unexpected manner when he suddenly married John Elliott's daughter, Esther who at 19 was two years younger than Martha. Within the week, Martha had consented to marry Elliott and in so doing became her former lover's step-mother-in-law.

For the following decade, the glamorous Martha accompanied her Senator husband along the corridors of power in Washington D.C. and the couple became the parents to two daughters and one son. John Elliot died at the early age of 52 and after ten years of marriage Martha found herself a widow still only 30 years of age. Within 10 months, James was also widowed when Esther died suddenly leaving him with a son. Martha and James eventually came together and after leaving an interval of five years after the death of John Elliott, they eventually married and in the best traditions of all dynastic sagas lived happily ever after.

James Dunwoody's father, Major James Stephens Bulloch had married his first wife, Esther Elliot in 1817. Little is known about Esther but little James was born on June 25th, 1823 and his mother gave him his middle name, Dunwoody, to commemorate her own mother's maiden name. James Dunwoody was their only child. James Dunwoody was nine years of age when his father married again in 1832 to Martha Stewart and the couple had three children. James Dunwoody's half-sisters were Anna (Mrs James K. Gracie and Martha, "Mittie", (Mrs Theodore Roosevelt Sr) and his half-brother, Irvine who was to have a distinguished career aboard the *Nashville*, *Alabama* and the *Shenandoah*.

In 1840, Major Bulloch built a neo-classical Greek mansion to the west of Roswell, 19 miles, north of Atlanta, Georgia. Martha would be married there on December 22nd, 1853, and her son would grow up to be the 26th President of the United States. "Teddy" Roosevelt was inordinately proud of his uncles and on a visit to the mansion in 1905, he gave a speech eulogizing James Dunwoody and Irvine and told of his pride in their achievements. The house still stands. James Dunwoody was only an infrequent visitor to the family home as 12 months previously, at the age of 16, he had enlisted as a Midshipman in the United States navy.

Theodore Roosevelt Sr had met Mittie on a visit to Bulloch Hall when she was 15 years of age and found him studious and boring. Three years later and he had turned into the love of her life. Their marriage was arranged for December, 1853 in Bulloch Hall and the celebrations went on for a whole week. One of Mittie's bridesmaids recalled the wedding celebrations many years later when she recounted every detail to an aspiring young reporter named Peggy Mitchell who was later to become Margaret Mitchell of "Gone With the Wind" fame. The beautiful and petite bride, barely 5ft tall went off to New York to set up home off Broadway with her new groom where she would eventually become the mother of Teddie, Anna (Bamie) and Corinne and later be the grandmother of Eleanor Roosevelt.

Bulloch Mansion

Bulloch Mansion was a continuance of the family cotton empire and boasted 19 slaves - a fact which would not have been lost on Sherman's soldiers when they ransacked the house during the war. The contents were taken but the fabric of the house was undamaged - it was said that the Masonic symbols present saved it from being destroyed.

As for James, the life of a Midshipman aboard sailing-ships little changed since the previous century was no sinecure combining hard physical work with rigorous theoretical exercises - not to mention dealing with hard-bitten seamen, older and more experienced.

James Dunwoody's apprenticeship was 5 years of solid grounding in every aspect of seamanship which culminated in him passing out 2nd in his class. He went on to serve under the renowned Farragut on the *Decatur* and later succeeded David Dixon Porter to the command of the *Georgia*, meeting many men along the way who would shortly become adversaries in the war. The *Georgia* carried mail to California during the Gold Rush. In 1853, James Dunwoody resigned from the U.S. Navy and moved to New York to pursue a career in private shipping - he had married Elizabeth Euphemia Caskie of Richmond 12 months previously, which may have accounted for his decision. James Dunwoody always had a good relationship with his sisters and brothers and Martha had by this time had Teddy and Anna so he often visited and as "Uncle Jimmie" he famously bounced the future President on his knee.

Harriot

The nature of Bulloch's work required a secrecy far beyond normal expectations and on many subjects things are only hinted at. The bare bones of Bulloch's family life are reasonably well- documented but further than that can only be guessed at. Add to this the fact that in the Victorian era "a woman's place was very much in the home" and the subject is more than opaque. However, although it may be "through a glass darkly" Harriot's actions reveal far more than reams of text.

Bulloch's marriage to Elizabeth was short-lived and in 1857, he married again to the widowed Harriot Cross (Foster) and the following year, their first child, James Dunwoody Jr was born in Louisiana and two years later in 1860 their daughter, Jessie Hart was born in New York. Harriot's husband was away on business a great deal and war clouds were gathering, until in January 1861, war between the States erupted and Bulloch was aboard his ship when the news broke. It was part of James Dunwoody's duties on behalf of the owners to sail a steamer called the *Bienville* to Southern ports along the eastern seaboard and it was while he was in New Orleans that he found out that Fort Sumter had been fired on and hostilities had begun in earnest. A number of members of the Southern "Board of War" soon boarded the *Bienville* and attempted to persuade Dunwoody to sell the ship which he refused to do out of loyalty to his employers. Persuasion turned to coercion and the impasse travelled all the way onto Jefferson Davis's desk whose response was; *"Do not detain the Bienville, we do not wish to interfere in any way with private properties."*

With this, Dunwoody sailed out of harbour to return the ship as quickly as he could, having refused to sell the ship despite his affiliations to the Southern cause. The incident said a great deal about both James Dunwoody Bulloch and Jefferson Davis.

Bulloch had already declared his loyalty to the South if war broke out and now he was as good as his word, resigning from his lucrative employment and offering his services to the Confederate Navy. Whether he consulted Harriot is not known nor is her reaction to the fact that their comfortable life in New York was now thrown to the winds.

There was another shock for Harriot to absorb when following quickly on the heels of Bulloch's resignation he was ordered to travel to England as quickly as possible and on the 11th May, 1861 Bulloch sailed across the Atlantic. It is difficult to imagine Harriot's emotions at this time in her life - just 4 months previously she had two children, a home and a husband with a secure income and here she was now alone with two children and an uncertain future. Even more traumatic for Harriot was that Bulloch had sailed just one week before the birth of the 3rd child, Henry.

Harriot remained in New York with her three children throughout the Summer of 1861 and sometime in late September she took ship for Liverpool. An Atlantic crossing in those days was a hazardous affair and for a woman on her own, travelling with two toddlers and a babe in arms says a great deal about her courage and her loyalty to her husband. But she must have felt bereft to discover on landing that her husband who was on the *Fingal* had probably passed her ship going in the opposite direction and she would have felt even more disconsolate if she had known he would be away for a further six months - "Ships in the Night" summed up their relationship to perfection.

Waterloo

Circa 1800, in the township of Crosby, the yet unnamed hamlet was a quiet fishing-village, five miles outside Liverpool town centre. Travel to Liverpool or Southport was by horseback, on foot or latterly, the horse-omnibus - it was in the 1850s that a train-line was laid down into Liverpool.

The Liver Hotel

The year 1815 was a landmark in the history of the tiny fishing village when not only did Wellington's resounding victory resonate throughout the land but somebody discovered that Formby shore had golden beaches and crystal clear water. Sometime during The Industrial Revolution, the bosses had found that not only the aristocracy benefited from days at the seaside but more importantly, a week's excursion to a beach resort each year made their workers more efficient and Formby shore was one of the forerunners in a trend towards seaside resorts which would burgeon and grow all through the Victorian era. Formby never really got beyond being a place for the upper classes - only the well-heeled could afford the stylish Crosby Seabank Hotel which was built in 1816 to cater for their needs. On June 18th, 1861, there was a grand dinner to commemorate the Battle of Waterloo and the opening of the hotel, with the more adventurous of the clientele taking advantage of the bathing machines which were rolled down to the sea where the bathers could swim in privacy. The fishermen's cottages adjacent to the hotel were sadly demolished in the name of progress, and around 1820, a row of early Victorian terraces were erected with the appropriate title of Marine Terrace.

The area was perfect for the bourgeoisie of Liverpool who could work in the city and live in the country and the little town grew larger in a very short time with a building programme in the 1840s which saw street after street and row upon row of houses built in that particularly sturdy style immediately identifiable as Victorian. By 1850, the tiny fishing village had been transformed into a fashionable Victorian enclave for an exclusively upper and middle class clientele with every street having some connection to the Battle of Waterloo - Blucher Street, Wellington road, Hougoumont and so on. And the township was of course called Waterloo. The road to the rear of the town runs to Liverpool and Southport and is an old coaching road. On the Waterloo corner is the 200 year old coaching inn called the Liver Hotel. The lych-gate at the front reveals that it was once converted into a church but by 1861 had since been converted back again. It was here that James Dunwoody Bulloch had been lodging since his arrival in Liverpool far from prying eyes but within easy reach of his office in the Fraser, Trenholm complex.

Formby shore as it is today.

Harriot's first priority on arrival in Liverpool was to find a comfortable home for herself and her three infants. A coaching inn was no place for a lady but a house on Marine Terrace was perfect and sometime in October, 1861, Harriot moved into no 2 Marine Terrace where the children would undoubtedly have been delighted by the close proximity of the sea and sand-dunes to play in. James Dunwoody would have been impressed by her energy and resourcefulness. Today, the sea is a safe distance from Marine Terrace but in the days when Harriot lived there and the fishermen before her, the sea lapped at the cottage doors during exceptionally high-tides.

Bulloch returned from America in March, 1862, presumably to a riotous welcome from a family he had not seen for nearly a year. The family stayed in Marine Terrace for the following summer until the lease ran out and they took up a new residence in no. 3 Wellington Street in October, 1862.

The house on Wellington St was an unpretentious end-terrace, just around the corner from their previous home and was memorable for being the birthplace of the couple's last two children, Stuart Elliott born in 1863 and Martha Louise in 1864.

Harriot now had five children to look after which was far from being exceptional in the Victorian era when families of twelve and more were not uncommon but his family must have been a source of great comfort and a welcome diversion to James Dunwoody and his great responsibilities. It is never recorded as to how Harriot and James Dunwoody became accustomed to the vastly different climate of England but it must have been quite a change from the warm and sunny climate that they were accustomed to.

Raphael Semmes was a visitor to the Bulloch home prior to sailing on the Alabama. He was extremely complimentary about Bulloch's family and almost envious in his admiration for Harriot. Semmes was also surprised at the modest house that such an important man had chosen and at the same time admired the frugality with which Bulloch spent Confederate money. The folk-history persists that Semmes and Bulloch met for several evenings to discuss business in the Liver Hotel and it is probable that Bulloch recommended the Liver as a lodging for the future Captain of the Alabama.

Several sources insist that Semmes visited the Prioleau's at Allerton Hall during the same period. Bulloch was enigmatic about who had the honour of launching the 290 but it was almost certain that it was Harriot. There was a comical and ironic interlude when Harriot's hat blew off and it was retrieved and returned by Bulloch's shadow, Maguire himself.

Dunwoody Bulloch would have been delighted to walk along Formby shore where several years previously troops bound for the Crimean War had trained. Armaments such as the cannon on the left were tested - the picture is from the 1860s and is a Mackay gun on trials. The Mackay gun was invented by James Mackay and constructed by the Mersey Steel and Iron Works.

In 1917, Siegfried Sassoon walked this same beach and was reputed to have thrown his Medals in the river. He only threw the ribbons away.

In late 1865, Harriot moved house once again - this time to the far end of the same street at no 12 Wellington Street. Next door at no. 10 lived Moses P. Robertson, Bulloch's secretary. Confederate agent, Charles L. Hobson had lived there also until his tragic drowning aboard the maiden voyage of the blockade-runner, *Lelia,* in February, 1865. The children were christened in St. John's church at the end of the street - but only after the war ended.

Waterloo Sunset

By 1871, the Civil War had been over for six years but Bulloch's name was one of those on the proscribed list and he had made his home permanently in Liverpool, earning his living ironically enough importing cotton with his offices in Rumford Street, across the road from what was once the nerve-centre of the Confederate presence in Liverpool, Fraser, Trenholm. He had successfully applied for British citizenship in 1869 and is rumoured to have travelled to New York on more than one occasion accompanied by Irvine.

The family had moved once again, still in Waterloo, to a larger house in Cambridge Road called Clifton. The house stood in its own grounds and was

Clifton

quite impressive but for Harriot it was a place where tragedy struck and Henry died suddenly at 9 years of age. Henry died of Scarlet Fever which was one of many diseases of Victorian England adding to the high mortality rate; even up until the 1940s and beyond, the Fever Van was a dreaded sight in Liverpool streets. Henry's death was particularly poignant, falling on his brother Stuart's 8th birthday.

From this distance in time, merely relating the facts does not reveal the grief that the whole family must have felt, but Henry's death must have been a dreadful shock for all of them and and in particular for Harriot who was at the very centre of heart and home. They had all become an integral part of life in Waterloo, attending church and the children attending school - their private school was yet another Victorian house at no. 9 Waterloo Road, Alexandra Terrace where the children were taught by Madame Micheline de Zastro. Jefferson Davis visited the Bulloch's in 1868 and placed his two sons, Jeff and Billy, in the school for the duration and a ten year old Teddy Roosevelt visited and "exchanged words with the young Davis boy." It seems the exchange was something to do with Southern loyalties and the future President later regretted the incident. It was a shock when Madame de Zastro died in the Christmas period of 1870/1871, a mere two months before the worse tragedy of Henry's death.

Teddy was of course not travelling alone. In May 1869, Mittie sailed on the side-wheel steamer, *Scotia*, with her whole family for a year abroad, visiting Egypt and doing the Grand Tour. But her first point of call was a visit to see James Dunwoody and Irvine who showed them around Liverpool.

The indefatigable Mittie repeated the trip in October, 1872 and Teddy Roosevelt returned to Liverpool in 1881 where "Uncle Jimmie" helped his nephew with the writing of The History of the War of 1812.

The death of Henry and to a lesser degree, the death of Madame de Zastro,was a pivotal point in the Bulloch's family life. Up to this point, Harriot's integration into the life of a Victorian housewife had been a commendably smooth transition from her life in America - she was not to know it but from now on their lives would be a very slow decline with further tragedy interspersed with intervals of family landmarks of a happier nature.

St James cemetery circa 1860 - two minutes from the Bulloch home. Several sailors from the Alabama are buried here.

Sefton Park

Although the Bulloch family had moved house several times, it had always been within the confines of the township of Waterloo but seventeen years after Harriot's move into the area and all the subsequent difficulties of integration into a new way of life, in 1878, the family decided to move once again. The reasons for the Bulloch family's many moves can often be put down to leases being ended and it would be easy to point to Henry's death as a reason to move from Waterloo but it was all of eight years after his death which makes it unlikely. Whatever the reason, once again Harriot was moving house along with all the stress which that entailed. Their home on this occasion was yet another Victorian house at no 63 Parliament Street which overlooked the depths of St. James's Cemetery, a sylvan glade replete with the gravestones of ship's captains and seamen. Once a quarry, St. James's was surrounded by picturesque paths and walkways with views across the city and from the pristine Georgian houses on Gambier Terrace could be seen the neo-Greek Oratory. The beginnings of the Anglican Cathedral were fifteen years hence and the views across the river were panoramic with Miller's ship-yard and Lairds still turning out ships at prodigious rates.

Despite the charms of Parliament Street, in 1886, the Bulloch family moved once again - this time further out from the city centre to no 30 Sydenham avenue. Like all the Bulloch family homes, Sydenham Avenue was an archetypal, middle-class Victorian house, modest by some standards but infinitely beyond the means of an average working man at that time. The house was on a narrow wooded Avenue in a select area adjacent to Sefton Park which had been landscaped in 1872. Sefton was one of the foremost parks in the country when it was first laid out, containing all the elements that went to make up a Victorian park with its magnificent Palm House, grottoes, statues, fountains, lakes and riding area à la Rotten Row, and it would surely have been inconceivable if the Bulloch family had not strolled around its beautiful surroundings, time and time again. In conjunction with many of the Bulloch neighbourhoods, Sefton Park and its environs today has an air of faded elegance, a Miss Havisham of the horticultural world, but a mark of how regal it used to be, is that when James Dunwoody and Harriot lived there it was compulsory to wear collar and tie before entering the park. The

76 Canning Street

modest church of St. Agnes on Ullet Road was 5 minutes walk for the family each Sunday.

The year 1888 was a bitter/sweet affair for Harriot and James Dunwoody with the happy event of Jessie's marriage followed a few months later by the devastating news of the death of James Jr. Jessie was the eldest daughter of the family and married comparatively late for those days at the age of twenty-eight. Her husband, Maxwell Hyslop Maxwell, was the son of a wealthy tobacco merchant and City Councillor. The family home called Hamlets is now Belvidere School. The marriage took place in April, 1888, and the couple set up home in a large, Georgian Terrace at no.76 Canning Street - Irvine Bulloch had an office across the road at no 77.

Just a few months later in August, 1888, the family's happiness was marred by the unexpected and devastating news that James Jr had died while on a trip to Lynchburg, Virginia, in the United States. It seems that medieval diseases were not restricted to Victorian England as James Jr was reported to have died of typhoid fever now an affliction largely restricted to Third World countries. James Jr was unmarried and left no heirs and was buried in a local cemetery in Lynchburg. It was an unfortunate irony that his aunt, Mittie had died of the same affliction four years previously.

As for Stuart Elliott, he was aged 25 when his brother died and following the example of his brother-in-law, Maxwell Hyslop Maxwell, he joined the British army and served 6 years in the Guards.

The End Of An Era

With two sons dead, another on the other side of the world and a daughter married, the halcyon days when Harriot was the centre of a bustling and vibrant family were well and truly over, while James Dunwoody's mercantile adventures were now restricted to the pages of his Memoirs. The death of Harriot on July 3rd, 1897, of peritonitis was a dagger to the heart of James Dunwoody - for nearly 40 years she had fulfilled the role of faithful wife and mother while he pursued his career. She had supported James Dunwoody in everything he did and remained a pillar of the family throughout, adapting to wherever her husband's career took her and their children.

James Dunwoody lasted 5 years after Harriot's death . His last home was 76 Canning Street where Jessie nursed him until his merciful release from the trauma of a particularly painful cancer on 7th January, 1901.

Jessie's home was just across the street from the home and offices of Irvine Bulloch who lived in 77 Canning Street in a row of Georgian houses.

Several years after the death of James Dunwoody Bulloch, Jessie and Maxwell along with Martha (who never married) moved into the luxurious surroundings of the grandiose Adelphi Hotel. The hotel was built in 1912 on the site of a previous Adelphi and its luxurious surroundings included a lobby which replicated the ballroom of the Titanic and within these palatial confines, in the very heart of Liverpool city centre, one by one, the last of James Dunwoody's family went to their deaths. Maxwell died in 1938, Jessie in 1941 and Martha in 1947. It was, truly, the end of an era.

Pen Portraits

Prologue

The two pivotal characters in the story of the Confederacy in Liverpool are of course, James Dunwoody Bulloch, whose unique work for the Confederacy defied all his efforts to remain anonymous, and Raphael Semmes whose undisputed mastery of the *Alabama* made her deeds famous around the world. Swirling in and out of the lives of both men, sometimes for years often for days, was a cast of characters which could have been drawn from any or all of Dicken's novels. They ranged from the treacherous Clarence R. Yonge to the unshakeably faithful John Low, from cunning lawyers to shady detectives, from wide-eyed midshipmen to cut-throat sailors and from highly-skilled ship-builders to Liverpool wharf-rats, as John Newland Maffitt described several of his crew. They inhabited a world of building yards, waterfront dives, whispered conversations and seamen's tales of fair winds and far-off lands where women and drink were there for the taking. Like characters in a play, they sometimes play the lead, sometimes play a cameo role and often are just extras but all of them without exception go to make up a colourful and lively crew aboard the good ship Liverpool in the days of the Civil War.

Captain John Low

At one stage of his career John Low was ranked as a First Lieutenant and it was the perfect description of not only his position aboard ship but also his role in life. Low was never destined to be a major player in the story of the Confederate navy - he left that to others - but as a right-hand man who could be relied upon in any situation he had few peers. When the chips were down or an extraordinary effort required then Low was your man, always playing back-stop to whoever he served, with unflinching fidelity and flair; happy to take orders but ever ready to use his own initiative whenever the situation required. In every narrative concerning the Confederate navy, Low's name will inevitably pop up at various stages.

John Low was born in Aberdeen in 1836 and was too young to comprehend the tragedy of losing both his parents while still a baby. Relations in Aberdeen and Liverpool raised him, up to the day that he left Liverpool in 1852, aged 16, and went to sea on a mail-passenger ship, the *HMS Shalimar* from Liverpool to Sydney. Even at such a young age, his ability as a seaman was there for all to see and within two years John Low was employed as the ship's mate. Low's uncle Andrew had a business in Savannah, Georgia and suggested that he try working ashore in the shipping business. Within the space of seven years, Low had set himself up in a shipping partnership which specialised in naval supplies and cotton transportation which gave him access to the financial, political and social high-flyers of Savannah. His marriage to Mary Elizabeth Wall of Culpepper County, set the seal on his success and it seemed that his future was a foregone conclusion. However, as in the case of Bulloch and many others, the outbreak of the Civil War was to change all that and in 1861, at the age of 25, Low joined the Georgia Hussars. Low's naval career may have been short but it was outstanding enough to come to the attention of Stephen Mallory and Low was ordered to Liverpool and instructed to report to a James Dunwoody Bulloch who would give him further orders. Bulloch wasn't slow in recognising John Low's qualities and when the *Fingal* sailed from Greenock in October, 1861, Low was aboard ship with orders to ensure that Captain Anderson picked up Dunwoody Bulloch from Holyhead. As things turned out, it was fortunate that Low was aboard the *Fingal*, as Captain Anderson turned out to be "unsuited to his work" as Bulloch delicately put it at a later date. Anderson was below decks drinking when the *Fingal* ran into a storm on the way to Holyhead and the crew were left to their own devices when the ship struck the coal-carrier, *Siccardi* and sank her. It was Low who rowed ashore in the teeth of a gale and in the pitch black of night and dripping wet, awoke Bulloch by the light of a lantern to relate the bad news. Bulloch later gave a graphic account of this scene in which still half-asleep he envisaged the loss of not only the *Fingal* but the invaluable cargo it was carrying. The *Fingal* proved to be sturdier than Bulloch feared and there was no damage to the little ship. It was, however, imperative to leave the area as quickly as possible and Bulloch sailed as quickly as he could, leaving Fraser, Trenholm to sort out the financial mess. Captain Anderson remained in charge of the *Fingal*, to all intents and purposes, but in reality John Low was in charge of the ship when it crossed the Atlantic and successfully ran the blockade.

Low remained with Bulloch in the South for the following frustrating 6 months until together they joined the *Annie Childs* and once again ran the blockade this time outward bound. The launch of the *Oreto* (*Florida*) was Bulloch's next priority and once again it was to John Low that he turned to when he required a trusted agent. Low's orders were to aid Captain Duguid

The Alabama in the teeth of a gale

in sailing the *Oreto* to Nassau and ensure a smooth hand-over of the ship to Captain John Newland Maffitt. Bulloch's instructions were, as usual, detailed and precise and every other paragraph emphasised John Low's speedy return for the next mission that was planned which was the launch of the *Alabama.*

John Low came aboard the *Alabama* as Fourth Lieutenant; and highly recommended as Low came, Captain Semmes was faithful to the officers who had served him on the *CSS Sumter* but as others before him had found, in John Low he had acquired an officer the equal of any aboard. When the *Alabama* began to take prizes, Low was usually to be found at the head of the boarding party and more likely than not would be the man to torch the ship. John Low's finest hour was aboard the *Alabama* when early in her voyage the worthiness of both ship and crew were tested to the limit. On the evening of October 15th, 1862, the barometer dropped like a stone and the *Alabama* entered into the vortex of a Gulf Stream hurricane which could have easily finished the voyage of the *Alabama* in an instant - and very nearly did so. The storm grew steadily worse as night fell and by morning had gathered intensity to such a degree that the ship was tossed about like a toy between the mountainous waves. The howling winds had splintered the main topsail mast and the sails had been washed overboard when in an instant there was an unearthly pause from the merciless buffeting as the ship reached the eye of the storm but everyone aboard knew it was only a temporary respite and sure enough a half-hour later the *Alabama* re-entered into the maelstrom. Hour after hour, the ship rode the storm until the unthinkable began to happen and slowly she began to topple onto her side. Every man aboard ship knew only too well that once over on her side it was certain death for all of them. The *Alabama* was teetering on the edge of a precipice and looking into the abyss - her voyage ended before it had really begun.

It was in that instant, with just minutes to spare, that John Low, unordered, took it upon himself to grasp the helm and wrestle the ship back from the brink of disaster and for the following two hours he remained at his post until the *Alabama* passed out of the cyclone. Low had saved them all from a watery grave with his quickness of thought and initiative and Lieutenant Arthur Sinclair later wrote; *"Lieutenant Low's superb seamanship and coolness doubtless saved the Alabama from foundering due to the fury of the waves."* As pragmatic as ever, Captain Semmes' priority was to repair the badly damaged ship and the captured *T. B. Wales* provided the mast and sails for her repair - and the *Alabama* sailed on. On June 21st, 1863, the *Conrad* was captured in the South Atlantic and for once, Semmes was reluctant to burn the ship. The *Conrad* was a fine example of an American clipper and Semmes decided to make her a satellite of the *Alabama*. He put Lieutenant Low aboard as commander, allowing him to choose his officers, and commissioned the *Conrad* into the Confederate navy with the new name of the *CSS Tuscaloosa*. Low's orders were to follow the example of her mother-ship and destroy every Yankee ship afloat and to rendezvous with the *Alabama* at given destinations which were known only to Semmes and Low. Armed and dangerous, the speedy clipper-ship was given carte blanche to roam the oceans and sink and burn at will but try as he could Low could find very few Yankee ships still at sea. It was a measure of how successful the *Alabama* had been that commercial shipping from Northern ports was almost non-existent and although the *Tuscaloosa* stopped over one hundred ships, only one of them was a Yankee - the curiously named *Living Age* was subsequently bonded.

After a fruitless voyage of over 6,000 miles, the voyage of the *Tuscaloosa* came to an abrupt end in December 1863 when she put into Simons Town. Usually a safe haven for Confederate ships, the *Tuscaloosa* was seized on the orders of the British government and detained somewhat reluctantly as an uncondemned prize. After the usual flurry of diplomatic letters, Low found himself kicking his heels ashore and after weeks of waiting for the *Alabama* he decided to return to England and in January 1864, accompanied by Lieutenant William H. Sinclair he sailed for Plymouth aboard the mail packet the *Saxon*. Low's passage was paid by a sympathetic British Admiral.

In February 1864, Low made his way to Liverpool where on June 19th, after news of the *Alabama* had filtered through, he was disconsolate at missing the final battle. Indirectly, the *Alabama* was to claim one more victim of that battle - possibly the most poignant and pointless of all and one which John Low would have cause to regret. The news of the sinking of the *Alabama* resounded around the globe and was mourned greatly in the Southern States of America and not least at the home of Mary Elizabeth Low. News of the *Alabama* may have reached the South but news of John Low himself was lacking and Mary Elizabeth determined to discover what had befallen her husband, little knowing that his transfer to the *Tuscaloosa* meant that his name would not have been associated with the *Alabama* for that very reason. Mary Elizabeth left her 2 year old son, John, in the care of his uncle Andrew and sailed from Savannah through the blockade, arriving in Liverpool in August 1864. She fell ill with what was probably pneumonia and on the 20th November, 1864, just 4 months after her arrival, Mary Elizabeth was on her death bed in 6 Elizabeth Street, attended by her husband who she had found safe and sound at the cost of her own life; she was just 24 years of age. The quest of Mary Elizabeth Low has elements of a Greek Tragedy about it and is sadder still for being just a footnote in the greater drama of the Civil War in Liverpool. There was a strange irony in Mary Elizabeth's death in that Elizabeth Street was right next door to the old Liverpool Royal hospital. The street has now been shortened and the houses demolished but just two or three inches below the tarmac, the original cobbles are still in place. Herman Melville, Charles Dickens and even Jules Verne were all moved to write about the poverty in Victorian Liverpool and the attendant diseases which erupted from time to time. Cholera, smallpox and typhoid fever were common but measles, tuberculosis and scarlet fever were just as deadly at that time.

Low returned to duty when Bulloch found him yet another mission - this time he was to command the blockade-runner *Ajax* but by the time she was fitted out and launched the war was coming to an end and his career in the Confederate navy ended with it.

It was difficult to believe that John Low was not quite 30 years of age when he returned to his former employment as a businessman in Liverpool. The lure of the sea was still strong and for a short time he captained a ship called the *Knight Errant* owned by G. Fletcher and Co of Liverpool but it was a short-lived stay and Low took a position with Brewers Mill, a Liverpool cotton firm. Active again as a businessman, his duties took him to Leigh and Golborne where there were cotton mills and he remained firm friends with James Dunwoody Bulloch whose funeral he attended in Toxteth in 1901.

John Low's house in Sheil Road

His business travels flourished in more ways than one when aged 31, he met and married Catherine Morris, the 27 year old "Belle of Paddington" and they went on to have six children. All of the children lived to maturity except Marian Elizabeth Low who died on 24th April, 1884, aged just seven to become yet another proof of the high child mortality in Victorian times and the virulence of Scarlet Fever which was dreaded even up to and beyond the Second World War.

In 1892, John Low and Catherine went to live in 110 Shiel Road - at the time a prestigious house adjacent to the classy Newsham Park which he called "Encubar". Whenever Queen Victoria visited Liverpool she resided at Newsham House which was within a stone's throw of the Low's residence. The area is a little less salubrious than it once was but the Low's house is still standing - as solid and sturdy as its former owner.

In 1906, five years after the death of Bulloch, hundreds of mourners attended John Low's funeral cortege from his home in Sheil Road and followed his coffin to Emmanuel Church, West Derby Road from where he was taken to his last resting place in Golborne Cemetery by train from Lime Street Station. His train was met at Newton-le-Willows station by 100 boys from the Newton Farm School and the whole cortege travelled to Low's last resting place. He was 70 years old when he died after a life of adventure the envy of any man.

John Low's life was outstanding by any standards and his career at sea was rivalled by his acumen as a businessman. In his capacity as manager of the John Brewis cotton mill at Golborne he was not only eminently successful but was unique in earning not only the respect of the workforce but they actually liked him as well. The Leigh Chronicle of 1884 records his farewell party at The Legh Arms in Leigh where he was praised for his "gentle demeanour" and presented with a marble timepiece and matching ornaments. Leaving to take up work in an insurance business at Freshfield after 17 years in Golborne, his friends and neighbours also took the opportunity to praise him at another farewell ceremony where John Low and Catherine were lauded to the skies and presented with a decanter set and a solid silver cutlery service.

Accounts of John Low's life from every source whether it be his career at sea or his life as a businessman all have one thing in common - they all attest to Low's universal popularity. The fulsome praise that Low received from the workmen at Golborne was no small thing in an era when the working classes were commonly treated with disdain by their employers. During evidence given during the Geneva Claims, one of the seamen attested that during the voyage of the *Oreto*, he overheard John Low say to Captain Duguid that *"He treated the slaves on his plantation better than Duguid treated the men and that he would make a different arrangement when he came to port."* And he did. In that single sentence, John Low's philosophy is illustrated clearly.

A Liverpool Sailor - Warrant Officer Henry William Alcott

Arthur Sinclair who served aboard the *Alabama* for the whole of the cruise was an interested observer of the foibles of the officers and men who served alongside him and he has left a fascinating insight into the nature of all ranks who served aboard the ship. Sinclair is one of the very few who seem to have appreciated that the ordinary seamen were in fact quite extraordinary and without their unique skills the *Alabama* could never have left harbour. Apart from admiring the bravery of Michael Mars, the professionalism of James Brosman and extolling the virtues of carpenters and boatswains, Sinclair gave a mention to Henry Alcott, the sailmaker.

Henry Alcott

Alcott appears throughout Sinclair's narrative as a man thoroughly dedicated to his trade. Alcott would never have known that he was among the last in a long line of sailmakers dating back centuries and within a few short years he would have been an anachronism in an age of steamships but for the time being, aboard the *Alabama*, Alcott was an invaluable member of the crew. He proved his worth early in the cruise when working alongside the boatswain his skill and knowledge were invaluable in repairing the sails after the October hurricane. Later in the cruise when the *Alabama* was becoming worn and the copper was peeling from her hull, Alcott performed a task which was unusual in the previous century but virtually unknown in the 1800s the job was called "fothering" which involved a complicated procedure using the sail as a temporary plug until repairs could be made.

According to Sinclair's amusing summary, Alcott was: *"Like Pat's Parrot, slow of speech but profound of thought and hard to convince that canvas was not the most important part of the Alabama."* Sinclair also praised Alcott for his work in "the shot and shell department" after the battle with the *Kearsage* when Alcott was one of the crew who were picked up by the *Deerhound*.

Alcott sailed aboard the *Alabama* for the whole cruise and when the time came to look for new employment, he was not long in finding it aboard the *Shenandoah*, again making the whole cruise until she sailed into the Mersey and lowered the Confederate flag for the last time. References to Alcott aboard the *Shenandoah* point to him being an inveterate grumbler but that can be a trait often found in those who are conscientious. There's certainly no reference to any complaints when he is in charge of boarding parties taking whalers in the Arctic Ocean.

Alcott's home was a terraced house in Esmond Street, Anfield which was then a prestigious overspill of houses from the city centre built within a farm and country setting. The house itself was in effect a scaled-down version of the higher class of Victorian mansions which were dotted around the area and like its neighbouring houses was without electricity and gas with coal fires and candles supplying light and heat. It is a testimony to the Victorian builders that like many others of its type. Esmond Street is still standing and the houses are as sturdy as they ever were. In Alcott's day, his home would have been a very desirable residence.

Henry Alcott died in 1891 and was buried in what was then the newly constructed Liverpool Cemetery but is now known as Anfield Cemetery. With him went centuries of accumulated knowledge of a skill which is now rarely used except for specialist yachts and ships.

John Caren

A Manxman, also served aboard the *Alabama* throughout the whole campaign and was wounded in the battle with the *Kearsage*. He later worked as a cotton porter and was looked after in his daughter's home in 15 Monastery St until his death in 1914. The house in Monastery Street is a carbon copy of Henry Alcott's home and is just a short walk away. John Caren is also buried in Anfield Cemetery. He is buried in a pauper's grave and his only monument is the grass above.

Frederick Matthew Johns

There were at least twelve graves in St. James cemetery associated with the Confederacy but when the cemetery was converted into a park in the 1960's many were lost or broken or mislaid. The Confederate graves were not the only ones to have been "lost" - there are many other historical figures known to have headstones in the cemetery but are unable to be located. One of the very few intact is the headstone of Frederick Matthew Johns who was the Paymaster's Steward aboard the *Alabama* who lost his life in the fight with the *Kearsage*. Frederick Matthew Johns' father had a coal business in Howard Street.

Allan Stuart Hanckel
The Trent Affair

On the face of it, the Trent Affair is little more than a footnote in history, largely unheard of by most people and forgotten by others but at the time of its occurrence it was a cause célèbre and well worth recalling as an incident which could have led to incalculable consequences - it was a flame which if fanned could have easily burst into a conflagration.

Federal officers boarding the Trent

The early months of the American Civil War opened with manoeuvrings on both sides, both militaristic and political. In an effort to represent itself as a fledgling independent state, part of the Confederate strategy was to enlist the aid of European nations, notably Great Britain and France, both of which were inclined to sympathise with the Southern cause. On the orders of Jefferson Davis, Confederate commissioners, Mason and Slidell, were despatched to London and Paris and in the winter of 1861 were travelling aboard the British steamer *Trent* to take up their respective posts. Also on board ship were a number of lesser Confederate agents, one of whom, Allan Stuart Hanckel, was carrying papers for his new employers, the company of Fraser,Trenholm in Liverpool.

The series of events that culminated in the Trent Affair began surprisingly enough with Captain Raphael Semmes. Having converted the packet boat *Habana* into the *CSS Sumter*, Semmes was busy honing his new skills as Captain of commerce raiders by chasing and harrying United States ships throughout the months of 1861 from July onwards. Irvine Bulloch, Lt. P Armstrong, Lt. Arthur Sinclair, Anderson, Galt and Kell who would all form the nucleus of the crew of the *Alabama* were also learning a craft which would make the *Alabama* such a formidable raider. The torching of the *Golden Rocket* off the coast of Maine and the bonding of several other ships brought the *Sumter* to the attention of the Northern fleet and several United States warships were sent on a seek-and-destroy mission which led them on a merry chase down the eastern seaboard and the Caribbean. One of the ships sent on the mission was the screw-sloop *San Jacinto,* commanded by Captain Charles Wilkes. Wilkes was a native New Yorker and had served in the United States Navy for many years before the Civil War. In 1838, he had commanded a four year voyage of discovery, taking in

Australia, Singapore, Borneo, the Sandwich Islands and Oregon for which he had been awarded the National Geographic Society of London's Gold Medal. In October, 1861, while in port in Cuba, Wilkes learned of the two Confederate commissioners and that they had travelled from Charleston to Havana on board the blockade-runner, *Theodora.* Abandoning the search for Semmes to a much less mercurial objective, Wilkes gave chase, but subsequently learned that the commissioners were headed for St. Thomas to board the *Trent.* Perhaps if Wilkes had known that Semmes would one day soon become Captain of the infamous commerce-raider, *Alabama*, he would have continued on his original mission but history hinges on such decisions and in the event, Captain Wilkes aimed for what was immediately accessible and on November 1861, 240 miles into the Atlantic, he made the fateful decision to intercept a British ship going about her lawful business on the high seas.

A shot across the bows brought the *Trent* to a halt and a boarding party sought out the two Confederate commissioners, Mason and Slidell, and in a blatant flouting of international law, took the pair aboard the *San Jacinto* at bayonet point. Allan Stuart Hanckel was unknown to the crew of the San Jacinto and could only watch as the two agents were removed from the ship but Hanckel not only retained his own dispatches from the South but subsequently found the commissioner's papers and later delivered them into the right hands.

The power and prestige of the British Empire was at its apogee when Wilkes chose to affront one of its representatives and the political repercussions were not long in following, rising to a crescendo in the weeks and days to come, fuelled by the British press who then as now loved a good International Incident. On the other hand, *Harper's Weekly* were of the opinion that Captain Wilkes didn't go far enough and had every right to impound the *Trent* and take it into New York Harbour. Ultra-sensitive to perceived insults to its Imperial superiority, the British government demanded an apology and the release of the prisoners and to reinforce their orders thousands of British soldiers were shipped over to Canada and exports of arms to America halted. Was it possible that the indignation from a nation who had lauded Nelson, Frobisher, Drake and Kidd for doing the same thing, smacked just a little of hypocrisy. The stand-off lasted for weeks until President Lincoln resisted the pleas of the "hawks" and released the prisoners in the knowledge that the United States could never fight two wars at the same time. U.S. Secretary of State, William Henry Seward, was eventually instructed to release the prisoners but no apology was ever forthcoming and neither was the gold which had been taken from Mason and Slidell. Finally, the British government were perceived to have won a diplomatic victory but it eventually turned out to be scant reward. The short term loss was that the British government had revealed its overwhelming sympathy for the South and earned the distrust of the Federal government and in the long term the same Federal government later pursued the Geneva Claims far more vigorously than would have been expected, in revenge for the stance of the British as epitomised by the Trent Affair. Allan Stuart Hanckel continued on his voyage and worked throughout the Civil War as a trusted courier for both Fraser,Trenholm and Dunwoody Bulloch. He worked closely with Bulloch and often acted as his representative when he was away on business. Perhaps the Trent Affair had taught Hanckel to keep a low profile or perhaps working with Bulloch's clandestine business affairs had taught Hanckel to be extra cautious but whatever the reason, little is known of his subsequent career. Evidently, Hanckel was well thought of and married the daughter of one of the partners of Fraser, Trenholm, settling in England after the war far from his home in South Carolina.

His first recorded domicile was 35 Bedford Street North in 1865, followed by a residency in no 4 Derwent Square in 1868 - houses typically Victorian, large and spacious, as solid as rock and inhabited today. The house in Derwent Square is one of a row of large terraces facing onto a communal garden area and was once a prestigious and private area on the outskirts of the city. Now renamed "Lilies" the house has been converted into a hotel. Hanckel's next home was in North Drive, Victoria Park, where he would have been familiar with the venerable Monks Cross and the small lake opposite the Wavertree Lock-up which was considered a danger to the children who fished for sticklebacks and filled in around 1930. He called North Drive, Chicora, possibly after the blockade-runner of the same name or possibly because of the floral connotations it had in North America. In 1873, he moved to Formby in a house called Roselands after a short sojourn in Cronton where his wife died. Allan Stuart Hanckel is buried in Wavertree where the family tombstone is slowly mouldering away and fast becoming indecipherable simply stating that Allan Stuart Hanckel, a native of Charleston, died in 1904. His wife Susan Marion was the daughter of Alfred and Jane Wood and born in 1845 she died at the early age of 39 in 1884.

Chicora in North Drive, Wavertree

George Trenholm

James Morris Morgan (1845-1928)

James Morgan's autobiography of his adventures afloat, "Recollections of a Rebel Reefer" is a picaresque and highly entertaining account of life aboard ship, before and after the American Civil War. Arriving in Liverpool in 1862, as a 17 year old Midshipman in the Confederate navy, his youthful impressions are a little narrow and he is quite understandably vague about many of the historic events that are going on around him. Nevertheless, for a short time he pulls back the curtain and reveals a tantalizing glimpse into the world of 1860s Liverpool and all too soon allows it to fall, leaving so many questions frustratingly hanging in the air.

Morgan's first trip to Liverpool came about quite by chance when he was at the home of George A. Trenholm of the company Fraser, Trenholm after Trenholm had kindly helped the 16 year old who was alone in Charleston. Trenholm always had many distinguished guests and one of them was Commodore Maury who was about to travel to Liverpool on business on behalf of the Fraser, Trenholm Company. Out of the blue, George Trenholm asked the young Midshipman if he would care to accompany Commodore Maury to Liverpool to which he replied in the affirmative. The famed Commodore and the young Midshipman set out on the Fraser, Trenholm owned blockade-runner, the *Herald* headed to Bermuda and from there they sailed to Halifax, Nova Scotia on a Royal Mail steamer. From Nova Scotia, they took passage on the Cunard liner, *Arabia* bound for Liverpool. The Americans on board ship pointedly ignored the two Confederates but the impressionable Morgan was intrigued by members of the British Scots Guards who were returning from Canada (the Trent Affair had panicked the British Government into sending troops to Canada). Captain Richard Cooper was the envy of not only Morgan but the rest of the soldiers aboard the ship for the facial scar which marked him out - the scar had been caused by a Sepoy cutlass at the Battle of Lucknow. The Earl of Dunmore was also mentioned by the Midshipman for the dash and élan which caused him to run the blockade, simply for the hell of it.

Commodore Maury's business was with the Fraser, Trenholm company on Rumford Place and Midshipman Morgan accompanied the Commodore to the offices where he was well received by Charles Kuhn Prioleau who gave him letters of introduction to Dents, the chronometer makers and a tailor shop. James Dunwoody Bulloch invited the youth into his office and was surprised to find that Midshipman Morgan had been acquainted with Mrs Bulloch when she was Miss Harriot Cross of Baton Rouge. Maury and Morgan stayed in the luxurious surroundings of the old Adelphi Hotel that night.

Midshipman Morgan's escort duties to Commodore Maury came to an end when he was ordered to report to Lieutenant J.R. Hamilton C.S.N. for duty aboard the *Alexandra* which was in process of construction on the waterfront. Eager to see his future ship, Morgan hastened to the dockyards where he was surprised to see that the only parts of the *Alexandra* in place were the keel and ribs and more attention was being paid to the construction of a blockade-runner called the *Phantom* - Morgan doesn't mention the shipyard but both ships were built by W.C. Miller. As the year passed from Autumn to Winter, Morgan became increasingly morose: *"The days were shorter than I ever believed days could be - it was not light before mid-morning and dark again by half-past-two in the afternoon with the exception of foggy days and then there was no light at all. How I repented ever having abused that bright, burning Louisiana sun. What I would not have given for a sight of it now."* He would probably have been suicidal during a British summertime but for the time being Morgan wallowed in a morass of self-pity, complaining at his loneliness and his lack of money. The Adelphi days were long gone and he could only look longingly at the great hotel from his *"dingy lodgings in Upper Newington Street."* The *"storms and snow and cheerlessness"* of Morgan's everyday existence gradually brought Christmas, 1863, when he was invited to spend Christmas Day at Allerton Hall escorting the sixteen year old daughter of a Confederate General who was at school in England. Even this couldn't raise the spirits of the Midshipman who was pointedly ignored by the young girl; it would be interesting to hear her side of the story. In company with most great mansions at that time, Allerton had a walled, kitchen garden which supplied food all the year round and Morgan was somewhat impressed by the hothouses which supplied *"an abundance of flowers and tropical plants in December"*. The walled garden and greenhouses were still much the same until the 1960s when for a few short years they became a menagerie for children and afterwards fell into dereliction. Mr Prioleau handed Morgan fifty pounds sterling as a very generous Christmas present and the young man asked permission to visit Paris. Both the present and the trip would have cheered anybody but Morgan returned as unhappy as ever and anyone close to him may have had occasion to worry when he returned to *"my dismal life in Liverpool"*. By February, 1863, it was obvious to everyone that the *Alexandra* would not be sailing for a long time due to political pressure from Charles Francis Adams and Morgan was finally released from his winter ordeal in Liverpool and ordered to London. Whilst in London, the young man witnessed the wedding of the Prince of Wales and Princess Alexandra but it's not certain if he realized the connection between the ship and the Princess.

The CSS Georgia

Things began to look up for Midshipman Morgan when he was ordered for duty aboard the Confederate ship, the *Georgia* and it was obvious that despite all his complaints, the only thing really lacking was the company of other young men. The *Georgia* was originally a merchant ship built as the *Japan* in 1862 in Dumbarton, Scotland and purchased by the Confederate government for service as a cruiser. The small ship was not ideally suited for the role of a cruiser and after capturing 9 United States vessels it was decided that she should be taken out of service which is when Morgan found himself back in Liverpool. The young Midshipman's second encounter with Liverpool was no less encouraging than the first when the *Georgia* sailed up St. Georges Channel in a thick fog seeking a pilot in May, 1864. They soon encountered one of the several pilots who were always touting for work but as soon as he saw the Confederate flag flying this particular pilot refused the work with remarks to the effect that " He would be damned if he would pilot a pirate!" and vanished into the fog fervently hoping they would pile up on the rocks. The ship managed to make its way upriver alone (which was either very skilful or very lucky - the sandbanks are treacherous) and dropped anchor at Birkenhead. Morgan was of the opinion that his Captain was using him as a guinea-pig when he ordered him ashore in his uniform but the fact was that he did have contacts in the city which was a far more likely reason. Why a young Midshipman should go to the theatre on his first night's leave is a mystery although the theatre was known to be far more raucous than it is today but that's where Midshipman Morgan landed up. Morgan was a little wary of the reaction he would get dressed as he was in his Confederate Grey and became even more on edge when at the sight of him *"a whisper went through the audience"* but his fears were allayed when the whole of the audience gave three hearty cheers for the *Alabama* which even then was entering into legend. Making much of the audience reaction, the manager insisted that the Midshipman move to a box which was a relief as Morgan feared he was about to be thrown out. The evening at the theatre became even better when the Midshipman took a bow to rousing cheers each time the curtain went down and was later introduced to the cast. Morgan omits to mention the name of the theatre but it was almost certainly the New Theatre Royal in Williamson Square which later became an Ice Storage Depot (now demolished).

It's quite possible that the same audience would have reacted differently had they known that during its career at sea, the *Georgia* had captured the *George Griswold*, the United States ship which was instrumental in bringing much needed supplies to the starving Lancashire cotton workers and although the phrase was yet to be coined, it was an early example of *"winning hearts and minds."* According to Midshipman Morgan the *George Griswold* was manned by an *"all Negro crew"* and had carried a cargo of flour. It seems that some of this flour had found its way to Birkenhead where it was baked into loaves of bread and at the urging of the celebrated preacher, Henry Ward Beecher, thrown at a model of the *Alabama*. The issue was far more complex than Morgan could have ascertained in such a short time and in such varied snapshots of the situation.

Midshipman Morgan left the *Georgia* with sadness at having to depart his old shipmates and the ship was subsequently dismantled as a ship of war and returned to her original purpose of merchantman owned by a Liverpool shipowner named Jones for carrying mail between Lisbon and the Cape Verde islands. Unfortunately for her new owner, the ship was only in service for two months when it was captured at the mouth of the Tagus by the USS *Niagara*, sent to Boston and sold as a lawful prize of the US government. The owner never saw his ship again and was never recompensed for her loss. Morgan said that he came across his old ship in 1866 in Charleston Harbour in a decrepit condition and that she was wrecked in 1867. Morgan's memory fails him at this point as the ship went on to work in Canada in 1870 and was wrecked off the coast of Maine in 1875.

Samuel Walters (1811-1882)

Although he was born in London, Samuel Walters spent most of his life in Liverpool and is undoubtedly the prince of Liverpool maritime artists. Samuel's father Miles was a painter in his own right, moving his family to numbers 30 and 38 Pleasant street, circa 1830. Samuel enrolled in the Liverpool Academy where he began his career in maritime art.

In 1835, Samuel married Betsy Staniland Pulley and the couple went on to have 9 children. The Victorian penchant for having large families may seem a little profligate in this day and age but in Victorian Liverpool it was in reality a bulwark against the high child mortality which was prevalent. And true to the dictates of the era, 3 of the couple's children died in infancy.

By 1840, the family were living in 56 Stanhope street and Samuel had studios in Berry street and Bold street. As time went by and Samuel's business thrived, the family moved to Falkner Terrace {now Byng street} in what was then an idyllic rural area of Bootle, complete with a nearby beach. Jesse Hartley lived a few doors way and it was his encroaching dockworks which forced the family to move once again to 75 Merton road, Bootle.

Walters was a contemporary of all of Liverpool's great Victorians – Herdman, Hartley, Foster, Duncan, Huskisson et al and he has left a legacy of Liverpool waterfront in its heyday.

Samuel Walters and Betsy are together in death as they were in life, sharing the same unpretentious grave in Anfield cemetery, in a row of dozens of headstones all alike.

This painting is not by Samuel Walters but is by one of the many artists who adopted his style – which is the greatest compliment that any artist can receive.

The Grand Southern Bazaar

St Georges Hall circa 1860

A Splendid Time is Guaranteed For All

William Gawin Herdman's famous picture of St George's Hall illustrates Liverpool's Forum as it was in mid-Victorian times around the time when the Bazaar took place - visitors could see the Art Gallery and Museum still being built. St Georges's Hall was commissioned in 1844 with the original architect, Harvey Lonsdale Elmes, winning the architectural competition. It was completed in just a decade and is acknowledged as the finest neo-classical building in Europe if not the world. The Church of St. Johns to the rear of the building, was demolished in 1897, while pictures of the Hall can always be dated by the marble frieze, reminiscent of the Elgin Marbles, to be seen within the triangular portico. Any pictures of the portico minus the marble frieze, are always after 1945 when it was deemed to be unsafe and taken down - where it is now is anybody's guess but rumours persist that it was broken up for road ballast.

The Hall had only been open a decade when on the 18th October, 1864, one of the strangest events in its history took place and a motley gathering of Southern supporters came together in a fund raising event, following the example of a similar event, held a short time previously in New York on behalf

of Northern prisoners of war. The list of people taking part read like a Who's Who of the British aristocracy with a multitude of Marchionesses, Marquises, Baronnesses and Ladies from across the country, never before seen together in one place. The event had been organized by Charles Kuhn Prioleau who as the manager of Fraser,Trenholm and Company was eminently suited for his role as Treasurer and the Hon.Sec.was James Spence who had been a Southern activist throughout the Civil War.

Out-of-towners stayed in the Adelphi or at the home of F.S.Hull in Birkenhead and the really well-connected stayed in Knowsley Hall. The grand occasion was not to raise money for the war effort but to aid prisoners-of-war, orphans and widows, left destitute by the conflict; it was in effect a tacit acknowledgment that the South was reeling with exhaustion and the war was coming to an end. The premonitions were correct and the war ended formally six months later.

A Little Help From My Friends

The Hall was divided up into stalls with each stall named after a Southern state and every stall manned by a group of volunteers, all female and most of them having some connection to the South - the male patrons of the event had silver buckles inscribed with the motto *"Aide toi et Dieu t'aidera"* which was originally inscribed on the helm of the *Alabama*. The fact that the bazaar had been advertised in the Times gave some indication of how prestigious the event was perceived to be and in a surreal exhibition of togetherness, a whole host of Victorian socialites rolled up their laced sleeves, gathered up their skirts and began to sell the donations to an awed host of potential buyers. Harriot Bulloch took the Georgia stall and Mary Elizabeth Prioleau took the South Carolina stall while Mrs Slidell looked after the Mississippi stall. The presence of Mrs Laird told a tale of its own; John Laird's early declarations that the *Alabama* was a neutral ship had, by this time, long been discredited and throwing caution to the wind, he came out in support of the bazaar. Rumblings of discontent in Parliament and growing criticism of Laird also signalled a subtle shift in allegiances now that the South was almost certain to lose the war. Most of the other ladies were less easily recognisable and their allegiance to the Confederacy was not so clear - further investigation revealed some colourful histories;

The ladies numbered well over 30 in number but among the plethora of titles, not one of them could aspire to the name at the top of the list and Her Imperial Highness the Princess Murat must have been the source of many a curious glance. The Princess's maiden name was Catherine Willis Gray, a great-grandneice of George Washington and she was married to Achille Murat, the son of Marshal Joachim Murat and Caroline Bonaparte, Napoleon's sister.

When the Napoleonic Empire fell apart after 1815, Achille travelled to the New World where he settled in Tennessee, became city mayor and married Catherine. Catherine Willis Gray Murat not only inherited a grandiose old world title, on the death of her husband in 1847, she was granted a pension for life by Napoleon III. Catherine died in 1867, and is buried next to her husband in Tallahassee; an unlikely union both in life and in death. During their duties as volunteers working in the Great Hall, there is no mention that the couple ever visited the last resting places of Napoleonic prisoners of war, interred in the cemetery to the rear of the Hall and just 100 yards distant.

The Countess of Bentivoglio was the widow of Arthur Middleton, the scion of a distinguished American family that traced its roots back to the early immigrants. Middleton had met the Countess when he was in Italy and they had married in Rome.

Lady Georgiana Fane was 54 years of age when she attended the bazaar and despite a reputation for being *"incredibly beautiful"* in her youth, she had never married. Lord Palmerston was one of her suitors but she turned him down. The truth was that Lady Georgiana had eyes for only one man and in a cry that echoes down the years she wasted the best years of her life in an obsessive pursuit of the Duke of Wellington. She had first formed an attraction for the Duke in 1815, when she danced with him in Paris in a celebratory ball after Waterloo - she was just 14 years of age. The Duke was far from immune to her charms and although Wellington was married their relationship blossomed into an affair which lasted into Lady Georgiana's late 20s. She fully expected to marry the great man when his wife, Kitty Pakenham, died in 1830, but Wellington found himself surrounded by eligible females and coldly put his mistress to one side. From that day onward, her whole life was devoted to writing letters to Wellington on a daily basis, expressing her increasing bitterness and disappointment over and over again, a practice which continued until the day he died in 1852. Charles Greville took Wellington's side and ungraciously derided the besotted Georgiana as *"cracked"* - some things never change.

Liverpool City Crest

The Wellington monument which now overlooks St George's Hall was not erected until a decade after the bazaar; how Lady Georgiana would have reacted at seeing it each day only she would have known. She had no particular Southern affiliations and her attendance at the bazaar was probably another of her eccentricities.

The Marchioness of Bath was married to a fabulously rich man who inherited the estate of Longleat, which became the family home long before it was turned into a theme park.

Lady de Hoghton's Southern affiliations were easily discernible - her mansions and lands outside Blackburn contained a long-established cotton factory within its boundaries.

Mrs Slidell was the wife of the Confederate diplomatic ambassador John Slidell who accompanied by James M. Mason was at the centre of the Trent Affair when the Northern warship *San Jacinto* boarded the English ship, the *Trent*, and forcibly removed Mason and Slidell (November 1861). The Trent Affair was the ensuing international incident which for a while had Britain and America teetering on the brink of war.

Lady Beresford Hope was the wife of the extremely rich Conservative M.P. and common to Victorian days they had a family of ten children. One of the Friends of today's St Georges Hall, Mrs Beresford Hope, is a descendant of the Lady who originally attended the bazaar.

Mrs Klingender lived in Waterloo and was the wife of a merchant whose business in the city centre sold many items to Fraser, Trenholm and Co for use on the Confederate ships.

All the other helpers could be found within the pages of the Peerage.

The Hendersons Will All Be There

The journalist from the *Mercury* covering the bazaar in Liverpool, wrote several paragraphs explaining that the event was non-political and purely from a charitable perspective, Northern and Southern partisanship should be put to one side - which is precisely what happened, with donations subscribed by most of the leading stores throughout the city; Stoniers supplied china, Jeffereys supplied carpets and Messrs Dreapers and Sons

Titan at left of Willis organ

managed the entertainment. The *Mercury* journalist then spent most of the next four days rhapsodising over it all. He was probably glad to take a rest from articles on Jem Mace's forthcoming bare-knuckle bout, the flock of sheep grazing in the grounds of St. Luke's Church and the increasing numbers of cotton merchants declaring bankruptcy.

The Southern Bazaar was never a low-key affair as might have been expected but on the contrary was a colourful and noisy carnival, part fairground and part Paddy's market, attracting vast numbers of excited buyers who paid a half-crown admittance and then swarmed through the building from early morning to late evening. The stalls each had an arched, ornamental entrance and they were individually designed in flamboyant bunting and brightly coloured Victorian drapes with British, French and American flags gaily flying above them. Overlooking the strange gala were the sombre marble statues of Liverpool's Pantheon, unseeing and inscrutable, with Roscoe sitting immediately opposite Gladstone, on the opposite side of the Hall.

The journalist from the *Mercury* seemed to be enjoying himself more than anyone and reported on the entertainment in glowing terms. The diorama of the city of Liverpool was popular but most people eventually found their way to the "mermaid" who was sitting in a tank of water giving paranormal insights into the future and calling up disembodied spirits not always of a serious nature. The Lord Mayor was curious enough to ask for a "reading" which attracted quite an audience. There was something particularly British about upper-class people such as His Worship the Mayor putting themselves on public display to be laughed at by the public at large and the "mermaid's" insights vied in popularity with several other wonders. Automatons were always a feature of Victorian entertainment and the singing bullfinch could be heard trilling around the hall from time to time but the "female Blondin" was the main attraction and at intervals danced her way across a high-wire to a sea of upturned faces (an automaton Pierrot balances precariously across the high wire each day in the Musee Grevin, in Paris, to this day and is always the star of the show). If things quieted down a little then the Willis organ, the largest in the country, boomed out or Master Willie Pape, "a prodigy of musical talent who has played before Royalty" played the pianoforte in the background and for those who liked their entertainment of a more cultural nature then an Operetta Company played in one of the adjoining rooms.

We're Sorry But It's Time to Go, We Hope You Have Enjoyed The Show.

The range and the quantity of the items for sale was astonishing and as soon as a stall became depleted of wares, it was immediately replenished from the numerous gifts that had been donated from Paris, London, Liverpool and even sympathetic Northerners from New York sent items. Prices were negotiable but a large doll's house was priced at £70 which was an astronomical sum in those days, the model of Milan Cathedral in pearl was even more expensive and rings and brooches made by Southern prisoners of war went for prices far beyond their intrinsic worth. Much of the material for sale seemed to be from the mansion houses of the wealthy patrons, with statuettes of the Prince and Princess of Wales, elegant silver collections, decorative clocks and even a supply of game birds from a Scottish estate. A model of the *Alabama* was on the Arkansas stall, with live rabbits, a wax magnolia and a model of a cotton flower in all its stages of development were on others.

Surprisingly, the most valuable item of all was not the gold or the jewellery it was a tiny Shetland pony, donated by an Irishman and raffled over and over again as each winner returned it to the sponsors. One item not for sale was held by the Vicomtesse de Dampierre and displayed on the Virginia stall. It was an ornamental sword supplied by Webb and Bonelli of Bond Street and inscribed: *"Presented to Major General Robert E. Lee from the Virginian stall of the Southern Bazaar at Liverpool, October 18th, 1864".*

Titan at right of Willis organ

The whole event raised £22,000 which was an inordinate amount of money in those days and everybody was happy to see it go to a good cause. The coming together of North and South and the atmosphere of bonhomie throughout the event was a constant theme as reported in the newspapers and was perhaps symbolic of what would soon be happening in America. Both sides in the conflict were war-weary and the North would soon achieve its aims of abolishing slavery and preventing Southern separatism. The real struggles were still to come and for the freed slaves would never really be resolved for a further century in the small civil war of the battles of the Civil Rights Movement. Still, it was a start, and perhaps in some small way the Southern bazaar presaged the coming together of North and South where it really mattered - in America.

The House in the Square

Charles Kuhn Prioleau

The company of Fraser,Trenholm based at 10 Rumford Place was a branch of the long-standing Charleston cotton firm of John Fraser and Co. When Civil War broke out, Fraser, Trenholm were ideally situated to help the Confederacy and their offices near to the waterfront, inadvertently but enthusiastically became a virtual Confederate embassy within the city of Liverpool. The company very quickly became deeply involved in the Confederate cause, purchasing ships, handling vast amounts of money and aiding Confederate agents such as Anderson, Huse and Bulloch in any way they could. The company's value to the Confederacy was inestimable and without Fraser, Trenholm's active goodwill the Confederate agents would have found life extremely difficult. The United States later asserted that the Liverpool branch of Fraser,Trenholm was set up in anticipation of the forthcoming war and although there's no proof of that belief, it's easy to see why the northern administration came to that conclusion.

As a senior partner in the company, Charles Kuhn Prioleau was obliged to keep a low profile and as a matter of expediency had adopted British citizenship. Nevertheless, from the very beginning, the offices were subject to intense scrutiny by agents of the U.S. consulate, just around the corner. Charles Kuhn Prioleau was undoubtedly the major player in matters concerning the Confederacy and even a cursory examination of the voluminous files on record reveal extensive communications of every nature between Prioleau and the Southern agents. There are also many letters from Charles's family in Carolina detailing the hardships of the war. It is Prioleau's name which is on every letter heading and it is possible that Prioleau was responsible for the company's deep involvement with the Confederacy in Liverpool; Prioleau, as a native of Charleston, South Carolina, was intensely patriotic and even when there were only rumours of the impending Civil War, in 1860 he had sent a British-made Blakely cannon to his home state as a gift. The Galena cannon was purchased from George Forrester and Company's factory of Vauxhall and was cutting-edge armament at the time. The gun played a part in the attack on Fort Sumter on April 12th, 1861 which presaged the outbreak of war. Prioleau's practical aid probably brought him and his company to the attention of Stephen Mallory but whatever the reason, Fraser, Trenholm and the Confederate navy became one and the same thing. The gift also added credence to the Northern claim that Fraser,Trenholm was a pre-emptive set-up.

The offices in Rumford Place were a hive of activity during the Civil War and Confederate agents were frequent visitors employing the expertise of Fraser, Trenholm to the utmost. However, the business was not only active on behalf of the Confederacy, they were also a considerably successful import and export firm, specialising in cotton - hence their great interest in the later promotion of blockade-runners. Prioleau himself, was by any standards a very rich man and a member of that elite band of Merchant Princes earning their fortunes from the thriving Liverpool mercantile trade. In 1861, Prioleau lived in Darby Road, Garston, which was a leafy suburb of Liverpool and still retains a regal air but the fine houses are now mostly new. His wife was Mary Elizabeth Wright whose own family were financially well-off (her father was a cotton merchant) and for a short time they rented the historic Allerton Hall while 19 Abercromby Square was under construction. Mary was reputed to be a great beauty and even in the short time that they lived in Allerton Hall she earned the soubriquet, the Belle of Allerton Hall. There was, and still is, a tiny garden near to the house which was filled with azaleas and perfect for contemplation, which was known up to and beyond the 1960s as The American Garden.

Allerton hall - present day.

Mary Elizabeth's father was himself a cotton merchant and as such his business suffered during the Civil War. There is a strong suggestion that Mr Wright was enlisted by Dunwoody Bulloch as an agent in ship purchasing which makes a great deal of sense given that his credentials would have been impeccable and allied to the fact that he was English. His name is mentioned in a clandestine meeting in Wood's Hotel, High Holborn, London where Wright met Lt. William Conway Whittle jr of the Confederate navy in negotiations concerning the Sea King. It seems that Wright had been instrumental in the purchase of the Sea King using money supplied by Fraser, Trenholm and of course signed for by his son-in-law, C.K.Prioleau. Soon after the meeting, Whittle sailed on the Sea King which sailed down the Thames and out into the Atlantic where it took on its true identity of the CSS Shenandoah. It goes without saying, that Wright would have been looked upon favourably whenever cotton was in supply via Fraser,Trenholm owned blockade-runners.

Child riding a wild turkey.

At the time that the Prioleau's knew the Hall, the house had an army of servants and the gardens were immaculately kept. Great houses such as Allerton Hall always had a walled garden within their estates and Allerton was no exception, providing exotic fruit and vegetables all year round, grown on walls warmed by fires at their base and greenhouses growing all manner of fruit out of season - a visiting Midshipman Morgan gave an account of the "hothouses" which impressed him. The walled-garden today is a sad shadow of its former glory, overgrown with weeds and the rotting skeletons of the "hothouses" and a neglected, circular pond awaiting water and goldfish as it it used to be. The house however, is a thriving "Pub in the Park" bearing several oil-paintings of unknown origin - one of the paintings is an intriguing portrait of a lady dressed in mid-Victorian style crinoline. Nobody can put a name to the lady who is quite beautiful and the painter's name has been obscured by poor framing but it's interesting to sit and speculate as to who she could be.

Charles and Mary went on to purchase so much property that they sustained far more gardeners and servants than family. The numerous letters to Charles from his retainers asking for instruction as what plants to grow or matters of staff discipline, written in formal, headed letters, reveal the typical Victorian upstairs-downstairs dynamics which existed between Charles and his retainers and just how much he had assimilated into an English lifestyle. Besides extensive properties he had left behind in South Carolina from which he received long letters from his family, Prioleau owned a cottage on the outskirts of Liverpool which he rented out and a large house in Carlisle called Balkail House where Mary spent a great deal of time. The mail in those days must have been far better than it is today, as Mary wrote daily to Charles never forgetting to express her undying love in one sentence and berating Charles for not writing in the next. It's easy to see why Charles was perhaps a little lax in replying as much of the content of Mary's letters was full of banalities such as curtains and carpets interspersed with the odd invoice from a Parisian couturier when Mary took herself off shopping to Paris.

Palmetto with snake peering around base - to be found on the ceiling of the lobby.

The most evocative of the Prioleau's homes is 19 Abercromby Square, a spacious town house within a row of terraced houses in the Georgian style surrounding a typical Victorian garden which they moved into circa 1862. The Abercromby house is redolent with Charles's influence and is almost a shrine to his Southern roots with its many subtle decorative features reminiscent of South Carolina. Even before one enters the house an alert observer can spot the stars at the top of the Georgian porticos and just within the foyer is a painting of a Palmetto and snake, the symbol of Prioleau's home State. The circular staircases leading up to the central skylight draw the eye to a glass ceiling with a star in the centre and in each corner and cornice there are sculptures of Crescent Moons, ladies' heads bearing Bonnie Blue Stars, yellow Jessamine and extravaganzas such as babes riding turkeys. The piece-de-resistance of the whole piece is a large, circular mural painted on the ceiling of what was once the dining room. The painting is an unusual departure from the Southern theme and is probably a result of Mary's influence to put something of her own stamp onto the house. It depicts a number of subjects dressed in classic Greek or Roman attire and engaged in various acts such as drinking or chatting and at first glance appears to be a whimsical folly. However, the painting is outstanding for the reason that the lady handing a posy of flowers to a bearded gentleman has been identified as Mary Prioleau, the Belle of Allerton Hall herself and what is more she bears a remarkable resemblance to the lady in the painting in Allerton Hall, down to the lace shawl she holds over her arm.

Mary's letter-writing to Charles never ceased and apart from her usual preoccupation with domestic problems she grumbled about the smoke and pollution in the area. As a matter of fact, she may have had a point as every house poured out a constant stream of smoke from coal-fires and William Roscoe's first botanic garden which was not far away had been forced to move further out of the city for that very reason only three decades earlier. The many years of smoke billowing from houses right across the city had a postscript in the 1980s when the soot-blackened buildings across Liverpool were all subject to a sand-blasting operation which revealed the honey-coloured sandstone as it was when the places were first built. William Roscoe was instrumental in enhancing the square when John Shepherd, the curator of the original botanic gardens at Crown Street, was instructed to design and oversee the central square

Painting of the Ceres.

gardens. The gardens with their gazebo in the centre were exclusively for the use of residents and each one had their own key to gates. One of the Prioleau's neighbours in Abercromby Square was Charles MacIver who with his brother had played a great part in forming the Cunard Line; whether the families ever met is not known but they must have passed each other many times.

No 19 Abercromby Square later became even more historically important when a new Bishop of Liverpool, Bishop Chavasse, moved in with his family. Bishop Chavasse laid the foundation stone to the Anglican Cathedral and was acclaimed in his own right but it was his son Noel Chavasse who is chiefly remembered as a double V.C. winner during the First World War. There is a Blue Plaque commemorating the fact that Noel Chavasse lived in the house but it is largely forgotten that the Prioleau's ever lived there.

What Bishop Chavasse thought of the Southern motifs scattered throughout his home is not recorded but he was obviously perceptive enough to realize that they were of historic value and the house stands today virtually unchanged from the day it was built. In 2008, during Liverpool's Capital of Culture year a bronze statue of Noel Chavasse was erected as opposite to his home as possible. The statue was sculpted by Liverpool artist, Tom Murphy, and depicts double VC winner, Captain Chavasse, between a wounded soldier and a stretcher-bearer.

The purchase of a magnificent yacht, the *Ceres*, purchased in 1864, and membership of the prestigious Liverpool Yacht Club (adjacent to Miller's dockyard) set the seal on the Prioleau's wealth. The yacht named the *Ceres* was built in Glasgow in 1859 for a Robert Buchanan Stewart by the company of Tod and McGregor of Glasgow and was the first ocean-going yacht seen on the Clyde. Prioleau purchased the yacht in 1864 for the astronomic sum, for those days, of £5,500. Because the yacht was capable of travelling great distances, had retractable funnels and utilised both sail and steam there were rumours that the yacht was yet another cruiser or blockade runner which may or may not have been true but there is no record of the yacht ever having been used for such a purpose.

Abercromby Square in 1860.

Elizabeth Lynch Hamilton.

Although the Prioleau's numerous properties occupied much of Mary's time, she was always active in helping the Confederate cause and never more so when she accompanied her husband in working on the Southern Bazaar. The Southern Bazaar was held in the magnificent St. Georges Hall and consisted of many different stalls each representing a Southern State of America. The event raised the staggering sum of £22,000 and went to help Confederate prisoners of war held in the notorious Northern prisons in appalling conditions - Elmira was synonymous with squalor and dreaded by southern troops. The aftermath of the Civil War not only caused embarrassment and financial liability to the British government but ruined Fraser, Trenholm via litigation following the Geneva claims - the company paid a high price for its patriotism.

In 1867, Charles Kuhn Prioleau moved his business affairs to London and the family assimilated themselves into life as an English upper-class family in the capital. The main reason for his move away from Liverpool was the constant harassment that he suffered at the hands of Bulloch's nemesis, Thomas Haines Dudley who was energetically gathering evidence for the Geneva Claims. The Prioleau family have a long and distinguished lineage which is too detailed to go into here but it is worth noting that Charles's father Judge Samuel Prioleau was born in Charleston in 1784 where he had an Admiralty law practice and a sketch of his background may give some clues as to Charles's subsequent path in life. After serving at the Bar, Judge Prioleau eventually became an eminent maritime lawyer which may have accounted for Charles Kuhn Prioleau's maritime interests. Judge Prioleau was a child of the South and financially secure and it would have been extraordinary if he had not kept slaves. There was an unfortunate incident in 1822, when his slave Peter Devereux revealed a planned slave insurrection which was suppressed and the ringleaders executed. Judge Prioleau became a rich man and Charles would have been no stranger to luxury. Judge Prioleau's first wife was Hannah Motte Hamilton the couple married in 1811 and after only a short time together, sadly, Hannah died in 1819, leaving Judge Prioleau and their son, James Hamilton Prioleau.

Judge Prioleau.

Judge Prioleau later married Hannah's sister, Elizabeth Lynch Hamilton and they went on to have five more children - only one of whom, Samuel Prioleau lived and died in Charleston. Hannah Hamilton, Elizabeth, and Alice Edith are all buried in Liverpool. Given that Judge Prioleau died in 1839, Charles' mother and sisters must have thought it advantageous to accompany Charles to Liverpool when he set up as manager of Fraser, Trenholm. It's unusual in Victorian times for girls to remain unmarried but, despite reports that she was *"a striking girl"*, Hannah Hamilton remained single and died in 1875. Alice Edith also remained unmarried and is buried in Liverpool and there is no record of Elizabeth marrying and she died in 1871 also in Liverpool. Charles' mother, Elizabeth Lynch Prioleau preceded her daughters and died in 1860 in Liverpool.

The clandestine operations of Fraser,Trenholm necessitated anyone connected with the Confederacy keeping a low profile and many files were later destroyed which is why the nature of the Prioleau family's affairs in Liverpool is sketchy and awaits many gaps to be filled in.

Charles and Mary had 7 children - 2 of the 6 boys joined the British Army; Lynch Hamilton was born in 1861 and attended Sandhurst in 1881 while his brother, Louis St. Julien Prioleau, born in 1869, became a major in the British army. Louis died in 1919, serving with the Norfolk Regiment in Egypt.

Charles died in 1887 and is buried in Kelsall Cemetery, London. Mary lived ten more years after Charles and died in 1897, in Sainte Croix, Bayonne.

The ceiling of 19 Abercromby Square in what was once the dining room. Mary Elizabeth Prioleau is at the bottom left of the painting, handing a posy of flowers to a heavily bearded gentleman who is probably her husband, Charles Kuhn Prioleau.

It's almost certain that the surrounding figures are friends of the Prioleau's but none of them have as yet been identified and neither has the artist.

Picture portrayal of the "Pride of Liverpool"

Several artists have been inspired to paint the Liverpool pilot boats during the "Follow me" incidents. There have been years when gales were so severe that ships have been forced to wait outside the Mersey until the storms abate. The picture here by Samuel Walters portrays the Pride of Liverpool leading a flotilla of ships along the Crosby Channel after the gales of January 1866. The flag at the pilot boat's foremast is the " Follow me please" pennant

Portrait of a Lady

Mary Elizabeth Wright (1840-1897)

Liverpool - circa 1860

Abercromby Square

William Roscoe's family home at the top of Mount Pleasant and the workhouse at the top of Brownlow Hill were in their day the outer limits of Liverpool. Although the inhabitants of the workhouse were hardly likely to take an interest, the view from Roscoe's house was an uninterrupted panorama stretching down the slopes of Mount Pleasant, across the rooftops of the churches, houses and warehouses and onto the river with its myriads of ships coming and going as they caught the tides.

To the rear of Roscoe's family home the slope levelled off onto a plateau containing the Mosslake, an ancient wetland, unchanged for centuries and thought to be unsuitable for any kind of building work. But by the turn of the century (1800) Liverpool was spreading outwards at an alarming rate, attitudes were changing just as fast, and for engineers about to build the first rail system across the much larger mosslands of Lancashire, the challenge of the Mosslake wetlands held few fears.

Once Liverpool Corporation had agreed for work to begin, John Foster senior drew up plans for the square as early as 1816. The wetlands were drained a decade later and by 1835, two thirds of the houses had been completed. The architecture of the houses was typical of the Georgian style adopted over the previous century and similar squares can still be found throughout Great Britain – Dublin's Merrion Square is an outstanding example. Georgian squares invariably consist of sturdy houses with pillars either side of York stone steps leading up to solid front doors – all of which gives them a slightly forbidding appearance. They were in fact designed and built for a merchant aristocracy and were far beyond the means of even the most industrious of the working classes. The frontages of the houses in Abercromby Square are deceptively small but once past the front door, the houses have an Alice Through The Looking-Glass effect and large rooms on several floors with stables to the rear go to make up extravagantly large households which required a staff of servants to keep them running smoothly. The gardens in the centre were an essential part of the features of any Georgian square and those of Abercromby were designed by William Roscoe's gardener John Shepherd, the curator of the Botanic gardens in Crown Street, which in 1830 were just about to be moved further out to Edge Hill. The gardens with their distinctive gazebo were the sole province of the householders of the square who paid one guinea per annum and were each provided with their own key.

The square was named after General Sir Ralph Abercromby (1734 – 1801) whose distinguished career came to an end after the Battle of the Nile (1798). Following Nelson's comprehensive defeat of the French fleet at Aboukir Bay, in 1801, General Abercromby sailed aboard the *Foudroyant* at the head of a fleet of ships containing 14,000 men. The soldiers fought their way along the coast and defeated the French at Alexandria but Abercromby was shot in the leg and taken back to the *Foudroyant* where he died several days later.

There are several memorials to Sir Ralph Abercromby scattered across England and Scotland – the most distinctive is in St. Paul's Cathedral and the most poignant is in the Upper Barraca Gardens overlooking Grand Harbour, Malta. The *Foudroyant*, once Nelson's flagship, also had a varied career and was almost as famous as Abercromby himself. Built in 1798, the famous ship came to a bizarre end wrecked on Blackpool shore in 1897, after an incredible 99 years in service.

Over the years, Abercromby Square has at different times, been home to many distinguished Liverpudlians including; Henry Booth, pioneer of the railways, James Newlands, Liverpool's Bazalgette, whose radical sewerage system and work alongside Dr. Duncan did so much to eradicate cholera and typhus throughout the city, Charles MacIver, who pioneered the Cunard Line, Lord

Russell of Liverpool, stalwart of the Daily Post for 50 years and author of the denouncements of Nazi war crimes in the Scourge of the Swastika (1954) and Japanese war crimes in Knights of Bushido (1958), Florence Melly who devoted her life to education in the city, Robert Gladstone, a cousin of William Ewart Gladstone and not least Sir Thomas Brocklebank of the famous shipping line. William Earle had a mansion on the corner of the square and Oxford Street and across the road St. Catherine's Church had been consecrated in 1831. The Earle mansion has long gone and St. Catherines was bombed beyond repair in 1941 – the Senate House now stands where the church once was.

Reminders of Home

One of the last houses to be built in Abercromby Square was that of Charles Kuhn Prioleau and his wife Mary Elizabeth. The couple married on 3rd May 1860, in Walton Parish Church - Charles was aged 33 and Mary Elizabeth gave her age as 20. Soon after the wedding, Charles commissioned the architectural firm of Culshaw to draw up plans for the house which would eventually become 19 Abercromby Square. The first plans were dated 1862 and the house was completed in 1864 when the Prioleaus moved in; the intervening years had been spent in historic Allerton Hall, a suitably fitting background for Mary Elizabeth's legendary beauty where she became known as the Belle of Allerton Hall.

Boy on a stag - ceiling 19 Abercromby Square

Although the neighbouring houses in Abercromby Square were decorated to each owner's requirements and many were famed for their tasteful designs, none of them approached the innovations that the Prioleaus introduced into their new home and in an uninhibited celebration of all that he stood for, Charles decorated the house in a glorious mélange of Confederate motifs, mosaics and sculptures. The circular mural on the dining room ceiling was always the most intriguing of the many paintings around the house and it was always an oral tradition that two of the characters dressed in Roman attire were in fact representations of Charles and Mary Elizabeth themselves. The scrolled wooden frame had at the sides of the circle the knotted inscription CKP – Charles Kuhn Prioleau. There was also speculation that the two carved heads on the staircase were sculptures of Charles and Mary Elizabeth but none of this was proven.

The only room that was not dedicated to the Confederacy was the large room immediately to the left of the entrance where Victorian sensibilities would have rejoiced in the allegorical figures representing Moral Philosophy. The

Prioleaus were only in the house a short time when in 1865, the Confederacy came to its inevitable conclusion and by 1870, they had left for London, leaving behind the still active agents of Thomas Haines Dudley and the scattered files of Fraser,Trenholm.

Over the years many visitors have craned their necks to view the mural on the ceiling and speculated on those tantalising images but they have all left frustrated by the enigmatic murals and the carvings on the staircase. After nearly a century and a half of speculation by the erudite, the knowledgeable and the simply curious, who all came to the same frustrated conclusions, it was generally accepted that the clues left behind when the Prioleaus left Liverpool would forever remain undeciphered. But in 2009, a totally unexpected turn of events came about which brought into the light many of the answers to questions that had remained unanswered for years.

The Confederacy Abroad

Oil painting of Charles Kuhn Prioleau

The first five years of Charles and Mary Elizabeth's marriage coincided, broadly, with the years of the American Civil War and Charles' fortunes fluctuated in tandem with the rise and fall of the Confederacy, although he worked tirelessly for the Southern cause right until the final days.

Charles was a native of Carolina and served in the United States army during the Mexican War. The Civil War was approaching fast and Charles was still a young man when he moved to Liverpool, as a partner and manager of Fraser, Trenholm and Co. at 10 Rumford Place, circa 1856.

It was during those heady days as war became an inevitability and the South was most defiant, that Prioleau had purchased a Blakely rifled cannon from Forresters of Vauxhall Road which was shipped to General Beauregard. The cannon, known as the Galena Cannon, on the 12th April,1861, fired on Fort Sumter in the opening rounds of the war between the States. In respect of the fact that the CSS *Shenandoah* arrived at Birkenhead on the 6th November where Captain Waddell surrendered to Captain Paynter of HMS *Donegal* of the British Navy, it could be justifiably said that the first and the last shots of the American Civil War had begun and ended in Liverpool.

The partnership of John Fraser and George Alfred Trenholm had originated in Charleston but in the months leading up the American Civil War, they established an office in Liverpool, along with several minor offices in the Caribbean. There is little doubt that the firm were establishing bases in order to aid the Confederate war effort, mainly of a naval nature, in an astute plan which discomforted the Federal government throughout the war; Charles Kuhn Prioleau, as managing partner, held a pivotal role in the whole operation. Working closely with James Dunwoody Bulloch, Charles was instrumental in securing the purchases of the *Alabama* and the *Florida* and dozens of blockade-runners, all bought either for Fraser, Trenholm or on behalf of the Confederate government. Prioleau acted as a banker for the Confederacy and if his duties had ended there they would have been onerous enough but Rumford Place inadvertently became a clearing-house for Confederate agents; James Dunwoody Bulloch kept an office within the building, sailors came and went and Confederate agents received their orders from there – it was in fact the nerve-centre of Confederate activities in Europe and Charles Kuhn Prioleau was the pivot around which all things revolved.

The *Many Faces* of the Betsy Ames

Among the many ships that were bought or paid for via the offices of Rumford Place Charles Kuhn Prioleau could not resist naming one of them after his wife, although he took the precaution of using her maiden name. And for a brief period of time Mary Elizabeth had the distinction of having a ship named after her. The ship was to be utilised as a blockade-runner and had started life as an American, privately owned brig named the *Betsy Ames*. The *Betsy Ames* was unfortunate enough to be captured, by the Confederate schooner, *Sallie,* in October,1861, during the early months of the war when enthusiasm and confidence were running high. She was subsequently designated a legitimate prize of war and sold on to Fraser, Trenholm and Co. As the *Betsy Ames*, the brig ran the blockade out of Charleston and reached Liverpool in April,1862, where she was renamed the *Mary Wright*. Mary Elizabeth's pride in such an honour was to be short-lived as the clandestine workings of the Fraser, Trenholm organization dictated that the ship be renamed once again in order to thwart the numerous agents employed by Thomas Haines Dudley. The *Mary Wright* adopted yet another female pseudonym and the ship was renamed the *Lilla* with a man named Richard George Bushby registered as the sole owner. It was undoubtedly a complete coincidence that Bushby, as a merchant, had his offices next door to Fraser, Trenholm at no. 9 Rumford Place. Bushby lived at no. 29 South Hill Road and besides his work as a merchant he was also Vice Consul for the Grand Duchy of Oldenburg, a north German independent state.

The Quaker City

In May,1862, the once *Betsy Ames*, the fleeting *Mary Wright* and now the *Lilla* finally began her career as the Confederacy's latest blockade-runner – an occupation which was to be as short-lived as every other facet of the ship. After just one month at sea, in July,1862, the *Lilla* was captured without difficulty by the U.S. gunboat, *Quaker City.*

Returned into the custody of the Federal government, the *Lilla* was immediately reclaimed by its original owners and after court proceedings in a Massachusetts court house, the ship was returned to its rightful owners, whose first act was to name the ship by its original name and the multi-named ship once again became the *Betsy Ames.*

In a bizarre postscript to the odyssey of the most ineffective blockade-runner that the Confederacy ever owned, at the conclusion of the Civil War, a poverty-stricken Fraser, Trenholm went to a court of arbitration for restitution of the ship they claimed to be legally theirs by right of purchase. The case dragged on for years and ended up as little more than a political football in which the Confederate cause came off worst.

The Leaving of Liverpool

The first five years of Charles and Mary Elizabeth's marriage were undoubtedly the most frenetic of times for both of them; for Mary Elizabeth there was the move to Abercromby Square and all that went with it and then there was the entry into the world of the first three of her seven children; and for Charles there was the heavy burden of his responsibilities at Rumford Place. The early successes of the Confederate armies and the buccaneering successes of the *Alabama* and the *Florida* had soon been followed by a lingering descent into desperation and when the South was eventually defeated, it also meant the end for the Liverpool branch of Fraser,Trenholm and Co.

Charles Kuhn Prioleau's loyalty had been unconditional but when the Confederacy collapsed, his unswerving devotion to the Southern cause, of necessity, became secondary to the demands of his growing family; his first son, Lynch Hamilton Prioleau had entered the world in 1861 followed in quick succession by Charles Arthur in 1862 and Richard in 1865.

Rumford Place sign

Charles eventually paid a heavy price for his patriotism and was left facing innumerable problems – not only was he owed a staggering £170,000 by the now defunct Confederate government, he was also hotly pursued by his creditors in Liverpool and to add to his troubles he was constantly harassed by the agents of Thomas Haines Dudley, whose tenacity knew no bounds. After a multitude of court cases Charles was eventually declared bankrupt and he at last came to the conclusion that his future and that of his family lay elsewhere. At the end of the 1860s, Charles and his family left Liverpool behind and moved to Twickenham where he began again, forming a banking-house named Prioleau and Co. In 1869, Louis St Julien was born and after four sons, in 1872, the couple finally had a daughter that they named Margaret. In 1874, it was business as before, when George Trenholm Prioleau was born in 1874 and eight years later in 1882, the last of the Prioleau's seven children was born and named John.

The New Neighbours

The new owner of 19 Abercromby Square had also been a Southern loyalist; Major Norman S. Walker, aged 40, was an associate of James Dunwoody Bulloch and had served in the Confederate War Office in Bermuda. In much the same situation that all Confederate supporters had found themselves after the war, Walker found it expedient to remain in England, and by 1870 he had moved his wife and 6 children, his mother and 8 servants, into his new home. Major Walker remained in the house for longer than the Prioleaus had done but by 1877 his firm of Gholson, Walker and Co was foundering and finding himself in financial straits, Walker sold the house to the city of Liverpool.

From 1877, the new owners leased the house for five years to the Haitian Consulate until in 1880 a conversation between Queen Victoria and her favourite, Benjamin Disraeli, decided who would be the new tenant. The newly-established diocese of Liverpool was in need of a Bishop and Disraeli had convinced Victoria that the Reverend John Charles Ryle (1816-1900) was the ideal candidate. Ryle was a commanding figure, standing 6 foot 4 inches tall with a flowing Old-Testament beard; his presence could hardly be ignored and in 1882, he moved into 19 Abercromby Square, as the first Bishop of Liverpool. Disraeli's instincts proved to be correct when Bishop Ryle went on to become a forceful leader of the Church of England whose written works are still available in print. It was Bishop Ryle who first instructed that the name "Bishop's Palace" be painted on the stonework at the front of the house. Ryle's headstone in All Saints Church, Childwall, can be found near to two other eminent Liverpudlians of the Victorian era, Sir Andrew Barclay Walker and Charles MacIver.

On the demise of the formidable Ryle, the diminutive Francis James Chavasse (1846-1928) moved into the house with his family. As the second Bishop of Liverpool, one of his first instructions was that the "Bishop's Palace" inscription should be allowed to fade, and in 2009, only a vague impression can still be seen. Bishop Chavasse's household consisted of 16 servants who were kept busy by the needs of the family, the comings- and-goings of numerous newly ordained clergy and invasions of student theologians.

Gilded Sculpture of Charles

Miss Jean Mitchell worked as a housemaid for the Chavasse family from the age of 14 (leaving in 1913) and she has left a graphic account of life in a Victorian house of the era. Her account tells of the room containing the Moral Philosophy murals being used as a chapel, where Mrs Chavasse played the organ but most of all she outlines the outstanding kindness of the Chavasse family to all they came into contact with – a complete contrast to penny-dreadful accounts of upstairs-downstairs tyranny; a favourite subject of novelists which rarely fails to sell books. Bishop Chavasse's dislike of the "Bishop's Palace" inscription was indicative of the reservations that he always had about the trappings of the church which even extended to the building of the Anglican Cathedral; it was, therefore, ironic that in 1904, it was his finest hour when he accompanied King Edward V11 and Queen Alexandra as they laid the foundation stone to the Cathedral and it was even more of an irony when on his demise, Chavasse was buried within the Cathedral itself.

The strengths of Bishop Chavasse as a minister lay in his ability to converse and work with people on all levels but his understated abilities have since been eclipsed by the celebrity of his son Noel Chavasse. Noel was the twin brother of Christopher and both were outstanding scholars and sportsmen – both of them competed in the 1908 Olympics in London. During the First World War, Noel and Christopher and their two brothers all served on the Western Front and it was during this baptism of fire that Noel entered into the military Hall of Fame. Serving as a doctor and a British army officer he had already earned a Victoria Cross at Mametz but it was during the inferno of Passchendaele, that he earned a second V.C. – becoming only the third man ever to do so. Noel Chavasse lost his life in 1917 at Passchendaele, toiling as always in the service of others. In 2008 a statue of Noel Chavasse sculpted by Tom Murphy was erected opposite his family home in 19 Abercromby Square; it had taken all of 90 years for his bravery to be commemorated in this way with subscriptions raised by those who were passionate that his memory should never be forgotten.

In 1923, Dr Albert Augustus David was appointed third Bishop of Liverpool but declined to live in 19 Abercromby Square and the house was purchased by Charles Sydney Jones, a partner in the Holt shipping line who owned other property in the square. Soon after purchasing no 19, Jones generously donated the house and all his other property to Liverpool University and No 19 has been a part of the university ever since.

Sir Nicholas Pevsner once visited the house and admired the architecture and fittings and in particular he liked the staircase leading to the upper rooms. The staircase to the basement and the servant's quarters is hardly in keeping with the one that Pevsner commented on but it contains two large, distinctive old-fashioned blackboards and although they have nothing to do with the Confederacy are historical documents in their own right. They once stood in the hallway of the Royal Institution in Colquitt Street which was founded in 1817 for the advancement of Science and the Arts and contain the names of all the members over the years – Roscoe, Earle, Lawrence, Walker, Sandar, and all the rest of the great and the good of Victorian Liverpool are all displayed in white paint on the black background. Considering that the Royal Institution once welcomed Audubon and paved the way for the Walker Art Gallery and Museum, it is sad to see it lying empty in the perpetual shade of Colquitt Street. Sadder still are the blackboards which were once such a proud roll-call in the building and now remain in complete obscurity on the back stairwell in 19 Abercromby Square.

Gilded sculpture of Mary Elizabeth

Of all the unusual things that go to make up 19 Abercromby Square as something unique, there is one which is rarely commented upon and appears to be taken for granted; it is the fact that of all the people who have moved into the house over the years, not one has ever altered or erased any of the Confederate motifs and murals. The house remains frozen in time, just as Charles Kuhn Prioleau left it nearly a century-and-a-half ago and it remains a memorial to a unique era in the history of Liverpool and its connections to the American Civil War; a priceless walk-through history book and a colourful display of one man's nostalgia for his homeland.

How Quickly We Forget

Of the hundreds of seekers after the truth who have passed through 19 Abercromby Square and searched for some meaningful painting of the Belle of Allerton Hall or looked in every crevice and corner for some sepia portrait of Charles Kuhn Prioleau, most have sighed with regret and taken some solace in the belief that the pictures may never have existed in the first place. But for someone as strikingly beautiful as Mary Elizabeth to have never had some kind of likeness made was extremely unlikely and in retrospect it was just a matter of time before some kind of image turned up.

Of Charles' and Mary Elizabeth's 7 children, Lynch Hamilton attended Sandhurst in 1881 and married in London in 1894, Louis St.Julien became a Major in the British army, while little is known of Margaret, Richard and George Trenholm Prioleau.

Imshi in North Africa

Mary Elizabeth and Charles' youngest son John (Jack) Prioleau was a great friend of Viscount Northcliffe (the originator of the Daily Mail in 1896) and he provided articles to the newspaper, most of them based around his adventures abroad. Jack Prioleau's book "The Adventures of Imshi" published in1922 was an account of his adventures travelling across Europe and North Africa in his ancient bull-nose Morris. Written in the particularly English upper-class vernacular of the day, the book is still a highly readable travel story. At the time the book was written, tourism was the province of the privileged few and accounts of Marrakesh, Tangier, Algeria, Genoa and even Seville and Madrid were read avidly. Jack Prioleau's cheery stories of the then exotic inhabitants of each country and his difficulties with the car and border controls are detailed in a good-humoured, easy-going text which was popular with middle-class Daily Mail readers and the name of his car "Imshi" which is Arabic for "Get out of the Way – Fast!" says more about its driver than the car.

Charles' and Mary Elizabeth's second child, born in Liverpool in January, 1862, was Charles Arthur Prioleau. Charles Arthur married Violet Bradshaw in 1895 and he died in 1912 – Violet went on to live until 1947.

Charles Arthur and Violet had four children with the third child Reginald Anthony (always known as Bill) born in 1900 and living until 1980. Reginald Anthony married Kathleen Saunders (born 1902) in 1925 and she outlived her husband by fourteen years, on her death in 1994. They left behind two daughters – Judith Violet born in 1930 and Grace Antoinette, born in 1933, both of them still alive and well in 2009.

When Charles Kuhn Prioleau had adopted British citizenship prior to the Civil War, it was no more than an act of expediency and he undoubtedly had visions of returning home to an independent Southern republic. As things turned out, all manner of events dictated that he would remain in England for the remainder of his life – not least the fear of prosecution in a Northern court. If Charles had difficulty in completely assimilating himself into an English way of life his children certainly did not and succeeding generations of the family have never regarded themselves as anything else but English. Grace Antoinette would have certainly done so; born in 1933, on the estate of the Duke of Richmond and Gordon near Chichester where her father was the racehorse trainer for the then Duke, Charles Gordon Lennox. Grace (better known as Toni) had lived most of her life in the South of England.

By the early 1980s the Civil War was a distant memory and the halcyon days of Charles Kuhn Prioleau had passed into the mists of time when Toni Prioleau unexpectedly came into an inheritance from her uncle, Guy Prioleau. The contents of the inheritance were in France and turned out to be so substantial that it required no less than two pantechnicons to haul her uncle's worldly possessions back to her home in England. While the majority of the treasury of furniture, documents, photographs and paintings were from Violet Bradshaw, her maternal grandmother, there were some accumulated possessions of several generations of the Prioleau family which were a tangible link to the past. Toni Prioleau faced the bittersweet task of sifting through the disorderly contents of her uncle's house, and in doing so she assumed the mantle of custodian of the artefacts of her family history.

There was one painting which was to be the most poignant of all Toni's possessions and one that she would come to treasure above all others. One massive crate was used to pack up a full-size oil painting containing the long-sought image of Mary Elizabeth Prioleau, exceeding all expectations in its dazzling portrayal of the erstwhile Belle of Allerton Hall. The belief that there was a picture of Mary Elizabeth had finally been realized and in addition to the fine oil-painting there were also two other pictures – shown left and right on this page.

In 2006, in a major upheaval in her life, Grace went to live in America, to be near her daughter and her grandchildren and the picture of her grandmother travelled with her. The picture of the young girl who once lived in Breeze Hill, Walton, now has pride of place on the wall of Toni Prioleau's home in Maryland.

A mark of the renewed interest in the likenesses of the previous owners of Abercromby Square is that the only known picture of Charles Kuhn Prioleau appeared at virtually the same time, after emerging from years of storage in Ireland.

The Keeper of the Scrolls

What strange forces were at work when Dian Thys (Maury) met Frost Prioleau in 1953 is a mystery yet to be resolved but for a descendant of the Maury family and a member of the Prioleau family to meet and eventually marry is surely a thing beyond coincidence. Stranger still is that Diane and Frost are both descended from ancient and venerable Huguenot families, traceable throughout centuries past – Frost is descended from the Prioleau family and Diane from the Maury family.

Matthew Fontaine Maury (1806 – 1873) was a deeply religious man who worked on behalf of the Confederacy during the Civil War, at one stage inventing an electric submarine which was effective against Northern shipping. He travelled extensively throughout Europe purchasing ships for the Confederate Navy, at the same time petitioning France and England to intervene to stop the fighting and fleetingly visited Charles Kuhn Prioleau and James Dunwoody Bulloch at Rumford Place – he lodged at the old Adelphi Hotel. Maury had been fascinated by the winds and currents of the world's oceans from an early age and his studies were subsequently translated into several dozen books which became essential reading for any serious mariner; James Nicol Forbes' record-breaking voyages aboard the clipper *Marco Polo* in the 1850's were attributed to studying Matthew Fontaine Maury's books. Maury's soubriquet of "Pathfinder of the Seas" was just one facet of a glittering career which is too long to be detailed here.

Matthew Fontaine Maury was a comparative *parvenu* when placed against the greater canvas of the family history which included his grandfather, James Maury (1746 –1840) who had even greater links with Liverpool. James Maury was the first diplomat and the first American Consul to be appointed overseas and his Consulate in Paradise Street was the first American Embassy in the world. Maury had been appointed by no less a personage than the then President George Washington and his tenure lasted from 1790 until 1829. Maury's title may have sounded rather grand but the job was no sinecure in the days when Paradise Street was known throughout the world as a sink of iniquity or a "Paradise Street" on earth, depending on your point of view. Until 1815, the waters of the Old Dock lapped at the cobblestones of Paradise Street itself and sailors could virtually step straight from the deck of a ship into the centre of Liverpool to be greeted by welcoming grog shops and some of the most persistent prostitutes to be found anywhere.

James Maury lived at no 4 Rodney Street where a plaque hangs outside his former home and his portrait by Gilbert Stuart Newton hangs in the Town Hall.

The American Eagle restored

The Embassy in Paradise Street was always known by the American Eagle over the doorway – probably acquired as a figurehead from an American sailing ship. Even in the days when the Embassy was abandoned and the house was later a coffee shop, pawnbrokers and pub, the frontage was always distinguished by the Eagle which was still in place when the work on Liverpool 1 began circa 2005. After 200 years of rain, snow, occasional sunshine and salt spray off the river, the Eagle was ready to fall apart until the Liverpool Conservation Centre which has proved its worth time and again, restored the Eagle to its former gilded glory and an opening ceremony took place in October 2008, to celebrate both the restoration of the Eagle and the former Embassy. Princess Anne opened both Liverpool 1 and the American Eagle.

Some weeks later in November, 1998, Frost and Diane Prioleau flew 7,000 miles from California – Diane to see the Eagle and the portrait of her ancestor and Frost to visit the places where Charles Kuhn Prioleau had worked so hard on behalf of the Confederacy. Their devotion to their mutual ancestors was rewarded by a reception by the Lord Mayor of Liverpool and an assurance that both their ancestor's part in the history of Liverpool remained a subject of on-going research. While Charles Kuhn Prioleau's story takes centre-stage in the Liverpool theatre of the American Civil War, looked at from a much larger perspective, Charles's war is little more than a chapter in the on-going saga which is the Prioleau family history. The Prioleau family tree is a patriarch of family trees which has been lovingly nurtured by Frost Prioleau who has discovered that its multitude of branches has been found to have extended across centuries and across the globe. Solid research and many hours of diligence have brought long-forgotten members of the Prioleau line into the light and over many years, Frost Prioleau has taken on the role of family genealogist and produced no less than seven books, painstakingly preserving the Prioleau family history.

There is an undoubted serendipity in the affairs of the Prioleau family as evidenced by recent events; the globe-trotting Frost and Diane had planned a trip to Morocco and were booked to travel in the month of December, 2009, when the holiday took on a relevance which was previously unplanned. Jack Prioleau's 1922 book on his travels with his Morris car had long been out of print until Frost inadvertently stumbled across a copy and their Morocco trip has taken on a whole new importance as Frost and Diane plan to follow in the tyre tracks of their ancestor, following the trail of "Imshi" and the youngest son of Charles and Mary Elizabeth Prioleau.

The portrait of Mary Elizabeth was by Chevalier Louis Desanges (1822-1887), a highly respected artist who had previously painted 50 battle scenes depicting Victoria Cross winners in action and had latterly turned to the more lucrative painting of portraits. Entitled "Mrs Prioleau" Desanges' colourful painting hung in the Royal Academy in 1871.

In 1985, Toni Prioleau had the painting restored by Messum's of London and it has traveled with her to every home that she has ever lived in since. In the picture on the bottom Toni Prioleau is holding a parasol which once belonged to Charles Kuhn Prioleau's mother, which she used when she traveled around Liverpool by carriage. The painting was originally believed to be a portrait of Elizabeth Lynch Prioleau but has been formally identified as an authentic picture of Mary Elizabeth Wright.

The Tragedy of The Lelia

Stormy seas

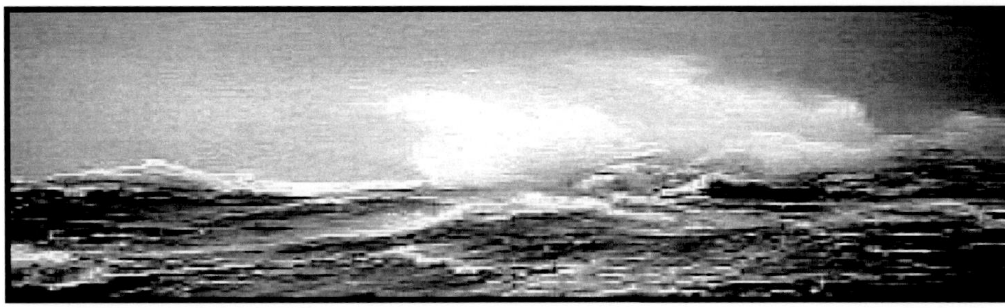

The Naval Officer

The Sinclair family are a distinguished dynasty of seafarers whose lineage can be traced all the way back to 1745, the year that Captain Arthur Sinclair decided to leave Scotland and try his luck in the New World. Ever since the first of the line settled in Virginia, the Sinclair name has appeared frequently in maritime annals as each succeeding generation has taken to the sea. However, the Sinclairs have also had the disconcerting custom of naming each first born son "Arthur" and since most of the male side of the family have gone to sea it can be confusing for anyone wishing to chronicle their adventures. For the sake of this narrative and also because it is a fascinating subject in its own right, a short summary of the main players is in order:

The second Arthur Sinclair (1780-1831) served in the United States Navy in an action-packed career which included service in the War of 1812 and a campaign against Barbary Pirates whose stock in trade was white slavery. The Barbary Pirates were unscrupulous North African slave traders who raided American and English ships for likely candidates for a lifetime of forced labour in the Moroccan cities of Fez and Marrakesh, selling their wares on the slave blocks of Tunis. Whenever trade was slow, the Barbary Pirates raided the fishing villages of Cornwall and many a youth was dragged from his family to live a life of servitude in an alien land. For a native-born Virginian, the irony of going to war against the institution of white slavery was probably lost on Arthur Sinclair. Sinclair's career was long and distinguished but there was an embarrassing setback during his service on the Great Lakes. In 1813, Sinclair commanded the *General Pike* and in 1814 he was aboard the *Niagara*, commanding a force of United States navy ships on Lake Huron. The United States ships were besieging Mackinac Island, had captured the British ship *Nancy* and were on the verge of completing a rout of the British forces when a totally unexpected and daring manoeuvre by the British snatched a victory from the jaws of defeat. The British and native American contingent on Mackinac had been reinforced by the crew of the *Nancy* who had evaded capture by the Americans and together they silently rowed towards the *USS Tigress* in small boats, and in the blackness of night the small force overwhelmed the crew and captured the ship. Adding insult to injury, the British turned the guns of the captured *Tigress* onto the *USS Scorpion* and captured that ship also. The humiliating defeat did little to affect Commodore Sinclair's career and he continued undaunted for the remainder of his life. Commander Sinclair's name lives on in many ways; a measure of the esteem he was held in naval circles was the naming of the destroyer *USS Sinclair* and his great grandson Upton Sinclair fought battles of a different nature with books such as "The Jungle" (1906), a hard-hitting exposé of corruption in Chicago's turn-of-the-century cattle industry. It's a sobering thought that when Arthur Sinclair entered the navy in 1798, the battle of Trafalgar was a decade into the future and right up to the end of his career in 1831 and beyond, the American Civil war was unthinkable, especially for something so firmly embedded into the Southern way of life. Arthur Sinclair's career could be said to have laid the foundation of his descendant's future roles in the Civil War, although he could never have envisaged such a tumultuous change in affairs.

Arthur Sinclair snr as a young US navy officer.

The third Arthur Sinclair (1810 - 1865) was born in 1810 and encouraged to go to sea by his father, Arthur enrolled in the United States Navy as a midshipman at the tender age of 13. In the year 1835, Arthur achieved the rank of Lieutenant and in the same year he married Lelia Imogen Dawley at Norfolk, Virginia. Arthur's younger brothers served in the United States Navy and his sister married yet another navy man. In 1852, when Commodore Matthew Perry sailed on his historic expedition to Japan in order to cement Japanese/American trading associations, Arthur Sinclair continued the proud family traditions and was part of the famous voyage in command of the store ship, fittingly named the *Supply* - aboard ship was Arthur Jr, as Midshipman. The Japan expedition was followed by command of the *USS Vandalia* on service in the Pacific. When the Civil War broke out, Arthur remained true to the South and after signing on to the Confederate navy commanded the *CSS Winslow* and saw action at the Battle of Hatteras Inlet. In August, 1861, Sinclair took charge of the *CSS Mississippi*, a prototype ironclad built at the shipyard of Nelson and Asa Tift. The *Mississippi* was the first ship that came out of the Tift's new shipyard and what she lacked in style the *Mississippi* made up for in power with engines designed to propel a ship of metal cladding up to 3ft in thickness. Construction began in October, 1861 but by April, 1862 the ship was as yet unfinished and worse still, Farragut's assault on New Orleans had led to the proximity of United States naval personnel, with the very real danger that the ship would fall into enemy hands before she had set sail. Arthur Sinclair was desperate to retrieve his ship from danger and employed tugs to haul the *Mississippi* downstream. The Spring tides prevented him from carrying out his plan and a frustrated Sinclair left orders that the ship was to be torched before falling into enemy hands - his orders were carried out a short time later and the *CSS Mississippi's* career ended before it had begun.

Sinclair's next ship was also an ironclad which came to an ignominious end - fortunately Sinclair had taken up another post by that time. When James Dunwoody Bulloch and Lt. John Low sailed the *Fingal* into Savannah in November, 1861 on the most successful blockade-run ever carried out, they fully expected to return on the same ship. However, the blockade was such that they were unable to escape and finding another method of escape they left the *Fingal* behind. Such was the desperation of the Confederacy for ships of any kind, the decision was taken to convert the *Fingal* into an ironclad and once again the Tift's were called upon to carry out the work. The result was the *CSS Atlanta*, an overweight hybrid, difficult to steer, inordinately hot below decks and totally unsuited for the tasks demanded of her. Arthur Sinclair was in charge of the *Atlanta* from February, 1863 to May 1863 when he relinquished command to Lt William Webb who ran her aground and had no choice to surrender her to the *US Weehawken*. After this dêbacle, there was no doubting the wisdom of the Confederacy in turning to Liverpool shipyards for their needs.

During a posting to Richmond April, 1864, working alongside the marine scientists experimenting with mines and submarines, Sinclair was placed in command of a ship called the *Squib* carrying a primitive torpedo (which was in effect an explosive charge on the end of a shaft at the bow of the ship) and his success in exploding it against the *USS Minnesota* led to his promotion to Commander. In September, 1864, Commander Sinclair was assigned to a new ship, the blockade-runner, the *Mary Celestia* which had run the blockade several times between Bermuda and Wilmington under Captain Mike Usina. Sinclair was off the coast of Bermuda when the pilot ran the ship into a reef and the *Mary Celestia* sank with the loss of one life - there were suggestions that the pilot had been bribed to sink the ship but nothing was ever proved. The *Mary Celestia* had been built by the Liverpool shipyard, WC. Miller and

Sons and there was a certain inevitability that Commander Sinclair would one day find his way to what was in effect the base for Confederate ships. On his posting to Liverpool, Sinclair was accompanied by his engineer, Charles Middleton for a new command which would prove fateful for both of them.

The Blockade-Runner

The Confederate cruisers *Alabama* and *Florida* may have captured headlines around the world as thieving pirates or heroic buccaneers, depending on which camp you were in, but when it came to profiteering then the clever money was on the blockade-runners. Liverpool businessmen, ship-owners and even Fraser, Trenholm were not slow to realise there was a great deal of money to be made running the blockade and when even a single voyage could recoup the cost of a ship, there was no shortage of investors. From 1863 onwards, a steady stream of blockade-runners slipped into the Mersey from the numerous ship-yards on both sides of the river. Built to a specific template, with the accent on speed and camouflage they sailed low in the water, burned the least smoky coal, had retractable funnels and anything else that could be thought of to suit their purpose.

On one memorable day in February, 1865, the yard of Jones Quiggin and Co, in front of a fanfare of dignitaries and a huge crowd of interested watchers, launched no less than five blockade-runners. Four of the ships, the *Widgeon*, the *Snipe*, the *Curlew* and the *Plover*, were identical, all 225 ft long, 24ft breadth and 645 tons in weight and all of them were built for the Confederacy. The fifth ship, intended for an Egyptian company for work in the Red Sea, was called the *Noor-el-Huda* (Light of the Day) and was considerably smaller than the other four.

Even at this late stage, the Confederacy still went to extraordinary lengths to conceal the ownership of their ships, purchasing in the names of British subjects or under other aliases, but their efforts seemed wasted when the Liverpool *Mercury* and the *Courier* openly stated the destination and purpose of each ship coming down the slipways. More than that, in between reporting on Jem Mace relinquishing his boxing crown and William H. Seward's long and heart-rending defence of the indefensible, the taking of the *Florida*, there were regular and detailed accounts of all of the blockade-runners out at sea; the *Charlotte* was reported to be carrying 1024 bales of cotton, the *Owl* had 700 bales and the *Colonel Lamb* had 1800 bales and so it went on. In the days leading up to mid February, the newspapers all carried ominous warnings of gales.

Typically, a blockade-runner would leave Liverpool with a cargo headed for Nassau or Bermuda where they would unload and and re-fill their holds with all manner of goods meant for the Confederacy, ready for the 600 mile trip to Wilmington. Evading capture was comparatively easy for an experienced Captain and the Northern naval administration complained bitterly at the number of ships evading capture. The winter months were especially easy for the blockade-runners as the large Northern warships were forced to stand off the coast for fear of smashing their ships on the massive breakers at that time of year. Once in Wilmington, the supplies would be gratefully received and the holds filled for the return to Liverpool - usually with cotton which was selling for high prices.

Rhett Butler was a blockade-runner; Margaret Mitchell's portrayal of the devil-may-care boulevardier whose source of wealth was shrouded in mystery was quite in keeping with the common conception of what a blockade-runner looked like at the time. Her caricature may have had more than an ounce of truth where the merchants were concerned but the true blockade-runner kept a low profile, was an experienced seaman and above all, loyal to the Confederacy. Commander Arthur Sinclair had all of these attributes and more.

The Colonel Lamb Blockade Runner, Built at Liverpool

W.C. Miller and Wife

The Ship-Builder

William C. Miller and Sons shipyard was situated on the Liverpool waterfront right next to their greatest rivals Jones Quiggin and Co. Although it is now a tranquil marina the original dock complex is still recognisable and with a little imagination it's not difficult to visualise the clanging of hammers, rivets glowing hot, the shaping of timbers and all the ordered confusion and clangour of a busy shipyard. Of all the shipyards on both banks of the Mersey, Jones Quiggin launched by far the greater number of blockade-runners, all of them having their own chequered histories in their own right, but W C. Miller's yard had the distinction of launching the very first of the many ships built for the Confederacy out of Liverpool.

The commerce raider the *Florida* left Miller's yard on the 22nd of March, 1862, and was second only in celebrity (some would say infamy) to the *Alabama* built by Lairds, not long afterwards. Despite the world-wide fame of the two most infamous commerce raiders on the high seas, by far the most numerous ships thereafter ordered by the Confederacy were blockade-runners and Jones Quiggin led the field, constructing in 1963, the *Banshee*, the *Lucy*, the *Wild Dayrell* which were followed by a regular succession of ships right up to the end of the Civil War. There were several other yards, such as Potters and Bowdler Chaffer turning out blockade-runners but Miller's was second only to Quiggin’s when it came to numbers with the *Phantom*, the *Let Her B* (later *Chicora*), the *Mary Celestia*, *Abigail* and *Ray* to their credit. All of these ships had varied histories but not one of them came close to approaching the disastrous fate and grievous losses engendered by a blockade-runner that Miller's named the *Lelia*.

William Cowley Miller was an ex-shipwright from Plymouth who brought his family to Liverpool where he found a post as foreman in a ship-builders. Miller set up his own business in 1836 with a Thomas Miller Mackay who subsequently left to make a career in ship-owning. It was fortuitous for William C. Miller that 3 of his 6 children were of an age to help out in the shipyard which flourished under the talented direction of Miller himself. His high regard among shipping circles and his election as a councillor for South Toxteth may have been elements which led James Dunwoody to first approach him. Foremost among his children in learning the trade was Thomas Lodwick Miller (born 1835) and it was understood that one day he would succeed his father in the family business. W.C. Miller was typical of men who made their living on the waterfront, in having his home near to his work. His Georgian, terraced house at 107 Parliament Street is still standing and is just a short walk down the hill to the marina which was once the shipbuilding yard. The family later followed the trend for moving out to the perimeters of the city and purchased a house in the swish Cressington Park which was within a private estate, guarded by a Lodgekeeper and where a stroll down to the river led to a private promenade.

Regarding his relationship with the Confederate agents who approached his ship-yard, William C. Miller's first consideration was of course to make a profit and there's no evidence that any of his actions were politically motivated but inevitably his involvement became a little more complicated: his son-in-law James Alexander Duguid was the man who Miller had recommended to captain the *Florida* (then the *Oreto*) when she first sailed to Nassau and Duguid captained several other Confederate ships as a sort of delivery agent. However, it was Thomas's involvement that was to cause Miller the most grief although his role aboard the *Lelia* was one that he might have taken anyway as a representative of the company. It was custom and practice for an official of any ship-building firm to travel on the maiden voyage of any ship to ensure that the ship handled well and that all was in order for the purchaser and on the voyage of the *Lelia* it was Thomas who had been appointed to travel as far as Holyhead (Anglesey).

Thomas C. Cuddy.

The Travellers

Commander Arthur Sinclair was just one of a handful of Confederate naval personnel due to travel aboard ship. Most of them were travelling back to the South for fresh orders in the struggle against the North which was gaining ground at an alarming rate. Although they were experienced seamen all, with Fireman Peter Laverty and gunner Thomas C. Cuddy celebrated for their years aboard the *Alabama* and its last fight with the *Kearsage*, on this trip they were travelling as passengers. Commander Arthur Sinclair was also designated a passenger aboard the *Lelia* but in reality he was captain in all but name and would officially take charge of the ship as a Confederate vessel when they reached Bermuda. He would have undoubtedly been inordinately proud of the fact that the ship he was to command had been accorded the singular honour of being named after his wife with the letters “Lelia, Liverpool” freshly painted on her bow. He would have also have been doubly proud when he was presented with a watch by the manager of Crenshaw and Co, which was unique in having attached to the chain a gold compass and a gold locket containing a lock of Lelia Imogene's hair.

The greater part of the ship's company were made up of seamen from Liverpool, closely followed by an Irish contingent. Several Scots and one or two from other countries were also signed on. It was custom and practice to keep a Confederate ship's crew in ignorance of their destination until the last minute and then sign the crew on in the service of the Confederacy but it was an open secret that the *Lelia* was bound for blockade-running and they would all have been looking forward to a lucrative number of voyages.

Captain Thomas Buxton Skinner, a native of Virginia was the man chosen to take the ship as far as Bermuda but there's little doubt that he would have conferred with Commander Sinclair in most things. On the morning of departure, anchored off Rock Ferry, they would almost certainly have discussed the weather which had been the subject of newspaper reports for all of the preceding week with gales forecast on a daily basis. In the days to follow, the newspapers would be littered with column after column of ships wrecked all around the coast of Great Britain, and the fateful decision to set sail, undoubtedly decided by Commander Sinclair and Captain Skinner, would place the *Lelia* foremost among all of them. To be completely fair to Commander and Captain, on the morning of their departure, although the winds were strong, it was only later in the day that they approached a ferocity which one of the survivors later described as unprecedented. Hindsight is a wonderful thing but when the *Lelia* slipped anchor and sailed down the river on the morning of Saturday, 14th January 1865, her fate was sealed.

The Shipwreck

An analysis of most disasters usually reveals a combination of events which by themselves would be sustainable but taken as a whole they become an irresistible hammer blow. In the course of the post mortems and Board of Trade Reports in the aftermath of the disaster, given so clearly and honestly by the few survivors, a list of potential dangers unfolded one by one, until, looked at retrospectively, it was almost an inevitability that a disaster would occur that day. Day after day, the newspapers had fluttered and flapped their warnings in the wind - warnings which went unheeded. The ship's carpenter was too inebriated to accept a vital delivery of stores which became lost just when they were needed most; the ship's anchors were stowed improperly which would never be a problem in normal conditions; there were inadequate safety procedures in other quarters which would be highlighted too late for the crew of the *Lelia*. Finally and most poignantly, when help was at hand in their hour of distress, conflicting signals saw it turn away, leaving them alone on a raging sea.

From Rock Ferry to the North-west Lightship is just a short distance out of the mouth of the Mersey but even in that comparatively short space of time the *Lelia* was shipping water from the huge waves breaking over the bows. Worse still, the anchors were stowed in such a way that even more water entered through their open hatches and it was stated by several sources that a large wave had lifted an anchor off the deck and one of the flukes had penetrated the deck on landing. By midday, the sea was becoming even rougher and it was imperative that the sea-water should be prevented from entering below decks and what was there drained away as quickly as possible. Part of the mislaid carpenter's stores were blocking fitments and on deck, the crew were forced to use blankets and anything else they could find as substitutes. Below decks, another vital component of the missing stores was a key for the steam-pump sluice-valves which allowed water to drain from the ship - the absence of the key effectively made them redundant.

Great Orme, 1860s

The very fabric of a blockade-runner required that she lay low in the water but the waves breaking over the deck of the *Lelia* were not draining away and little by little she was sinking lower into the sea. William Williams, the pilot, was of the opinion that she might make it to Holyhead, on the island of Anglesey, but by the time the ship was in sight of the Great Orme, a landmark, mountain overlooking the Welsh town of Llandudno, it was obvious that the ship was in dire trouble. In sight of the Great Orme, Captain Skinner discussed with the pilot the wisdom of going any further, when the matter was decided for them with a large wave smashing into the ship causing her to shudder from stem to stern. The ship was so down at the head that she refused to answer the helm and it was only by the use of the sails that they were able to reverse their course, but once faced towards Liverpool the ship gathered speed. Nevertheless,the water sloshing around near the bow was an alarming four feet deep and it was ironic that it was the carpenter who was ordered to deal with the problem by taking a sledge-hammer and knocking out a metal plate in the bulwarks. Some would say that it was poetic justice when he was unable to carry out the task and was later washed overboard.

The return journey began to be a race against time and the question was whether the *Lelia* could make it back to port before the incoming seas swamped her; each minute brought her nearer home and each minute the *Lelia* sank lower into the sea during an afternoon fraught with anxiety. There were very few ships that had braved the elements that morning - the Cunard steamer *SS Cuba*, bound for New York was the only one out of Liverpool but there was another out of Bristol called the *Sovereign* and spotting the distress signal from the *Lelia* of the ensign upside down and that she appeared to be in trouble, the Sovereign turned back from her course and followed the distressed ship. Despite the weight of water holding her back, the *Lelia* was sailing too fast to be caught and it was thought that Captain Skinner believed the *Sovereign* to be also returning to port, so that when the *Sovereign* turned back on her original course the chance of rescue had gone. Realizing the mistake, the crew of the *Lelia* raised clothing and fabric into the rigging but it was all in vain and they could only watch in despair as the chance of rescue disappeared over the horizon. It is not beyond the bounds of imagination for images of Gericault's horrific painting, The Raft of the Medusa to come to mind at such a pivotal moment - made even more exquisitely poignant in the knowledge that they would have undoubtedly been saved by the *Sovereign* if Captain Skinner had slowed the engines of the *Lelia*.

With five or six miles to go before once again sighting the North-west Lightship, the *Lelia* finally conceded defeat to the towering waves and the raging gale and as the waters of the Mersey washed over her deck and poured below decks where the hatches had burst, she foundered and stopped. At the mercy of the elements and unable to steer the ship, Captain Skinner was forced to order what would have been unthinkable a day previously - abandon ship, six miles from the Lightship and fifteen miles out from Liverpool.

Imaginative sketch of the Lelia by William Woods.

The Cruel Sea

The time was around 4pm when the order was given to lower the boats. The Mersey could never be said to warm up even in mid-summer but even the strongest swimmer would never survive for long in the icy February water - throw in a howling gale, mountainous waves and a peppering of sleet and the outlook for anyone in the water was grim, to say the least. To add to the difficulties, the light was fading fast and at that time of year, it becomes dark soon after 5 pm. Despite everything, there was no choice but to lower the life-boats and a mixture of the two pilots, several passengers and several crew members were joined by Commander Sinclair, making fifteen in all, and the first boat was lowered safely to sea-level. Having accomplished the difficult task of lowering the boat while the *Lelia* swayed heavily from side to side, the fifteen men would at this point have felt reasonably secure in the knowledge that some hard rowing would bring them to the Lightship and safety but it was not to be; as the *Lelia* pitched and wallowed in the troughs and swells of the rolling sea, the lifeboat was struck by the protruding sponson (a section of the cowling over the side-wheel) which smashed into the small boat. All of the witnesses to this distressing scene later attested that the boat was swamped and those on board were thrown into the sea with no chance of rescue and no chance of survival in the unforgiving, icy sea and none were seen again - not on that day, anyway.

The order was then given by Captain Skinner to lower the second boat and a total of twelve crew members clambered aboard, with some trepidation no doubt, after witnessing the wreckage of the first boat. They were right to be fearful, as the lowering of this boat was not without its moments of danger as the davits bent and the boat began to fill with sea water. The second steward fell into the sea and was pulled back by one of the ten firemen aboard as the lifeboat finally pulled away from the side of the *Lelia* and the crew began the long row towards the Lightship.

The third boat to be lowered contained eighteen survivors, including Thomas Miller. Once they had pulled away from the now stricken *Lelia*,

William Wood's sketch of the Liverpool pilot at night

a seaman named Tynan Danford Obey later testified that the mate suggested making for the shore but Obey himself warned that the boat would be smashed to pieces in the heavy surf. Thomas Miller took Obey's advice and ordered that the men pull for the Lightship. Whether things would have turned out differently if Miller had ignored Obey is open to conjecture but as things turned out, Miller himself could have been no worse off, and given that much of the shoreline is sandy beach even if the boat had been swamped the crew would have stood a fair chance of swimming the short distance to shore.

There is some understandable confusion as to the lowering of the fourth boat and one witness claimed that this boat was attempted to be lowered second but fouled in the tackles with Captain Skinner abandoning the attempt at that point to go onto boats that could be lowered. Whichever was the case, Captain Skinner now turned his attention to the fourth and last lifeboat which was indeed fouled in the rigging. Prior to this, when Captain Skinner sent the third boat successfully on its way, a helmsman named Andrew Brodie had implored him and a seaman called Michael Curry to join them - an offer which they both declined. From a shipload of 59 in total, Captain Skinner had loaded 45 men into the boats and the only reason for his remaining was loyalty to the remaining 13 men aboard the *Lelia* and Curry remained out of loyalty to his Captain, when he could easily have gone to the safety of the lifeboat. The two men were still seen to be struggling to free the final lifeboat when the third boat pulled away and as they settled down to a long haul to the Lightship, the final thing that they all saw of the *Lelia* were three rockets from the deck of the crippled ship, shooting into the night sky.

Captain Skinner has never really received the credit for all that he did on that fateful day as, true to the traditions of the sea, he determined to stay aboard his ship until the last man was safely away. Accompanied by the faithful Curry, Captain Skinner clearly intended to remain aboard the *Lelia* until every man had gone and he paid for it with his life. In the face of a monumental disaster, Captain Skinner's efforts were nothing less than heroic, and even when he knew that death was inevitable his final act was to launch the rockets which would never be enough to save himself but could aid the men in the lifeboats. It can only be conjecture as to why Captain Skinner never received

Wood's version of The Pride of Liverpool leading 12 ships in after the 1866 gales.

any formal recognition but on the one hand it's unlikely that the United States would honour his actions and on the other hand the British government would be reluctant to recognize an American national and a Southerner to boot. This is all just a guess and it is perfectly possible that the whole thing was forgotten as political events overtook the sinking of the *Lelia*.

The Lightship

If the men in the two lifeboats, which had successfully cleared the swaying *Lelia*, thought that they were now safe, they were in for a rude awakening. Quite apart from the fact that they faced a six mile haul in heavy seas with the gale at its worst, from the murky depths of the Mersey, the carpenter had left them one last proof of his inadequacies when it was found that the rowlocks were missing. Thomas Miller in the larger boat ordered improvised locks made from the boat hooks while another crewman used his hands to hold the oars in place, and in this way they made their way after the smaller boat which had left earlier. The larger boat overtook the smaller boat and at 5.45 pm when it was now pitch black, the crew at last pulled alongside the flanks of the Lightship and what they believed to be the end of their ordeal. But the storm was still raging and fate had one last card to play as the survivors anxiously reached for the ropes hanging down the sides of the Lightship; a huge wave took the lifeboat and flipped it over as if it were a toy and eighteen men were tossed into the icy sea. The boatswain, Smith and the seaman, Obey, who were eyewitnesses to what followed, both managed to scramble aboard the keel of the lifeboat and they watched helplessly as their shipmates were lost to the howling gale and the heaving sea in the blackness of the early evening.

The most poignant loss was that of Thomas Miller who was only inches away from safety only to be snatched back into the freezing sea as cold and exhaustion overtook him. The Lifeboat was never designed for rescuing men from the sea and the high bulwarks meant that rope-ladders and ropes were needed to throw down to the men bobbing helplessly, their strength ebbing away as the minutes passed. There were never enough ropes and Andrew Brodie was scrambling to safety up one of them when he was pulled back by the mate, frantic to reach safety. Thomas Miller swam to the same rope and the three men clung on with the Lightship crew unable to pull their total weight aboard ship. The mate succumbed to the numbing cold and slipped away and Brodie shouted to Miller to hold on while he pulled on a lifebuoy he had been thrown and all that was required was for the two men to be hauled out of the water like fish on a hook. The rope was slackened and both men were lowered to the waterline in readiness to haul away, but as the line was pulled in Brodie was alone and Thomas Miller was nowhere to be seen. Of the eighteen men so near to rescue, only Smith, Obey, Scott and Brodie made it aboard the Lightship. The waters of the Mersey could never be described as warm even in mid-summer but in mid-winter in the midst of a storm they are a freezing, elemental force of nature which numbs the mind and exhausts the body and even the strongest swimmer will succumb sooner or later. It was that icy sea that took away most of the crew of the first lifeboat and now it was about to do the same to the second. As the smaller lifeboat containing twelve survivors drew close to the Lightship, four of the crew leapt the short distance toward the ropes dangling so tantalizingly near and all four of them ended up in the sea. And the unforgiving waters of the mid-winter Mersey claimed another four seamen. The remaining men in the lifeboat managed to reach the deck of the Lightship successfully and joining the four members already saved, they made up a meagre twelve in number rescued from the two lifeboats out of a total of thirty who had set out from the stricken *Lelia*. Of the fifty-nine who had set out that morning, those twelve were the only survivors.

There are days when the natural world is in such a rage that it can be seen thrashing angrily around looking to assert its strength over anything or anyone foolish enough to challenge its might. At times like these, it would seem the wisest course to remain indoors and allow unbridled nature to scream and howl and beat its breast as long as it liked, until it grumbled its way back to where it came. While we can only stand and admire the courage of the tiny Lelia braving the might of the gale on that fateful day on the 14th January, in retrospect, a greater respect for the forces of nature and a little more awareness of the fragility of even the finest ships, would have seen the histories of fifty-nine families take a different course.

But to be entirely fair to the captains of the Lelia, this storm was unlike any storm seen before on the river. It had an almost siren quality about it; seductive enough to lull ships in port into a false sense of security and viciously erupting into full fury when they reached the open sea. It lured the Lelia to its doom and on the following day returned to the waterfront searching for more victims.

The Liverpool Lifeboat

There were (and still are) several Lightships at the mouth of the Mersey. Their primary function is to act as a floating lighthouse warning ships away

The Blazer as the lifeboat overturned.

from the shallow, silted areas dotted around the river. The North-west Lightship was typical of a Victorian lightship in that it was tiny, high-sided and anchored in position with a crew of a mere handful of men who would live in small but comfortable quarters for the duration of their shifts which involved maintaining the light burning at all times. The North-west Lightship was anchored off an ancient lake which was now full of sandbanks called the Hoyle Bank. The Lightships were never designed for rescue work and their high sides and lack of rope-ladders would have frustrated the crew in any attempts they made to pull people out of the water. Fortunately, they were rarely called upon to carry out any rescue work and the twelve survivors of the *Lelia* would have made the tiny ship very cramped indeed.

In the early hours of the following morning while the twelve survivors of the *Lelia* huddled exhausted in the warmth of the crew's quarters (they were later fulsome in the praise of the Lightship crew's hospitality), a passing steam-tug, the *Blazer* passed by and was hailed by the Lightship crew. The Lightship crew asked if the tug, captained by John Parry, could take the survivors back to Liverpool, but after several attempts he was forced to abandon the attempt as the heaving seas made it too dangerous to get near the Lightship. The *Blazer* headed back to Liverpool for help and as the dawn came up, Liverpool learned of the disaster of the *Lelia.* It was the beginning of another eventful day which would also end in tragedy.

The Liverpool Courier reported that news of the Lelia disaster created a "considerable sensation" at the Exchange and Underwriter's Rooms but it was even more of a shock for the relatives of those aboard the ship and despite the adverse weather conditions a crowd of friends and relatives began to gather at Prince's Landing Stage awaiting news of their loved ones. The news also galvanized another group into action and the crews of the Liverpool Lifeboats no 1 and no 2 also began to gather, ready to do what the *Blazer* was unable to do and bring the survivors back to land. Even in the 1860's, the Liverpool Lifeboat Institution, despite the constraints of the era, was quite a sophisticated organization and the Mersey Docks and Harbour Board which survives to this day, retained seven lifeboats and the crews to go with them available at a moments notice. On this occasion, no 1 lifeboat and no 2 lifeboat vied for which boat could be ready first and with no1 boat winning, several of the crew of no 2 boat jumped aboard no 1 to supplement their crew. In those days, the 30ft long lifeboat was attached by a rope to a steam-tug and hauled out into the river and it was the *Blazer*, by dint of her involvement with the Lightship, which earned the honour of hauling lifeboat no 1 and the eleven lifeboat-men aboard. The crew were all experienced hands and had faced gales before and, like the *Lelia* before them, they seemed to think that the storm was subsiding. By mid-afternoon they were in the river being hauled along by the 100ft rope attached to the Blazer. The lifeboat crews of course trained rigorously for their demanding job and while they were under supervision they wore the standard cork lifebelt but whenever the crews went out into real rescue operations invariably they shucked off the lifebelts which were universally disliked as cumbersome and perceived in some instances to be downright dangerous. Standing orders required that the lifebelts were worn at all times and to ensure that nobody misunderstood, the regulations read "any person disobeying the regulations will be liable to forfeit the amount of a day's pay" as just a section of the edict. As they had done on so many occasions before, the lifeboat-men of no 1 boat left off their lifejackets as they headed out to sea, but on this particular occasion, sadly the price they would pay was to be far higher than a "day's pay".

By early morning, the shockwaves emanating outward from the disaster, had gone beyond the waterfront and struck the Miller family like a slap in the face. Not only was the *Lelia* wrecked, many people they were familiar with were missing and among them was Thomas Miller, the de facto head of the family. Brothers Henry and Edwin Miller were too impatient to just sit back and await the news and accompanied by brother-in-law James Duguid and Mr Keverigan, Thomas's father-in-law, immediately hired a steam-tug the *Royal Arch* and set out for the North-west Lightship. By sheer good fortune, which was in short supply that day, the *Royal Arch* came across another steam-tug, the *Slasher* which had braved the gigantic swell, pulled alongside the Lightship, taken off the twelve survivors and was heading back to the Liverpool Pierhead. Naturally enough, the Miller family were anxious to know if their brother had survived and impatient for news, they shouted across to the *Slasher* but an arm pointing to the depths told them all they needed to know of their brother's fate. Despite their extreme disappointment, the Miller's took the survivors aboard the *Royal Arch* and returned them safely back to Liverpool.

While the weather and the waves near to shore were nothing that they hadn't faced before, once out into the river, the lifeboat-men found that conditions were far worse the further out they travelled. As they neared the Lightship, in an area of sandbanks called East Hoyle Bank, with the *Blazer* pulling on the heavy rope, a heavy cross-sea suddenly struck the port bow of the lifeboat and the whole crew were thrown into the icy-cold, maelstrom. The unthinkable had happened, the lifeboat had capsized with no chance of being righted and the would-be rescuers were now at the mercy of the stormy seas - like the crew of the *Lelia* before them, the lifeboatmen found themselves fighting for their lives in an unforgiving and alien environment. However, unlike the *Lelia*, there was a ship close at hand and the *Blazer* turned immediately (the side-wheels could stop independently so that the ship could turn on a sixpence) throwing ropes out to the men in the water. Even in the short time that the *Blazer* returned to the rescue men were succumbing to the numbing cold and of the eleven who were in the water only four of them were hauled out of the heaving waves - one man was pulled through the stopped spokes of the sidewheel.

The February gales had lured out more prey into the river and claimed another batch of men who had the temerity to go out while the elements were still raging and once more nature had asserted her superiority in the most cruel and final manner. What made things worse on this occasion was that there is no doubt that if the lifeboat-men had been wearing their lifejackets then all of them would have had a realistic chance of being saved. But the worst thing of all was that their deaths were a particularly profligate waste when as the lifeboat-men were struggling for their lives, the *Royal Arch* was already heading back to Liverpool with the survivors of the *Lelia.*

The Aftermath

For those who had lost relatives in the disaster, their lives would never be the same. Although there were collections made for the ordinary seamen and the lifeboat-men, the amount was never enough to sustain a family and widows would inevitably marry again if only to provide for their families.

Fireman Peter Laverty and gunner Thomas C. Cuddy were particularly unlucky, having survived the whole voyage of the *Alabama* and the *Kearsage* fight only to lose their lives most unexpectedly and a mere few months before the end of the Civil War. In other circumstances and in another place, Captain Skinner and able seaman Michael Curry would have been eligible for bravery awards but their heroism has been subsequently

Lelia Bell

forgotten along the way. Thomas Miller was acknowledged to be the next head of the Miller shipyard and as his father was ageing, Thomas had been more and more involved in the running of the family business. After his drowning, the dynamism that had typified the Miller family business was no longer in place and the shipyard was never a major force again. And then there was CSN Commander Arthur Sinclair whose family were particularly grieved that he had been lost at sea and his body never recovered.

In the days to follow, The Liverpool newspapers reported that the gales were subsiding and ships which had been sitting it out now began to enter the Mersey, following the Pilot boats like so many ducklings. There had been wrecks all around the coast of Britain but in Liverpool the *Lelia* took precedence over all of them and for weeks afterwards, coroners reports, Board of Trade Enquiries and witness accounts began to put together the picture of how the *Lelia* had gone down. There was no mystery at all as to how the ship had foundered and none of the testaments differed in any way; every man told of the events as they are detailed above. As time went by, the newspapers gradually turned their attentions to other matters and apart from a flurry of letters critical of such things as "Should Lifeboats be tugged out to sea on the end of a rope?", the sensational shipwreck gradually faded from public consciousness.

Postscript

And there it would have ended if it had not been for a strange event on the last day of May, 1865, when the captain of the Fleetwood fishing-boat, the Elizabeth and Emma, fishing ten miles out into the Irish Sea, unexpectedly hauled in the remains of a man clothed in an overcoat and uniform. Within the pockets of the coat was an ornate watch, stopped at 4.10 pm, and there was no doubt whatsoever that the body of Arthur Sinclair had been found at last.

The funeral took place on 3rd June, 1865, in Fleetwood and Sinclair's two sons, Terry and Arthur Jr were present. Arthur was of course the eldest son and was the same Arthur that his father had taken with him, a lifetime ago, on the famous Perry Expedition to Japan when he was just fifteen years of age. Arthur had gone on to make his own way in life and when the Civil War broke out, he followed his father's example and joined the Confederate Navy. Arthur jr was aboard the CSS Virginia (the converted Merrimac) as captain's clerk when the iron-plated ship sank the Congress and the Cumberland in Hampton Roads and in the same ship in March, 1862, he was present at the first Ironclad battle in history when the Virginia met the Merrimac. In August, 1862, Arthur jr joined the CSS Alabama and as Lieutenant Arthur Sinclair he spent the following two years aboard the infamous rebel raider, culminating in his efforts in the fight against the Kearsage.

In his latter days, Lt Arthur Sinclair wrote of his experiences on the Alabama and produced one of the most readable and reliable accounts of the epic voyage. As a historical document, Arthur's book is invaluable, recounting the adventures and misadventures of the infamous raider but it is Arthur's pen-portraits of the crew - comical, tragic and insightful which go to make up a unique account of life aboard the Alabama in the days of the Civil War.
Lieutenant Sinclair married in 1857 and predictably his first born was named Arthur. The couple's second child was a girl and they named her... Lelia Imogene Sinclair.

A Hazardous Occupation

Blockade-Running - as an occupation

"Money flowed like water, men lived for the day and never thought of the morrow and in that small place was accumulated a mixture of mankind seldom seen before: Confederate military and naval officers; diplomatists using the blockade as a means of ingress and egress from their beleaguered country; newspaper correspondents and advertisers of all kinds - some rascals, no doubt; the very cream of the English navy composed of officers on half-pay who had come out, lured by the prospect of making some money and gaining an experience in their profession which a war such as this could give them and last but not least our own immediate circle."

The above quotation is from the autobiography "Running the Blockade" by Thomas E. Taylor and in those few words captures the essence and excitement of blockade-running. From the very beginning of the Northern blockade, merchant ships had slipped in and out of Southern ports, mostly for the cotton bales which the Confederacy used to purchase arms and supplies and given the huge profit margins there was never any shortage of recruits for blockade-running. As Taylor pointed out: *"Englishmen and Americans are particularly made for the dangerous calling."*

Although there's no doubt at all that the Confederate captains and crews were motivated by a devotion to the Southern cause, the fact remained that the work was made more attractive because they stood to make fabulous sums of money from their trade. Quite apart from the money made from their legitimate (or illegitimate, whichever way you look at it) cargoes, there were few who didn't have some lucrative sideline in unauthorized goods, lining their pockets with every trip. The blockade-runner was everybody's friend - mainly the Southern ports which were anxious for the arms and supplies, the cotton merchants who sold the compressed bales at exorbitant prices and the manufacturers of both. The people that Taylor neglected to mention, however, were those who stood to make the most - the ship-owners and consortiums who left it to others such as Taylor to take the risks and the kudos in their clandestine operations. The romance and heroics of blockade-running were not for the shipowners - they remained in the background, providing the ships which was considered to be a gamble given the high losses of shipping to bad weather and Northern cruisers. But the gamble was not as high as most people were led to believe, as a single trip selling arms and supplies and returning with hundreds of cotton bales could easily recoup the price of a ship for the merchants, who remained as enigmatic and shadowy, high-stakes players in the game.

The quotation at the beginning of the page could quite easily be attributed to the wharfs of Liverpool but Taylor is in fact referring to Nassau which was as he describes it exactly. As the jumping-off point for the Southern ports, it was a comparatively short 300 miles to the coast where a typical trip would involve lying in wait and at the opportune moment, usually at night, slip through the Northern ships and await unloading at Wilmington. The ship would then be loaded with cotton and after the dash through Northern lines, return to Nassau. Nassau was one of four main ports which were in effect Confederate bases for keeping the Southern armies supplied - there was even an outpost of the Fraser, Trenholm clearing house. Bermuda was secondary to Nassau and Havana and Matamoras were used less frequently.

Banshee by Samuel Walters

Although several ports were used by the blockade-runners, Wilmington, North Carolina was by far the favourite and most frequently used. The reasons were not difficult to find, consisting of several forts overlooked by the main defensive barrier of the formidable Fort Fisher. If the dangerous shoals weren't enough to keep the Yankee ships at a distance then the guns of Fort Fisher certainly were, with the British-made, 150 pound, Armstrong rifled-cannon a weapon to be feared. As a result, the blockade-runners stood off until night-fall and then slipped unseen into harbour via the wide channel between the Yankee ships and the shore.

Fort Fisher was commanded by the 26 year old Colonel William Lamb who was also the architect of the fort and had overseen its construction in July, 1862. The fort and its surrounding defence works was from the very beginning a formidable barrier to the Northern army and the constant flow of materièl in and out of the fort made it a prime target for Northern forces. The fort survived several attacks by Northern forces and when other ports fell, one by one, to the Yankee armies, Fort Fisher assumed even more importance and traffic increased accordingly, until by December, 1864, Fort Fisher remained the only port of entry remaining open.

In the following month, the Northern forces made a concerted effort to level the fort and on the 14th January, 1865, a naval attack combined an offshore bombardment with a landing force of 2,000 marines and sailors. The fort was the focus of some fierce fighting in which Colonel Lamb was severely wounded but the 600 defenders were eventually overwhelmed and the fort was taken, effectively sealing off the final lifeline of the Confederacy.

Blockade-Runners - as an art form

As the art of blockade-running became more risky and more refined, the days of enterprising merchant ships slipping in and out of harbour became less and less and it became apparent that there was a requirement for specialised ships to fulfil a particular need and the shipyards of Liverpool were in the forefront of constructing blockade-runners as custom-built ships specifically designed for one purpose only - to slip through the lines of blockading ships. A whole industry of blockade-runner manufacture sprang up and shipyards on both sides of the Mersey turned out ships which were essentially built to a template, varying only slightly in minor details. The two essential requirements for a blockade-runner were speed and lack of detection and the ships coming out of the yards reflected these factors in their lines which always had the ship lying sleek, long and low in the water an inevitability of the evolutionary process which would always end the same way no matter who designed the ships. The foredeck was distinguishable by a turtleback which facilitated water run-off and the funnels were often telescopic to change the appearance of a ship at a moment's notice. The ships were able to utilise either steam or sail and the boilers were made to burn the least smoky fuel. The bridge was in the centre of the ship, between the paddlewheels, and they were only ever lightly armed as they invariably anticipated being able to outrun any ships giving chase. The shipyards working on blockade-runners on the Birkenhead side of the river were Laird brothers and Bowdler and Chaffer and on the Liverpool side, W.H. Potter, W.C. Miller and sons and Jones, Quiggin and Co - between them, the Liverpool shipyards manufactured over 35 blockade-runners.

As the ships came out of the docks on their trials, they all looked very similar in appearance but once they left the Mersey, no two ships were ever alike in their varying fortunes. All of them had the same purpose but every one of them had a different destiny:

Blockade-Runners - in action

Banshee *(A female wailing as a portent of death)*

January 1863

The *Banshee* (1) is generally recognized as the prototype for all blockade-runners, having all the attributes of every ship that came hereafter. Jones, Quiggin and Co were the contractors for the Anglo-Confederate Trading Company who commissioned the ship with a consortium counting the Lord Mayor of Liverpool, Edward Lawrence, amongst its number. Shipping agent Thomas E. Taylor whose quotation opened this chapter, travelled to Liverpool to take charge of the ship accompanied by her Captain, Joseph W. Steele and he later wrote fondly of the *Banshee* and her exploits in his memoirs of the Civil War. Although Taylor described the *Banshee* as *"cranky and unsafe",* once across the Atlantic, her first foray into the blockade-running game was an unqualified success and Taylor spoke in glowing terms of the Captain, engineer and pilots as they ran into Wilmington *"laden with arms and provisions for the Confederacy."* They then returned with the holds brimming with £7000 worth of tobacco and 500 bales of cotton - that single trip had paid for the initial outlay and everything thereafter was a bonus. Taylor accompanied the *Banshee* as she ran the blockade seven times in all, often under fire and sometimes chased by Northern cruisers. On 22nd September, 1863, the *USS James Adger* gave chase on the return trip to Nassau and for once the swift blockade-runner found herself being outrun in conditions which favoured the Yankee steamer. Captain Steele ordered the cotton bales thrown overboard (which must have caused wailing of a different kind altogether) and the *Banshee* began to outdistance her pursuer until engineer Erskine reported that the main bearings were overheating and unless the engines were stopped then irreparable damage would be inevitable. Captain Steele was obviously determined to remain out of the clutches of the Yankee cruiser and with a mixture of salad oil and gunpowder managed to keep the bearings cool enough to maintain their speed. The Federal ship was only five miles distant when she gave up the chase, running out of coal and the stokers on the point of exhaustion. She had never fired on the *Banshee*, having only guns placed for broadsides. On another run, the Southern agent in Egypt had taken it upon himself to purchase a fine Arab stallion as a gift for Jefferson Davis and had it shipped to Nassau where the *Banshee* was chosen to take the horse on to Wilmington. The horse was nearly the cause of their capture and Taylor's description of the incident is inimitable.

"On a very still night as we were running in and creeping noiselessly through the hostile fleet, he commenced neighing (smelling the land I expect). In an instant, two or three jackets were thrown over his head but it was too late. He had been heard on board a cruiser very close to which we were passing and she and two or three of her consorts immediately opened fire on us. We had the heels of them however and our friend Colonel Lamb at Fort Fisher was soon protecting us playing over our heads with shell."

Taylor ran the blockade seven times aboard the *Banshee* but her luck ran out when Taylor left for pastures new. After one more successful run, on the *Banshee*'s ninth run on the voyage to Wilmington, she was captured by the *USS Grand Gulf* and the army transport *Fulton* on the 21st November, 1863. Overall, the *Banshee* had earned a 700% profit for her owners. In March, 1864, the *Banshee* was commissioned into the United States navy under her own name and ironically, took part in an attack upon Fort Fisher, serving out her time on Chesapeake Bay. She was sold in November, 1865, and entered into a commercial cattle-carrying operation in the Gulf of Mexico, under the name, *J.L. Smallwood.* In 1867, she was sold on to a British firm, renamed the *Irene* and remained in service until into the 1890s. Thomas E. Taylor's initial assessment was wide of the mark and although the *Banshee*'s blockade-running feats were praiseworthy, her longevity in service was a tribute to her builders, Jones, Quiggin and Co. The second *Banshee* was also built by Jones, Quiggin as a replacement for the original. This version, built in 1864, was 40ft longer than her predecessor and she also survived the war, although little is documented about her career.

Raw cotton being pressed and baled, ready for transportation

Sketch of Banshee 1

The launching of the *Banshee* begins the era of the blockade-runners out of Liverpool. The story of the *Lelia* has been documented on a previous page but the various adventures and destinies of the other blockade runners as much as they are known, are detailed on the following pages.

The Liverpool Blockade Runners

Fort Fisher after the defeat by Northern troops.

When the American Civil War first began, running the blockade was a lucrative venture well worth the small risk involved to the merchant ships which stood to make small fortunes with the inflated prices that the situation had brought about. As the war dragged on and became harder-fought, the stranglehold on goods going in and out of Southern ports became increasingly tighter and merchant ships were no longer free to come and go as they pleased.

But the South needed guns, ammunition, all manner of war materials and even basic items such as soap and food were becoming difficult to come by. Without these things the Southern war effort would grind to a halt and the struggle would be lost within months.

Out of necessity was born the ship called the blockade-runner specifically designed for speed, camouflage and evasion. Low in the water, retractable smoke-stacks, a turtleback deck allowing fast water run-off, smokeless fuel and powerful engines went to make up the typical blockade-runner. The ships were painted a dull grey and their usual method of entering a port was to lie up at night hidden by a headland and in the early dawn to slip between the Northern ships and the shore, unseen and undetected. The blockade-runners were of a unique design to counter a unique situation. Many of them were built on the banks of the Mersey and throughout the war a steady stream of these unique ships silently sailed out of the river to meet destinies which were many and varied. The fate of the Lelia has been outlined on a previous page as have the adventures of the Banshee, but they all have their tale to tell.

The Denbigh - **Built by Lairds**

The *Banshee* might have been credited in February, 1863 as the first purpose-built blockade-runner out of Liverpool but merchant ships had been running the blockade since it first began. Opportunist merchant ships of all nationalities operated out of Havana, Bermuda and Nassau but very few of them were of English make although many English captains and crew sailed the ships. The *Fingal* had been used as a blockade-runner on Dunwoody Bulloch's famous adventure but proved the point that non-purpose built ships were becoming unfit for purpose when the *Fingal* was unable to get out of port. The P.S. *Denbigh* was a rarity as it was one of the very few ships out of English waters to run the blockade without being purpose-built. The *Denbigh*, built at Lairds shipyard and numbered no 268, was constructed in the name of Robert Gardner of Manchester. From 1861, she ran the easy passage between Liverpool and Rhyl as a packet steamer but in 1863, she was transferred to the European Trading Company which was in partnership with Robert Gardner's firm who were Confederate agents. They obviously thought the *Denbigh* was suitable to run the blockade and she did get through on 6 occasions between Havana and Galveston; she was nicknamed *"the Mail Packet"*. Her career as a blockade-runner came to an abrupt end on the night of 23rd May, 1864, when she ran aground and was destroyed by Union gunfire. The crew were rescued by another English ship, the *Lark*.

The Alexandra - **Built by W C. Miller/Engines by Fawcett, Preston and Co.**

The *Alexandra* was ordered by Charles Kuhn Prioleau on behalf of Fraser, Trenholm and at first all went well when she was launched in March, 1863, and towed into Toxteth Dock for her engines to be installed. Unfortunately, the *Alexandra* fell foul of the backlash from the launch of the *Florida* when Thomas Haines Dudley and Charles Francis Adams had become apoplectic at what they perceived to be the British government's complicity in her sailing from W C. Miller's yard. The Consul and the Ambassador had transferred their attentions to the Alexandra and once again had forced the British government into carrying out the tedious process of the examination of the ship as to whether or not she was built for war. Once again the Custom's Officers declared that there were no armaments fitted and the Foreign Enlistment Act had not been breached. But the strange vacillations of the British authorities and the tenacity of the Northern agents forced the British to reconsider and the *Alexandra* was impounded which was an odd decision given that they had managed to

The Alexandra impounded.

allow the *Alabama* to escape the previous year and would soon allow numerous blockade-runners out of the Mersey on a regular basis.

Whatever the reasons for the actions of the British, the fact was that the *Alexandra* became the subject of protracted legal wranglings in which Fawcett, Preston and Company complained bitterly that they would have to lay men off and Fraser, Trenholm proclaimed their innocence, stating that the ship was nothing more than a pleasure boat.

The British were finally forced to admit defeat - there were no weapons and therefore there was no obvious breach of the Foreign Enlistment Act which was always the crux of any differences and an argument that FS. Hull had hung his hat on so successfully on Dunwoody Bulloch's behalf. However, it took 12 months before the argument was resolved and Fawcett, Preston's were recompensed with a sum less than they had asked for but the Alexandra was finally released in April, 1864 and changed her name to the *Mary.* But the *Alexandra* (or *Mary*) was fated never to fulfil her destiny and after sailing to Nassau in December, 1864, in the process of being fitted with a 12 pound rifled-gun stamped with the incriminating maker's name of Fawcett, Preston and Co, transported from the Liverpool foundry by the steamer *Powerful*, she was boarded by United States officials. Once again the ship was impounded and the tedious legal processes began anew, during which time the war was declared over and the crew of the *Mary* could only dream of what might have been.

The Phantom - Built by W C. Miller/Engines by Fawcett, Preston and Co.

The *Phantom* was purchased by Fraser, Trenholm, registered in May, 1863 and delivered to the Confederate Ordinance Bureau in July, 1863. She operated from Bermuda into Wilmington and her first two runs were successful. On her third run into Cape Fear, the *Phantom* was pursued by the *USS Connecticut* and ran ashore on 23rd September near to Fort Fisher. The crew followed the usual practice of torching the ship and escaped in the lifeboats.

The Lucy - **Built by W C. Miller/Engines by Fawcett, Preston and Co.**

A Fraser, Trenholm bought ship, the *Lucy* was registered in October, 1863 and sailed to Nassau by Captain James A. Duguid who had made the same journey on a previous occasion when he delivered the *Florida* in March, 1862. Duguid was the son-in-law of William Cowley Miller and acted as captain for several ships out of the shipyard, successfully carrying out his mission on every occasion. Among others Duguid delivered the *Lucy*, *Juno* and *Giraffe* (later the *Robert E. Lee*). The *Lucy's* record as a blockade-runner is outstanding which makes it a mystery why she is not better known - the only reason can be that the Captain and crew kept a low profile which may also account for her success. She began her career in November, 1863 and was captured in the same month of the following year after 21 successful runs.

The Wild Dayrell - **Built by Jones, Quiggin and Co. (engines probably Fawcett, Preston)**

The *Wild Dayrell* was bought in the name of Edward Lawrence (who later became Lord Mayor of Liverpool, hence Lawrence Road) for the Anglo Confederate Trading Company and registered in November, 1863. She ran the blockade 4 times throughout the month of January, 1864 and was lost on the first day of February, 1864.

The Mary - **Built by Lairds**

Registered in January, 1864, the Mary's career began in March, 1864, and she ran the blockade 7 times before being trapped in Mobile.

Let her B. *(later the Chicora)* - **Built by W C. Miller (sub-contracted by Jones, Quiggin and Co.)**

In many ways, the *Chicora* had the most remarkable history of all the blockade-runners - she certainly had the longest career and was a fine tribute to the ship-building know-how of W C. Miller and the engineering skills of Fawcett, Preston and Co. She was originally registered as the *Let her B* in March, 1864, and owned by the Chicora Importing Exporting Company. She undoubtedly had the most distinctive name of all the blockade-runners until the owners decided to change it to the *Chicora* but it wasn't just her name that was distinctive, the *Let her B* (or *Chicora*) was the last blockade-runner to get out of Charleston before it fell to Union troops on February 7th, 1865. She was actually on the point of entering Charleston when it was realised that Sherman's forces had overrun the city - the *Chicora* promptly turned around without unloading and returned to Nassau. The *Chicora* ran the blockade 14 times before the war ended and after the war she went as a passenger ship on Lake Superior from 1865 until 1869. In 1870, she was one of the ships which transported Sir Garnet Wolseley's expeditionary force to Manitoba in what was called the Red River Rebellion which was a land dispute with the Métis Indians. After working on Lake Superior for the Governor General, Lord Dufferin, the *Chicora* received a major refit and in 1878, eventually returned to work on Lake Ontario as a pleasure steamer, ferrying passengers on excursions from Toronto to Niagara-on-the-lake and along the panoramic Niagara river - two of those passengers were the Duke and Duchess of Cornwall. The Royal couple were probably ignorant of the fact that they were aboard an English-built ship which had fought for the Confederacy during the American Civil War. They later opened the Mersey Tunnel in 1934 when they had become George V and Queen Mary. The *Chicora* became a well-loved excursion ship for well into the new century and both passengers and ship's officers felt an affection for the ageing steamer. She had several competitors on the excursion trips with one of them being another ancient blockade-runner, the *Southern Belle* - built on the Clyde in 1864, the Clyde-built ship was scrapped in 1891, leaving the *Chicora* to steam along for many more years. In 1904, the *Chicora* had a major refurbishment and returned to service better than ever until her route was altered to Toronto to New York in 1914. The route proved to be unsuccessful and the *Chicora* found herself laid up and forgotten in Toronto harbour where in 1919, she suddenly sprang a leak and sank to the bottom of the 24ft harbour. To all intents and purposes, *Chicora* had finally come to the end of the road but her owners took the surprising decision to raise her from the depths and in November, 1919, she was lifted from Toronto harbour, dripping wet, bloodied but unbowed. By 1921, the old ship had been stripped down and sold to a transportation company who renamed her *Warrenko* and sold her on to a coal carrying firm. It was as an ancient coal transport that the *Chicora* ended her days, shuffling along the St. Lawrence river at half the pace she used

The Chicora on Lake Ontario

to muster and wearily carrying out her mundane task. But game to the last, the *Chicora* experienced something of the drama of her blockade-running days when in 1938 she was rammed by a freighter called the *Sprucebay* outside Kingston harbour and promptly sank into the waters of the St. Lawrence where the story might have ended but incredibly, the *Chicora* was raised once again and on Howe Island was dismantled. The *Chicora's* engineers invariably spoke in glowing terms of her engines which were still serviceable to the last and the Fawcett, Preston Foundry would have expected no different - but the fact was that the craftsmen who built the *Chicora*'s engines lived in mid-Victorian times and their creation had outlived them all. The *Chicora* sailed for an unprecedented 75 years when others lived mere months and in the case of the *Lelia* whose life was truly ephemeral, could only be measured in hours.

It would be tempting to believe that the *Chicora* inherited her name from the name of the company which owned her but the name has Indian connotations and means "Land of Flowers". Alan Stuart Hanckel named his house Chicora in memory of his homeland - the house still stands in Wavertree, Liverpool.

The Badger - **Built by Jones, Quiggin and Co. (engines probably Fawcett, Preston)**

The *Badger* was a sister ship to *Let her B* and had her trials in the same month of March, 1864. During the two ships' speed trials they reached 19 knots. Owned by Fraser Trenholm, the *Badger*'s career was nowhere near as distinguished as her sister ship, running the blockade once only in May and lost in September, 1864.

The Lynx - **Built by Jones Quiggin and Co. (engines probably Fawcett, Preston)**

Another Fraser, Trenholm ship which ran from April to September, 1864, the *Lynx* was known for being speedy and distinctive and for her two white masts and smokestacks. She ran the blockade 9 times, captained by Edward C. Reid. On her final trip from Wilmington she was carrying 600 bales of cotton, passengers and $50,000 in gold but was unfortunate to encounter 3 Union ships, the *Howquah*, the *Niphon* and the *Governor Buckingham*. The 100 pounder rifled cannon hit the *Lynx* 6 times below the waterline and twice to her decks and she beached 6 miles away from the shelter of Fort Fisher. All escaped, taking the gold with them and they left the *Lynx* in flames.

Renowned blockade Captain Simpson Adkins

The Fox - Built by Jones, Quiggin and Co. (engines probably Fawcett, Preston)

Registered in April 1864 to Fraser Trenholm, the *Fox* was commanded by Captain Simpson Adkins who ran the blockade 18 times from June until the end of the war. This picture of Captain Adkins is rare as there were very few blockade-runners who would allow photographs. Most preferred to keep a low profile for fear of repercussions. Adkins was renowned as a daring blockade-runner and survived the war to retire to Charleston where he liked to relate his adventures to anyone who would listen. The final run of the *Fox* was one of Adkins' most exciting tales in which he relates how the *Fox* was on her way into Galveston harbour and faced by no less than 25 Federal ships commanded by Commodore Sands. Most sensible men would have turned and made a run for it but Adkins was made of sterner stuff and headed straight for his destination as if the Federal ships did not exist. Head down and straight along the line of blockading ships, the *Fox* ran a gauntlet of fire which tore her woodwork to ribbons. Every ship in the blockade opened fire and for one hour and a quarter and a full seven miles, the *Fox* endured a battering which should have seen her sunk without trace several times over. By some miracle, the engines and steering gear of the steamer were totally untouched and the *Fox* sailed into Galveston to the astonishment of everyone who was present. There was nobody more surprised than Commodore Sands and under a flag of truce on the following day, he demanded an assurance that the Captain of the *Fox* was "an American". Sands knew that it would never have been sanctioned to supply the name of the Captain of the man who had escaped his guns but he was told that his man was a Confederate which satisfied his curious sense of honour - he couldn't stand the thought that he had been thwarted by an Englishman. Commodore Sands was fulsome in his praise of the *Fox*'s handling and in an unprecedented bout of generosity to the enemy he promised the *Fox* safe passage out of Galveston. Two nights later, the *Fox* slipped out of harbour with a load of cotton.

The Fox

The *Mary Celestia* - Built by W C. Miller/Engines by Fawcett, Preston and Co.

Registered in London, April, 1864, for Crenshaw and Co (the erstwhile managers of the *Lelia*), the *Mary Celestia* was the last ship commanded by the ill-fated Commander Arthur Sinclair before he came to Liverpool to take up his command of the *Lelia*. She ran the blockade 8 times and sank on the 26th September when the ship ran into a reef under suspicious circumstances.

The *Hope* - Built by Jones, Quiggin and Co. Engines by the Victoria Foundry, Jack and Co.

Registered in July, 1864, for Fraser Trenholm, the *Hope* was a sister ship to the *Colonel Lamb*. The ship was regarded as one of the finest to come out of the Liverpool shipyards and great things were expected of her. With a length of 281 ft, 5 watertight compartments, the ability to carry 1800 cotton bales and 2, 350 hp engines fore and aft, the *Hope* was faster and stronger than anything the Union forces could put against her and yet on her second run, she was chased for 65 miles by the *USS Eolus* and cornered while trying to enter Cape Fear in October 1864. For once, the Union forces were able to capture the ship before she could be torched earning her crew $1,000 each.

The Hope at sea.

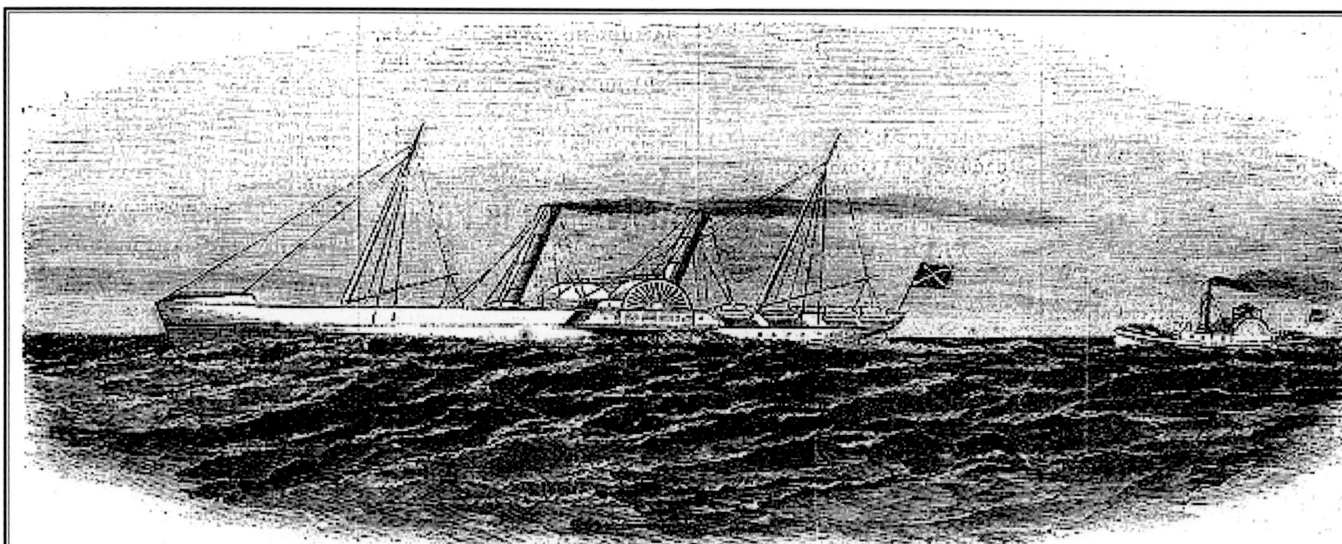

CAPTURE OF THE BLOCKADE RUNNER "HOPE" BY THE UNITED STATES STEAMER "ÆOLUS" OFF WILMINGTON, Oct. 22, 1864.—Sketched by S. M. Lane.—[See Page 790.]

The Owl - Built by Jones, Quiggin and Co. Engines built at Lairds.

Another Fraser. Trenholm acquisition on behalf of the Confederacy, registered July, 1864; for some reason, the *Owl* was painted bright red. The *Owl* ran only 4 times and on an early run into Wilmington in September, 1864, the *Owl* was unable to get out and in October was forced to make a dash out of port. The Captain and several crewmen were injured in the firefight which ensued but they returned safely to Bermuda. When Captain John Newland Maffitt stood down from his command of the *Florida* in August, 1863, due to a heart condition exacerbated by an attack of yellow-fever, he made his way to the Royal Hotel, Waterloo, not far from Dunwoody Bulloch's home (the hotel is still in business) where he spent some time recuperating. He later took his examinations for the British mercantile marine but in December, 1864, he was ordered by Stephen Mallory to captain the *Owl* and pick up the crew from the *Florida* which had been sunk in the preceding month. The *Owl* seemed to be dogged by ill-luck and she was almost captured at Wilmington, jettisoning secret mail packages and sustaining 12 casualties. The following port of Galveston seemed safe enough until she grounded in sight of no less than 16 enemy cruisers and was hauled off by a tug in the nick of time. Her luck finally ran out when she ran the last trip under the name of *Foam*, possibly hoping it would change her luck.

The Bat - Built by Jones, Quiggin and Co. Engines by Watt and Co. of London.

Registered on behalf of Fraser, Trenholm on August, 1864, the *Bat*'s career was to be short-lived and she was captured on her first run. In October, 1864, she attempted to enter the Fear River by night and was turned back by the blockading ships. Captain A. Hora attempted the entrance again two nights later and the ship was fired on by the *USS. Montgomery* resulting in the removal of the leg of an old *Alabama* hand by a 30 lb shot. Captain Hora surrendered and the Union surgeon attended to Match Medick who had survived the battle with the *Kearsage* only to lose his life aboard the *Bat* with 6 months only remaining until the war ended.

As the final days of 1865 went by and the war was drawing inexorably to its conclusion the beleaguered South was desperate for supplies. The blockade had become more of a stranglehold and less ships were getting through. Both sides had refined their strategies to such a degree that where running the blockade had once been a dashing race through a gauntlet of ships and the stuff of swashbuckling derring-do, it was now a skilful game of cat-and-mouse where the odds were becoming increasingly stacked in favour of the Union ships.

It was ironic that although the blockade-runners had evolved into sleek, fast and powerful craft, perfectly suited to their purpose, the sad fact was that more and more of them were being trapped in the mesh of encircling Northern ships.

Despite the overwhelming odds, the South fought on and while the blockade-runner's efforts became more and more frantic, the Liverpool shipyards were busy constructing ships as if the war would never come to an end. The fall of Fort Fisher was a dagger in the heart of Southern opposition and with her supply lines cut completely, it was just a matter of months before capitulation became an inevitability.

The Colonel Lamb - Built by Jones, Quiggin and Co.

Registered in September, 1864, on behalf of Fraser, Trenholm the *Colonel Lamb* was a sister-ship to the *Hope*. Captain Thomas J. Lockwood was something of a legend among blockade-runners and known as a daring and experienced captain who had commanded several successful Southern ships notably the *Kate* which had run the blockade many times and earned Fraser, Trenholm a fortune in the process. Lockwood's wife, Anna (née McDougal), was just as intrepid as her husband and as well as accompanying him on his adventures aboard ship she had once spent three weeks accompanying him at sea in an open-boat; Captain Lockwood needed to get his family from Charleston to Nassau and finding the blockade keeping all ships in harbour he decided on the most unusual and perilous method yet of getting past the Union ships which was to utilise a 16ft long whaleboat. Lockwood, Anna, their children (including a four day old baby) and several trusted oarsmen, sailed successfully into Nassau after three weeks at sea. Anna was at her husband's side when they arrived in Liverpool in Spring, 1864. Lockwood's orders

The Colonel Lamb at sea.

were to oversee the construction of both the *Hope* and the *Colonel Lamb* and to captain the latter ship when she was ready to leave the Mersey. It came as no surprise that Lockwood took an inordinate interest in the building of the *Colonel Lamb* and he was so intent upon customizing the ship to his particular requirements that she went all of 30% higher in price than the *Hope*. James Dunwoody Bulloch was always a man to cross all the "T"s and dot all the "I"s and he found it incumbent upon himself to complain to the fiery Lockwood who responded in a typically robust manner, telling Bulloch to mind his own business and that he, Lockwood, knew more about ships. There were probably a great deal more altercations and arguments but eventually the ships were ready to sail and Anna Lockwood was given the honour of launching her husband's new command, the *Colonel Lamb*. The ship sailed out of the Mersey in October, 1864, and headed for Nassau where she was fitted out and Lockwood began running the blockade once again.

There's no knowing how the *Colonel Lamb* would have fared as a blockade-runner as she ran only twice from November 1864, until the fall of Fort Fisher in January, 1865, which effectively cut the final Southern supply line and presaged the end of the war. Lockwood found himself and the *Colonel Lamb* redundant and in April 1865, he sailed the ship to Halifax where he could be found treating the locals to pleasure trips, something which he had done on previous occasions in other ships. Lockwood had once displayed the Confederate flag on one of his ships while in a neutral port (he greased the mast to make sure nobody could take it down) and the ensign flew defiantly above the *Colonel Lamb* while he was in Halifax but Lockwood ordered its removal when he heard of the death of Lincoln.

The sinking of the Bouboulina

All the care and attention given to the construction of the *Colonel Lamb* was irrelevant now that the war had ended and Lockwood returned the ship to Fraser, Trenholm in Liverpool.

Fraser, Trenholm sold the ship to a Greek shipping firm who renamed her the *Bouboulina*. Her first cargo was a hold -full of explosives which blew up and sent her to the bottom of the Mersey where she lies today the second of two blockade-runners in the river - the other being the *Lelia*.

The *Stag* - Built by Bowdler and Chaffer sub contract from Jones, Quiggin and Co. Engines by Stephenson of Newcastle for Fraser, Trenholm.

The *Stag* was another superlative ship, built on this occasion on the Birkenhead side of the river and like the *Hope* and *Colonel Lamb* great things were expected of her. She left the Mersey in August, 1864, fitted out in Nassau and took up her duties in September, 1864. She ran the blockade several times before falling into an unprecedented Northern trap and becoming one of the very few Southern ships to be captured intact.

In the days when the blockade-runners were more frequent and came and went at will, a system of signal lights from the shore batteries guided ships along the river and into port. Each ship was assigned a group of signallers who had a particular responsibility for their particular ships and the lights were an indication that all was well. The lights that greeted the *Stag* in January, 1865, also welcomed another blockade-runner called the *Charlotte* and the two ships made ready for unloading and another successful run. The lights that guided them in on this occasion, however, had been manned by officers from the Northern warship, the *Monticello*, and as soon as the *Stag* and *Charlotte* had weighed anchor those same officers and crew took both ships as prizes. The two blockade-runners had been unfortunate to enter harbour before the fall of Fort Fisher was known and the *Stag* and *Charlotte* fell victim to the jubilant Northern sailors.

The Deer - Built by W H. Potter sub contract from Jones, Quiggin and Co for Fraser, Trenholm.

Registered at Liverpool as late as November, 1864, the *Deer* ran only once before being captured in February, 1865.

The Lark - Built by Lairds for Fraser, Trenholm.

Left the Mersey in December, 1864 and ran 8 times. It should be noted that the *Lark* worked in the Gulf of Mexico where the blockade was far less stringent. Nevertheless, she earned fame of sorts when she came to the aid of John Newland Maffit's *Owl* when it was stuck on a sandbar off Galveston and working between Havana and Galveston she successfully fought off an attack by Federal ships.

The Wren - Built by Lairds for Fraser, Trenholm.

Left the Mersey in December, 1864 and ran 8 times. It should be noted that the *Wren* worked in the Gulf of Mexico where the blockade was far less stringent. The following ships were all blockade-runners but by the time they had been ready for launching, the war was over and they never ran although the *Ruby* was reported by the Liverpool Mercury to be off Nassau on the 17th January.

There's no doubt that James Dunwoody Bulloch was involved in the building of most of the blockade-runners, working on the orders of Stephen Mallory, and in collaboration with the managers of Fraser, Trenholm. Bulloch always tried to keep a low profile and remained a shadowy figure, working behind the scenes. Charles Kuhn Prioleau was an even more enigmatic figure and it is only in 2009 that a likeness of the man has come to light.

Jones, Quiggin and Co. were far and away, the most prolific builders of blockade-runners and on one memorable occasion in February, 1865, they launched no less than five ships in one day. Four of the ships, the *Widgeon*, the *Snipe*, the *Curlew* and the *Plover*, were identical, all 225 ft long, 24ft breadth and 645 tons in weight and all of them were built for the Confederacy. The fifth ship, intended for an Egyptian company for work in the Red Sea, was called the *Noor-el-Huda* (Light of the Day) and was considerably smaller than the other four. The launch took place in front of a huge crowd and later on there was a banquet where Jones, Quiggin and Co. were lauded for their industry and the observation that the company *"had launched more ships in this part of the country than any other firm ever had or ever would"*.

None of the above ships were used as blockade-runners but the *Widgeon* went into another war which was being fought out in South America. The War of the Triple Alliance was a power struggle between Brazil, Paraguay, Uruguay and Argentina and dragged on from 1864 to 1870 and the *Widgeon*, now a British merchant steamer, entered the fray as a troop carrier carrying Spanish troops. The Captain of the *Widgeon* was none other than the indefatigable Captain of the *Florida*, John Newland Maffitt and in a reprise of his days on the *Florida*, Maffitt once again faced his old nemesis, Yellow Fever. Reaching South America, Maffitt found himself acting as a nurse to the stricken troops but fortunately for him he was lucky enough to escape the virus. In 1869, Maffitt took a chance when he returned to his native country via New York and settled down on a farm in Wilmington but the lure of the sea was too strong and he took to ferrying Cuban Revolutionaries in the Ten Years war.

The Penguin

The *Penguin* was another of the blockade-runners built too late to actually run the blockade. She was built by Bowdler, Chaffer and Co. in Seacombe and subsequently sold to the Greek government for £14, 000 in 1867, in the same package as the *Colonel Lamb* (*Bouboulina*). The two ships were meant to take part in putting down the Cretan Revolution of 1866-1868 but both ships missed that war as well. While the *Bouboulina* ended her days abruptly and sank in the Mersey, the *Penguin* went on to be converted into a Royal yacht in 1869. In 1872, she was reported to have been fitted with a new boiler and up to 1907 she was used as accommodation at the Salamis naval base - and although the *Penguin* took no part in any martial affairs she did end her days near to the site of one of the defining sea battles of all time - Salamis.

The Penguin in her days as a cruise ship entering Venice harbour.

The 11 inch cannon in action aboard the Kearsage

The Taking of The Emily St Pierre

Homecoming

Captains of blockade-runners were by their very nature known to be daring and resourceful but they were also notoriously reticent when it came to recounting their various adventures. Snippets of information came to light here and there but most of the Captains engaged in blockade-running did so in a clandestine world of dawn sailings, secret operations and elusive trade routes. When the *New York Times* on one side of the Atlantic and the leading British newspapers on the other printed a detailed account of the voyage of a blockade-runner then it was bound to be something special and readers were agog at the unprecedented events that unfolded between the pages. The readers were not to know it but they would not read of events at sea between the North and South again in such detail until the Civil War had ended and the only reason they were able to have access to this story was because it was almost impossible to keep it under wraps. For once, the chronically secretive Fraser, Trenholm Company allowed itself a small display of satisfaction and Victorian jingoists were always ready to cheer a British victory no matter who it concerned. The story caused a sensation when it was first published and the story of the capture and recapture of the barque *Emily St Pierre* made a celebrity of its Captain.

The story of the *Emily St Pierre* caught the imagination of everyone who heard it and accolades came from near and far; from a donation of a shilling each from the 1145 residents of Tasmania to a case of shaving materials from a barber in Chapel Street, Liverpool. Captain Wilson had already received a handsome £2,000 reward from the ship's owners when he was called to a banquet in the hallowed halls of the Liverpool Mercantile Marine Association where he was presented with a gold chronometer and a magnificent silver coffee set, engraved with the thanks of the merchants of Liverpool. The engraver must have been taken aback when he was commissioned to engrave the coffee set - the inscription told nearly the whole story. But on that day in May 1862, 170 merchants and mariners of Liverpool waited to hear it all again from the lips of the man himself and Captain Wilson obliged to cheers which punctuated every incident.

The Emily St Pierre

Action and Reaction

The barque, *Emily St Pierre* was built at Bath, Maine in 1854 and subsequently purchased by Fraser, Trenholm and Company for use as a blockade-runner in the early days of the Civil War. Captain Wilson's orders were to leave port in Calcutta on the 27th November, 1861 and to make for South Carolina. According to Wilson, further orders instructed that if a blockade was in place then the *Emily St Pierre* was to veer off and sail to St. Johns, New Brunswick, but it's fairly reasonable to assume that Wilson intended to run the blockade. The ship reached Charleston on the 18th March, 1862 and 12 miles out at sea was approached by the Federal warship, the *James Adger.* Two boats were sent out to the *Emily St Pierre* and the officer in command took possession of the ship and arrested Wilson and his crew for attempting to run the blockade and import contraband in the form of saltpetre. Captain Wilson was rowed to the Flag-Officer, Goldboursh, where he protested his innocence, stated that he was unaware of the presence of the small amount of saltpetre and that the ship was British property. His protestations were in vain and Wilson was rowed back to the *Emily St Pierre* which was now a *"lawful prize of the Federal Government."* The whole of the crew of the *Emily St Pierre* were removed, leaving only Captain Wilson, the cook and the steward as the only original crew members of the ship, and the prize crew was put aboard, consisting of Lieutenant Stone, a master's mate, an engineer and 12 seamen. Lt Stone's orders were to sail to Philadelphia, 800 miles distant. Whatever possessed the Northern officers to leave Captain Wilson, the cook and the steward aboard, as the *Emily St Pierre* sailed for Philadelphia is open to question, but it was a fateful decision which would lead to embarrassment and humiliation far in excess of anything that Lt Stone could have conceived. During the first three days of the voyage, Wilson had time to reflect upon his own humiliation and slowly he began to think the unthinkable, which was to take back his ship. Left to his own devices, Wilson feverishly devised a plan for recapturing the ship and it became such an obsession that at 4 am on the 21st March, he awoke the cook and steward and pleaded his cause for joining him in the mad enterprise. In a whispered conversation in which Wilson vowed that he would take the ship or die in the attempt, the Dublin born, steward, Matthew Montgomery and the cook, Louis Schelvin from Frankfort-on-Main, joined in a pact which they all knew had little chance of success. Captain Wilson's plan could have been drawn from the SAS textbook and he later stated that the design of the ship might have been constructed with his guerrilla operation in mind. The fact was that Wilson had conceived a plan in which he incorporated every feature of the ship's design and took on the overwhelming odds in bite-size proportions - it was clever and ingenious in its simplicity and was aided in no small part by the monumental arrogance of their captors. The three conspirators wasted no time and in the early hours of the same morning they crept towards the cabin of the master's mate. Without awakening him, the trio took his revolver and sword and quickly bound, gagged and secured him in irons before he could fully comprehend what was happening. Returning to the alley-way, they entered the engineer's cabin and he received the same treatment as the master's-mate and the three secured more weapons. There was no going back now, but made bold by their success the trio now entered into the next phase of the plan and while Montgomery and Schelvin laid out a map below decks, Wilson clambered on deck where Lt Stone had the watch. Over the three days of their captivity, Wilson had built up an easy-going familiarity with Stone and Stone, in his

Captain Wilson

turn had realized the quality of Wilson's seamanship so when Wilson questioned Stone's navigation, the Federal officer was only too pleased to go below and take a look at the chart. Threatened with a belaying-pin by Wilson, Stone was told in no uncertain terms that the ship was not going to Philadelphia and he was also bound, gagged and placed in irons. The next target was the three men who were on deck - one of them "a perfect Hercules" and once again Wilson used guile instead of muscle to achieve his aims. Calling to the men that Lt Stone wanted a coil of rope from the hold, Wilson held the hatch as the three sailors jumped down to haul out the heavy rope, and immediately closed the cover when they were all inside. The helmsman who was watching helplessly, was told at gunpoint to keep quiet and Wilson, Montgomery and Schelvin who were now armed to the teeth next called the look-out, and in a departure from the usual procedures asked the man if he would help to sail the ship back to a British port. When the look-out refused, he received the same treatment as all the others. Wilson then undid the fastening on the forecastle door and called the watch below. The first two men were captured easily enough but the third came at the steward with a knife and was promptly shot in the shoulder by Montgomery himself.

The remaining four men were released from the forecastle one by one and taken into custody with the others, leaving the ship back in the hands of Captain Wilson and a trusted crew of two men to sail it 3,000 miles back to Liverpool.

Atlantic Crossing

Faced with sailing the *Emily St Pierre* back to Liverpool virtually single-handed, everything that had gone before seemed simple by comparison. Captain Wilson's cook and steward were ever-willing to help but their expertise was limited to their specific jobs which did not include running the ship and as a consequence Wilson asked if any of the Federal crew would be willing to take a hand. Two men stepped forward but they were poor seamen and Wilson began to carry out most of the duties himself which included navigating, taking the helm, climbing aloft and anything else that was necessary. On top of this, he had a hold-full of prisoners to take care of which was no small matter - the prisoners were fed at gunpoint with only one man allowed to approach the door to take the food for the others. Wilson was on duty night and day and set-up a canvas shelter near to the helm where he rested whenever the chance came along.

The cook and steward of Emily St Pierre

The *Emily St Pierre* sailed along slowly with Captain Wilson unable to put out the top-gallants and only just capable of setting any canvas at all given the lack of manpower. When the Atlantic weather turned foul, it was Wilson himself who climbed to reef the sails and it was Wilson who used the sextant and took the helm - he was everywhere at once and he was totally focused on his burning desire to return the ship to Liverpool. At one point in their odyssey, as if to emphasise just how necessary Wilson was to the running of the ship, one of the hands caused the tiller to break away and the ship was out of control in heavy seas. Wilson single-handedly secured the rudder and installed the spare steering gear and the *Emily St Pierre* was back on course. One of the seamen below hatched a plan of his own when he persuaded Captain Wilson to allow him to help with the running of the ship. He was caught trying to induce his fellow countrymen to overpower Captain Wilson and returned to the hatch in irons. After thirty days of mental and physical toil at sea, a bone-weary Captain Wilson entered the mouth of the Mersey and faced his final challenge before he could enter port and hand over his ship to the owners. When the pilot boarded the *Emily St Pierre* it was essential that the ship appeared to be running normally and that nothing was amiss. The danger of the pilot claiming salvage was real and would have undone everything that he had accomplished thus far. As it turned out, the pilot was suspicious of Captain Wilson's haggard appearance and the lack of a crew but Wilson's complaints at the excessive cost of the pilotage seemed normal enough and in that manner, on the 21st April, 1862, Captain Wilson sailed up the Mersey and anchored at his usual berth. Releasing his prisoners, Wilson's relief was palpable and in a display of good humour he remarked that "They were just in time to see the Great Exhibition."

The re-taking of the *Emily St Pierre* was a major embarrassment for the Federal government who at first demanded their ship and crew back and when the British government pleaded ignorance of the whole matter, they were reduced to pleading which fell on deaf ears, especially in the corridors of Fraser, Trenholm who afforded themselves a quiet smile.

A Scottish Seaman

William Wilson was born in Colvend, Dumfries, Scotland in 1815. According to local lore, the Colvend parish school was exceptionally good at turning out a regular supply of well-educated boys and when William Wilson and his three brothers decided to go to sea, they had a solid grounding in English and mathematics which stood them in good stead when they rose through the ranks. Basic education may be taken for granted in the present day, but to be literate in Victorian Britain was no small thing and the Colvend teacher, Mr Halliday, was a local celebrity for the quality of his teaching. In 1902, an old school friend, also a sea Captain, remembered William as a quiet and well-liked lad.

On leaving school, Wilson was apprenticed to a Mr McKnight of Barlochan and sailed as a cook on the brig *Elizabeth* of Dumfries. The *Elizabeth* worked as a trading ship on the Solway but she had an interesting history; once a French corvette, she had been captured as a prize by a British man-of-war and sold to a Dumfries merchant. There are huge gaps in the narrative of William Wilson but what is known is that he learned his trade as a seaman aboard the *Elizabeth* and gradually achieved the rank of Captain. We next encounter Captain Wilson at the height of his career when he is working for Fraser, Trenholm and Company out of Liverpool and the story of his famous exploit recounted above.

On 9th May, 1862, Wilson, his wife Margaret and daughter Jessie returned to Colvend for several weeks and once again he was invited to a banquet in his honour where to the accompaniment of cheers he recounted the story of the *Emily St Pierre* once again in Dalbeattie Town Hall. He was regaled with the usual long-winded speeches and silver presentations and after resting up in the serenity of his home for some weeks, Wilson returned to Liverpool.

Wilson had dined out for months on the back of the *Emily St Pierre* incident and there's little doubt he could have done so for the remainder of his days but experienced ship's Captains were in short supply and Fraser, Trenholm found him a new ship. Captain Wilson was placed in charge of a blockade-runner called the *Douglas* and in January, 1863, after a successful first run into Charleston, she was renamed the *Margaret and Jessie* in a tribute to Wilson's wife and daughter. Wilson made three further runs into Charleston and Wilmington until on a return run coming out of Charleston at midnight on May 27th, 1863, he was spotted by the vigilant Union warship *Rhode Island*. The *Rhode Island* gave chase and despite Captain Wilson alternating between steam and sail, he was unable to shake his tenacious pursuer and close to home, a fusillade of shells finally hit their mark with one shattering the boiler. Wilson was fearful for his crew and passengers and had little choice but to beach the ship on Eleuthera Island near to Nassau where the passengers and crew escaped as a crowd of ship-dismantlers began to gather like vultures around a carcass.

When the Civil War came to an end in spring of the following year, William Wilson retired a rich man; the two thousand pound from Fraser, Trenholm, alone was more than many men saw in their whole lives. Resourceful, experienced, cunning Wilson was all of these things aboard ship, so why he decided to invest his money in a business venture he knew nothing about, only he could tell us, but at the tailors and outfitters in Lord Street where he set up in partnership he was the proverbial fish out of water. Perhaps, his partner a fellow Scot, had persuaded him of the worth of the trade but whatever the reason, Wilson lost a great deal of his hard-earned capital to his unscrupulous partner.

Three years after the Civil War, in 1868, Captain Wilson was back at what he knew best. After commanding several ships, he took command of the *Glasgow*, of Glasgow bound for Aden with a cargo of coal. After rounding the Cape of Good Hope and just a few days from their destination, Wilson came down with a fever and before the ship could reach port, William Wilson died at the age of 53. It was ironic that after all his hair-raising adventures aboard blockade-runners, Wilson died during a routine trading run on a merchant ship.

William Wilson lived in Everton Terrace in one of the pretty hillside villas that dotted the slopes of Everton Brow and went to make the Everton of the time a picturesque and sylvan slope. Wilson's fame was celebrated in many ways and in many places and it was no surprise that at the bottom of the steps leading from Everton Terrace onto Netherfield Road was a pub named the Emily St Pierre which survived into the 1950s and the coming of the bulldozers.

*Isle of Man
Steam Packet Company
anniversary in 1980
showing the Douglas at sea*

The Douglas

A Manxman goes to war - the remarkable career of an Isle of Man boat.

To all intents and purposes, the career of the *Margaret and Jessie* had ended on the shores of Eleuthera Island on May 27th, 1863, when Captain Wilson and his passengers and crew left her to the tender mercies of the Nassau wreckers, but by good luck or good fortune, the *Margaret and Jessie* reappeared a short time later, refitted and with a new Captain. Robert Lockwood, the brother of the legendary Thomas J. Lockwood, was the new master of the *Margaret and Jessie* and he continued where Captain Wilson had left off.

Whether Lockwood or Wilson knew the origins of the *Margaret and Jessie*, or whether they were too busy to care, is not known but any Manxman or Liverpudlian who ever travelled on the Manx ferry would have been astonished to learn that she had ended up working for both sides during the Civil War.

The *Margaret and Jessie* had started out her career as the *Douglas*, built specifically to steam between Liverpool and the Isle of Man, by Robert Napier and Sons. She was built on Clydeside in 1858, a 211 foot long, 726 ton, iron-sided paddle-wheel steamship. The *Douglas*, as a packet steamer, was fast and luxurious; her fastest time between Liverpool and Douglas, Isle of Man, was 4 hours and 20 minutes and her cabins were adorned with landscapes of the Isle of Man, Liverpool and Scotland. In November, 1862, Fraser, Trenholm and Co. took an interest and purchased her for £24,000 in the name of Cunard, Wilson and Company and outfitted her as a blockade-runner with her first Captain, William Wilson, who began his command in January, 1863 and ended in May of the same year.

Captain Lockwood was extremely successful as commander of the *Margaret and Jessie*, making a further 15 runs throughout the summer of 1863. On the 5th November, 1863, Lockwood's luck ran out and the *Margaret and Jessie* was captured by the *USS Nansemond* and subsequently purchased by the United States navy. Converted to a gunboat, the once Manx packet steamer was commissioned with her grandest name yet, the *USS Gettysburg*, in May, 1864, with her main duty being the opposite of her previous role, enforcing the blockade on behalf of the Federal navy. In the final phase of the war, the *Gettysburg* captured three steamers and took part in the attack on Fort Fisher in January, 1864. She was decommissioned in June, 1865. The *Douglas* had a habit of reappearing from seeming obscurity and in 1866 she appeared once again working as the *Gettysburg* in the Caribbean and in 1874, she took part in surveying duties off the Atlantic coast. 1876, found her working in the Mediterranean where she was sold to a Genoan merchant in 1879 and could be plying between the islands still for all we know.

The Strand, circa 1860.
The Custom House can be seen clearly.
The picture illustrates how essential horses were to the operation of the docks up to and beyond the Second World War. The dock workers formed a great attachment to their horses and many years after the demise of the docks the horses are remembered fondly.

Engines of War

Fawcett Preston and Company

The President

The Quaker Engineers

Fawcett Preston and Company is a name which crops up on a regular basis on ship's specifications built by WC. Miller and Sons and Jones, Quiggin and Co., most especially during the Confederate years in Liverpool. The name can still be seen today stamped onto cannon and engine castings made by the firm and lovingly preserved by museums and enthusiasts around the globe. There's a cannon outside the courthouse in Warren Pennsylvania, another in Cherbourg museum and the United States army retains many of the historic Civil War artefacts. There are many others, both engines and guns, lying at the bottom of the sea, silently proclaiming their origins to nothing but the passing fish.

Fawcett's popularity among the yards that built ships for the Confederacy was in part due to its proximity to the waterfront, a stone's throw away from both Miller's and Quiggin's yards, but the real reason was a tried and tested record of excellence which was second to none. When WC.

Miller's yard was commissioned to build the first Confederate Cruiser, the *Florida*, it was Fawcett Preston and Co. who supplied and fitted the steam engines and it was Fawcett's who also cast the armaments which followed. The American Civil War years were a busy time for the engineering firm and the order books remained full for the duration of the war but the demands from the shipyards were nothing that they couldn't cope with - the fact was that the Fawcett's Foundry had been in existence for over a century before the Confederates came calling and would remain in business a further century after the Civil War had faded into history.

The origins of the Fawcett Foundry in Liverpool can be traced as far back as 1758 when an established engineering company in Shropshire with the impressive title of the Coalbrookdale Ironworks decided they needed subsidiary outlets to sell their goods. Outposts of the Coalbrookdale Empire sprang up in Bristol and London and in Liverpool. Coalbrookdale had been founded in the early years of the 1700s by engineers with solidly Quaker backgrounds and was at the epicentre of the burgeoning Industrial Revolution which would revolutionise social and economic life in England for all time. At the forefront in their new techniques in ironworking was Abraham Darby whose transformation of iron casting was of such sublime simplicity that it was almost laughable but his use of coke in the smelting process instead of charcoal as early as 1709 was fundamental to the fame that it brought to the acclaimed Ironbridge in Shropshire and to everything that followed. Charcoal had been used for years and would have no doubt continued to be used but for the lack of timber, England's forests having been pillaged for years to supply the demand for wooden ships, furniture and all manner of household utensils and the wood to make charcoal was becoming a rare and therefore expensive product.

The Phoenix foundry

George Perry, born in 1719 in Scotland, was the man chosen to head the Liverpool part of the firm and followed the long tradition of fine Scottish engineers. The site chosen for the new factory is now a maze of houses and offices but in 1758, it seems that even though the factory was just a short walk from the bustling waterfront, it was built within a rural area where snipe were still shot. Maps of Liverpool city centre in that era are always distinctive by the sudden transformation from dockland onto farmland and Perry's new factory was possibly the first precursor of urban sprawl. But George Perry's only concern was to turn his fiefdom into a viable business and his first

A Blakely cannon forged in Fawcett, Prestons

decision was to name his factory the Phoenix Foundry a name which would prove to be strangely prophetic, although not in Perry's time. The Foundry's stock-in-trade was the casting and sale of what would first appear to be a mundane household utensil a three-legged cast-iron kettle. But as comical as it first appears, the demand for the pot-bellied tripods (or tripots) was quite phenomenal and apart from selling them around the country by horse and cart, the factory supplied demand from all around the globe and mainly for the sugar industry. The pots ranged in size from small household models to leviathans which required machinery to move them. Examples of these pots of the 1700s can be seen as far afield as the West Indies, Hawaii or Africa or as close as Shropshire where they are dotted around the Coalbrookdale Foundry.

Perry must have become a little bored with his single item and began to experiment in boring out cannon from solid-metal castings. His experiments never amounted to much more than that and he kept the subject from his Quaker patrons who would have been appalled at any thought of weaponry being cast in their workshops. Later on, the Quaker's went so far as to refuse to supply timber for ships which would be engaged in the Slave Trade. Perry also took an interest in a girl from an old Huguenot family and later married Lydia Ann Lacroix in 1765; her name lives on in the street which bounded one side of the Foundry called today Lydia Ann Street. Having established the Phoenix Foundry, George Perry died in 1771, at the early age of 52 - he would never have envisaged that the humble pot-belly stoves produced by the factory would be the beginning of a major engineering firm renowned throughout the world.

The Apprentice

Perry's successor to the factory was Joseph Rathbone who was unfortunate to take up the reins when the Coalbrookdale empire was in financial difficulties. Much of this could be attributed to the Quaker resolve to refuse any contracts which involved making arms and while others prospered from the American War of Independence, the Coalbrookdale factories languished in a morass of debt and litigation.

Rathbone's tenure of the Foundry, now renamed Joseph Rathbone and Company was one of trial and tribulation with the management struggling to keep afloat in the stormy financial seas and for the following fifteen years the fate of the factory was in the balance. The Bristol and London outlets had closed and Liverpool was just hanging on. In the midst of this depressing atmosphere, a young relation of the Quaker family was quietly learning all he could of his trade as an apprentice engineer amongst a demoralised workforce and an uninspired management. William Fawcett was the name of the young man. He was the son of Joseph Rathbone's sister, Elizabeth, and one day he would play a leading part in dragging the Foundry back from its depressed condition. For the time being, in 1784, Fawcett came out of his apprenticeship and began to take an active part in the management of the factory.

Renaissance

Joseph Rathbone had died prior to 1793, the year that Coalbrookdale decided to relinquish their hold on the factory, and William Fawcett's star was well and truly in the ascendancy when he decided to go into business for himself and bought the factory for the sum of £2,300 - there's little doubt that the foundry would have faded into obscurity without the energy and creativity of William Fawcett. Fawcett was a breath of fresh air to the moribund factory and along with his engineering skills he brought creativity and vision which all combined to galvanize the factory into a new phase of its existence. Fawcett was also aware that the foundry must diversify or go under and his unprecedented decision made in 1794 that the foundry would begin to manufacture armaments coincided with the beginnings of the Napoleonic Wars. Fawcett had also received a Quaker upbringing and his decision was undoubtedly made with a great deal of soul-searching but his head ruled his heart and he stuck to his decision - from that day forward the foundry's fortunes increased accordingly and in due course Fawcett was disowned by his Quaker relatives. The schism between Coalbrookdale and Fawcetts was a defining moment in the history of both Foundries and from that day onward each diverged into the manufacture of their own specific items and both of them flourished in their own particular field.

The Hindostan leaving Southampton

Fawcett's naval guns, usually made to the Blakely design, were very soon a large part of the factory's output and further to George Perry's secretive potterings with boring out gun muzzles, there were 6 gun-boring lathes installed which were turned by a single horse whose life was one of interminable "going round in circles." Despite the cannon being purchased and used extensively by Wellington's armies in the Peninsula, despite an astronomic annual income for their manufacture of £10,000 and despite Fawcett's prodigious time and energy spent in the factory, the spectre of debt haunted Fawcett all his days and in the long run culminated in his bankruptcy in 1813. The foundry once again had new owners and George and Henry Littledale bought the place, lock, stock and barrel. The Littledale's were astute enough to know that of all the assets they had purchased William Fawcett was the finest of all of them and they had the good sense to retain him as manager, changing the name of the foundry to Fawcett and Littledale.

Steam and Sail

After 1815, and the Battle of Waterloo, cannon production slowed to a trickle but Fawcett was far in advance in his thinking and his latest ideas would soon lead the factory into the forefront of a different manufacturing subject altogether. Fawcett was a devout disciple of the Industrial Revolution right from the very beginning and even while the men on the shop-floor were casting cannon his mind was far into the future, inspired by his association with the son of James Watt whose tales of steam engines fascinated Fawcett.

Fawcett had been toying with the subject as early as 1800 and had gone so far as to make a working model of a steam-engine which was stood in the foundry for demonstration purposes. But Fawcett's ambition was to use the new technology as propulsion for ships which would prove more difficult than a mere model. The difficulties lay in persuading the ship-owners and Captains that the steam was literally the way forward but many were highly suspicious of change and produced viable arguments against the use of steam-engines in ships - they were quite right when they said the price of coal was prohibitive The first engines were not reliable and they took up valuable space on a ship and why should they pay when the wind was free. On the other hand, when there was no wind billowing the sails a steam-engine was a definite advantage and so the arguments went on. Some ship-owners would never be persuaded to take up the new technology and even into the 1870s clipper ships were flying along the Australian routes with ships specifically designed for speed and unencumbered by engines. Others such as the *Royal Charter* and other long distance ships utilised sail in mid-ocean and engines whenever necessary. After a while, a compromise was reached by some of the ship-owners whereby steam-ships would retain their masts and sails thereby having the best of both worlds and this situation retained until late into the Victorian era.

While all this was going on, Fawcett decided to pre-empt all the arguments and make a steam-ship of his own and in 1817 the *Etna* took to the Mersey as a ferryboat crossing from Tranmere to Liverpool at regular intervals. What the *Etna* lacked in beauty she made up for in reliability and Dawson and Company ordered another called the *Mersey* which was just as impressive. Not only were these two vessels the precursors of the famous Mersey ferries, as unlikely as it may seem they were also the blueprint for ocean-going passenger steamships which were not too far into the future. The technology was moving fast and from these humble beginnings, Fawcett's steam-engines began to power increasingly larger ships and between 1817 and 1850 manufactured no less than 230 engines for customers across the globe. The King of Wirtemberg's *Wilhelm*, sailed Lake Constance, the French Minister of Marine ordered the *Veloce*, Carling and Young of London ordered the *President*, sadly lost without trace in 1841, and Thomas Wilson of Liverpool built the *Royal William* on behalf of the City of Dublin Steam Packet Service the forerunner of the New York to Liverpool liner services. All of them were fitted with Fawcett steam engines which became more reliable and fitted larger and larger ships as time went by.

The factory was working at full capacity by the early 1820s, manufacturing all manner of equipment - sugar-cane roller-mills in the West Indies, waterwheels in South America, steamship engines, pumps, boilers and armaments all for a multitude of customers all over the world. Under William Fawcett's brilliant leadership the foundry had been transformed from a business dying on its feet into a dynamic and forward-looking engineering firm whose reputation travelled around the globe. It therefore came as somewhat of a surprise when Littledale's decided to sell two thirds of their share in the business. The Preston family were not slow to take up their offer and once again the factory fell into new ownership. Like the Littledale's before them, the new owners recognized that Fawcett was the heart and soul of their new purchase and retained him as general manager, with the firm going forward as before under the new title of Fawcett Preston and Co, a name which would soon be etched into their cast-iron goods for many years into the future and would still be over the factory entrance 150 years into the future.

Fawcett Preston and Co

If anything, the factory prospered even more under the new management and the next few years would be the halcyon days of both Fawcett's foundry and Fawcett himself. Fawcett's authority was unchallenged among his workforce

The Lady Mary Wood steaming off Ceylon

numbering 150 employees and the quality of the factory attracted the best of men at all levels. While the foundry ran as smoothly as his machinery, Fawcett forged ahead with new projects, driving the factory forward and leading from the front as he had always done. His daily tour of the foundry was always an occasion for the workforce to apply themselves exclusively to their work but he was never a hard man and looked upon his staff with respect and affection.

The steam-engines for ships which were just a short time previously such an innovation were now a routine part of the manufacturing process and Fawcett turned his attentions toward other applications for the new technology; in engineering terms there was very little difference between the sails of a ship and the sails of a windmill. They were both propelled by the wind and the obvious corollary to that logic was Liverpool's first windmill powered by a steam engine.

Fawcett's next project was the adaptation of steam propulsion to the watermill at Spital Dam in Bromborough; eighty years later in 1910, the same engine was still powering the watermill, quite near to where the company would one day make its new headquarters.

The foundry's fame had spread near and far and the newly formed Peninsular Steam Navigation Company (which would one day evolve into the famous P & O shipping company) were anxious to become a part of the revolutionary new processes and it was a Fawcett Preston steam engine which powered their first paddle-steamer. The ship was launched in 1828 by Caleb and James

Smith of Liverpool for the Dublin and London Steam Packet Company and Fawcett must have been a proud man when the Company named the ship the *William Fawcett* although he had previously been honoured by a Mersey ferryboat of the same name. The Steam Navigation Company went from strength to strength and larger and larger steam-ships were the result with Fawcett's supplying the engines for each ship. The *William Fawcett* was 206 tons but the next in line, the *Oriental*, was 1,787 tons and the speed of the transition was a measure of the Company's ambition which came to fruition when they became the famed P and O in 1840. The *Lady Mary Wood* of higher tonnage again was another of the Fawcett/Peninsular association, followed by the *Hindostan* of 2,017 tons and the *Bentinck*. All of these ships set records and made history for various reasons but the *Bentinck*'s maiden voyage became the finest endorsement ever for Fawcett, Preston and Co when the ship travelled 4,000 miles under steam without coaling. The *Lady Mary* might have sounded ladylike and William Makepeace Thackeray certainly thought so when he was a passenger around the Mediterranean but while in service on the Ceylon - Singapore - Hong Kong run she fought a gun-battle with Chinese pirates, emerging triumphant.

From an engineering viewpoint, William Fawcett's work from 1800 to the 1840s had seen him reach the pinnacle of his career as an engineer of the highest quality, spoken of in the same breath with such hallowed names as Lairds of Birkenhead and Forrester of Vauxhall. The foundry he had dragged back from the brink of extinction had become one of the finest in the world purely as a result of his industry and genius and although he seemingly managed it all with consummate ease, kept a large work force in work when times were really hard, and made fortunes for the owners, William Fawcett could never manage his own finances and his whole life was given over to paying debts accrued by bad investments. While others lived in mansions, Fawcett lived the whole of his life in a small Georgian house on the corner of York Street which was part of the foundry.

While the foundry enjoyed unremitting success for the whole of Fawcett's career, the reckoning came in 1844, a year which is undoubtedly the blackest in the whole 200 year history of Fawcett Preston and Co. The beginning of the run of misfortune began early in the year with a small fire which the watchman spotted early and in a sad piece of misjudgement thought he could extinguish without help. His buckets of water were to no avail and the arrival of the fire brigade soon had the fire under control until their water supply ran out and the flames leapt back into life. By the time they had pumped fresh supplies from the Mersey the fire was out of control and it was only

A limber and cannon manufactured for the Boer War

the intervention of 60 seamen from *HMS Redwing* whose energies prevented the whole neighbourhood from going up in smoke. As it was, the conflagration left the factory nothing but a heap of smoking ruins.

Adding insult to injury, the foundry's reputation took a rare battering from an unlikely source and one which was hardly deserved. In the previous year a Captain Robert Stockton of the United States Navy, flying in the face of accepted wisdom, had concluded that a wrought iron gun would be advantageous and placed the contract for his new weapon with the Mersey Steel and Iron Company who sub-contracted to Fawcett's whose job was to turn and bore a piece of the finest Yorkshire iron. For once, Fawcett's cavalier penchant for accepting any challenge no matter how difficult was their undoing although in trials on the north shore at Liverpool the 12 ton cannon fired its 219 pound shot without difficulty. The gun was named the Oregon and shipped to New York where a small crack was discovered in the rifle. Captain Stockton strengthened the gun with iron bands and it was fired a further 150 times without incident but anyone who knew of the weakened casting would surely have stood well clear. As things turned out it wasn't the Oregon which caused a problem but another gun manufactured to the same specification in a New York foundry which preceded the Colt 45 by being called the Peacemaker. Captain Stockton's obsession with firing huge cannon in front of admiring crowds would today bring him in front of not only a court-martial but also a psychiatrist but in 1844, an invited audience of 350 guests stepping aboard the frigate *Princeton* were only too happy to trust in the flawed Stockton and his flawed cannon. The first shot was a great success with great rumblings from the gun and huge spouts of water where the shell landed in the Potomac and Stockton was prevailed upon to fire another. To his credit, Stockton prevaricated but finally gave in to the many dignitaries present including the President of the Navy. The Peacemaker proved to be anything but when it burst asunder causing a great deal of damage and killing several of the guests including many of the naval dignitaries. The dêbacle seemed to be a long way removed from any involvement by Fawcetts but by some labyrinthine logic the explosion was traced back to the foundry and Captain Stockton put the whole thing behind him and went on to enjoy a distinguished career.

As the year dragged on and December arrived, if the factory thought their troubles were over then an even worse disaster arrived when William Fawcett, the beating heart and icon of the foundry, died at the age of 82. Throughout his life he was burdened with debt but despite his financial embarrassment

Fawcett had supported his half-brother's 11 children for years, a fact which speaks volumes about the man. However, his pride would not allow him to go to his grave owing another man and his debts were paid in full before he died. The funeral cortege numbered over 400 some of whom were fellow members of the Athenaeum, his only luxury, and a portrait was commissioned to hang in the Mechanics Institute in memory of the great man.

A Phoenix Rising

If any competitors thought that Fawcett Preston and Company would go into decline after the trio of blows which they had suffered, then they were to be sadly disappointed as the foundry lived up to the name given it many years before and arose from the ashes like the proverbial Phoenix. In fact, the management took a positive attitude to the fire and treated the blaze as a way of sweeping away some of the older and obsolete equipment and re-building a better and more modern establishment. Twelve months later, the factory was operating as if nothing had happened. As far as production went, the influence of William Fawcett was pervasive and his spirit lingered on and would always do so. The impetus and ideas he brought to the foundry would keep it going from strength to strength. As incredible as it may seem, the factory which had begun by forging and selling three-legged pots was still producing the same product, which was as popular as ever, during the mid-Victorian era. The fact was that Fawcetts were renowned for taking on work no matter how big or how small and for this reason the factory was constantly humming with activity. In 1849, the foundry even produced a steam locomotive for the East Lancashire Railway Company which was predictably called the Phoenix and was still running as late as 1890. The orders for ships never ceased and the *Leeds*, the *Antelope*, the *Merlin*, the *Medusa*, the *Medina* were followed by the *Countess of Ellesmere* reputed to be "the fastest ship on the Mersey" at that time.

In 1854, the Crimean War brought another challenge for the engineers at the foundry when the government ordered 80 mortars. The resulting guns were nearly as wide as they were long and someone christened them "malevolent frogs" but the stubby little guns were also described by their gunners as extremely durable and reliable. The foundry was as busy as it ever was in the mid-Victorian era and having attracted the finest engineers by its reputation, Fawcett's legacy lived on.

The Coming of the Confederacy

By the 1850's the foundry that George Perry had called the Phoenix was over a century old and within its walls life went on as it had always done but although Perry would have been familiar with the factory he would never have recognized the surrounding area. The original foundry had arisen in a rural setting where the elegant Georgian houses of Duke Street were just beginning to spread outwards from the city centre and considered to be a fashionable suburbia at the time. Such was the rural nature of the area that Gilbert Street and Lydia Ann Street did not exist until the 1760s and remained unnamed tracks until the 1780s. Within the ivory towers of Duke Street and the noisy cloisters of the foundry, each insulated from the outside world in their different ways, the people who made up those two institutions would have barely noticed the houses spreading slowly outward from the river in a tide of bricks and mortar. The population explosion from the 1750s onwards was unprecedented and swelled greatly by an influx of Irish fleeing from the Great Famine. Many of them were intent on reaching America but many others were fleeced of their money or never had any in the first place and they washed up on the banks of the Mersey, destitute and desperate. Vast numbers of three storey houses were thrown up to accommodate the demand and by the 1860s the factory was surrounded by a sea of houses and Duke Street was fighting hard to retain its elegance. The houses were built for the working classes and cramped enough even with the requisite numbers of people to a room but they were soon overcrowded when rapacious landlords crammed as many families in as they could in order to rake in more rent and very soon much of the area was a labyrinth of seething slums where cholera and typhoid erupted intermittently and tuberculosis was endemic.

William Fawcett's house in York Street in 1837

Streets such as Duke Street and Greville Street which had only been affordable by the rich were now cheek by jowl with some of the worst slums in Europe and it was almost inevitable that the "haves" and the "have-nots" would clash at some point but nobody could have anticipated in 1849, one of the most horrific murders in the history of the city. Greville Street was similar to Duke Street and home to a higher working class such as the ship's captain who was away at sea when Maurice Gleeson, a native of Limerick, broke into his home and slaughtered his wife, two children and the maid. Gleeson was hanged at Kirkdale Jail in front of a crowd of 30,000 onlookers and Greville Street, for many years was erased from the maps.

These were the streets that James Dunwoody Bulloch negotiated to reach the foundry when he first arrived in Liverpool in June 1861and began an association with Fawcett Preston and Company which would lead to many of their steam-engines and armaments being built for cruisers and blockade-runners bound for the Confederate navy. He almost certainly negotiated with Alfred Chapman who served Fawcetts for the same length of time as William Fawcett - 60 years. The ship-builders who they worked with were just a short walk away down by the river and W C. Miller and Jones, Quiggin and Company worked in conjunction with Fawcett's for the length of the Civil war, manufacturing ships which became famous for many different reasons and guns which were used on many different targets. No matter what the fate of the ships, everyone agreed that they were all of the finest workmanship. The construction of the *Florida* and the fate of the *Lelia*, both with Fawcett engines have already been dealt with in detail in other chapters and the stories of the many ships built for the Confederacy involving either W.C. Millers, Jones, Quiggin, and/or Fawcetts are detailed on other pages.

"If It Can Be Built, Then we'll Build It"

Although the Confederate years were memorable for many reasons, the fact remained that in relation to the age of the foundry the time spent on the engines and arms manufactured for the rebel government was a short hiatus in its history. There's no doubt that Fawcetts were well aware that they were building ships and guns for a foreign government but like everyone else approached by the Confederate agents, Fawcetts placed money before any questions of morality they may have harboured - apart from which there was a great deal of sympathy for the Confederacy in Liverpool and beyond. They would also have taken comfort from the fact that most of the equipment was supplied to the shipyards and Fawcetts was merely a sub-contractor. Despite the relatively short association with the Confederacy many of the Fawcett engines and cannon were

The Fawcett Fowler steam car

fitted to ships which enjoyed world-wide fame (or infamy depending on how you looked at things) which has done nothing to diminish the reputation of Fawcetts and has made much of their old equipment collector's items. After 1865, the foundry switched back quite easily to manufacturing the multitude of machinery they were accustomed to and while sugar-processing plant, steam-engines and pumps were routine the engineers were often challenged by eccentric orders which were rarely turned away and invariably built successfully. There was nothing unusual in visitors to the foundry seeing an engineer poring over blueprints for a press for making paving stones while another was busy with a mammoth, cast-iron waterwheel and yet another was putting the finishing touches to a distillation plant. Fawcetts delighted in every challenge and ship's propellors, bottling machines, pumps, condensers, presses and virtually anything that could be made out of cast-iron went to make up a day's work. The novelty and variety of the work were just two reasons why the very best engineers were attracted to the foundry and why the apprentices took pride in stating proudly that they worked for Fawcetts. The apprenticeship scheme was one of the finest ways of learning a trade and Fawcetts turned out a steady stream of engineers ranging from the merely excellent to the often eminent. None of them thought it unusual that they were required to work 6 days per week, making up 54 hours of standard time in practical experience at the foundry and all of them accepted that they attend night-classes for 4 nights per week in theoretical work - times were hard and it was a privilege to be learning a trade. By the turn of the century, the workforce numbered over 1,000 consisting of coppersmiths, brassfounders, ironfounders, millwrights, boiler-makers and craftsmen of every hue.

A Fawcett, Preston waterwheel deep in the jungles of Guatemala in the 1930s.

One of the foundries more unusual orders was for an automobile fitted with a steam-engine which on reflection was completely in keeping with William Fawcett's penchant for adapting steam-engines to everything that moved and the great man would no doubt have greatly approved. The resulting vehicle was a handsome automobile with the imposing title of The Fawcett Fowler Steam Car. The car was obviously built with loving care and a shining example of the adaptability of Fawcett's engineers but sadly it was to be just one of a kind; the combustion engine was king and the Fawcett Fowler Steam Car ended its days as a bizarre curiosity in an evolutionary cul-de-sac of the motoring world.

The First World War and Beyond

The First World War brought new demands on the foundry and the repair of ship's engines was accompanied by the production of high-explosive shells on lathes custom-built at Fawcetts for that singular task. The workforce swelled to 1500 and subsidiaries were opened in Edge Lane and Aintree all dedicated to the manufacture of munitions with all aspects of the work overseen by Fawcett's technicians.

Following the war, the working week was reduced to 47 hours and the factory returned to manufacturing more conventional machinery with a staff drastically reduced to 400. Life went on much as before and would probably still be doing so but for Liverpool Corporation's need for housing land and in 1935 the management were under pressure to sell the historic foundry. Many of the staff had worked in the foundry for years and had a sentimental attachment to the old place - their fathers had worked there and in some cases their grandfathers also. William Fawcett's house still stood on the corner, an enduring reminder of the driving force and patron saint of the foundry. But the harsh reality was that the foundry had grown old and 177 years of the incessant hammering of metal and the super-heating of forges, the clatter and the clamour and the ceaseless work had all gone to erode the crumbling fabric of the building. The management had been aware that they needed new premises for a long time, making Liverpool Corporation's overtures not too difficult to resist.

The site chosen for the new factory was "across the water" in Bromborough on the site of the old magazine where gunpowder had once been stored - Magazine Road testifies to its original usage. It seems that the cobbled streets of Liverpool had been dangerous as gunpowder was taken down to the river by horse and cart - the horses' hooves struck sparks from the granite setts and could have ignited the powder. Working on the premise that it was OK to blow up Birkenhead, the magazine was moved to Bromborough where the locals must have been overjoyed at the good luck that had befallen them. The magazine at Bromborough was subsequently deemed to also be unsuitable and the decision was taken to site the gunpowder in the middle of the Mersey within the holds of ships which seemed a good idea until the *Lottie Sleigh* blew up in 1864 and showered both sides of the river with a hail of iron and wooden shrapnel.

By 1936, the arduous process of moving house was completed and many of the staff also moved house onto the Wirral to be near to their work. The factory had barely started production before the rumours of war began to get louder and once again ships' engines and shells took priority and once again Fawcett Preston and Company took a leading role - this time in supplying materials for the Second World War.

The momentous decision made by William Fawcett to make armaments in the foundry had been its salvation and over the years from boring holes in solid metal the work had evolved and become refined into the production of shells of all shapes and sizes. The technicians had become masters of their trade and the expertise which once fashioned cast-iron cannon culminated in a frenzy of bullets and shells coming off a belt which worked night and day throughout the five years of the conflict. It was therefore ironic that a decision made 150 years ago should be the very thing that eventually brought the factory to its knees and the guns which were of such anathema to the Quakers were to play their part in defending the country from the evils of Nazism.

The end of the war found Fawcett's exhausted by their efforts with the workforce down to 300 and the daunting task of re-building facing them. Many of the technicians had gone to war and the machinery so invaluable in wartime was useless in peacetime and needed replacing. The task was overwhelming and in 1948 the management conceded that a new dynamism was needed to energize the foundry and took up an offer to amalgamate with another firm. Metal Industries was a larger and more powerful firm and in reality had swallowed up the foundering factory but they were astute enough to leave Fawcett Preston with its name and separate identity and in this way the foundry survived once again.

The Dolphin lamps on William Brown Street

Very few people on the Liverpool side of the river can recall Fawcett Preston and Company but on the Wirral peninsular, there are many who remember the Bromborough factory with great affection. They always called their place of work *"Fossets"* and so did their fathers and grandfathers and that's the name it has always been called since William Fawcett bought the factory in 1793. The unusual affection that the workforce always felt for this place has endured and has been a unique element of the foundry from its beginnings. Much of the information for this article has been drawn from an out-of-print book called predictably *"Fossets"* by Horace White O.B.E and in my battered copy, in one of the margins somebody has pencilled in - *"What great memories I have. W.H. App.1927 to 1932"* - which says it all really.

Liverpool Corporation's plans for a new housing estate were delayed due to the war but true to the spirit of the architecture of the 1960s they eventually demolished the factory making sure in the process that they erased all trace of the Phoenix Foundry from the face of the earth and then they replaced it with a nondescript housing complex. When the tracks each side of the factory were laid out into roads in the 1760s, they never had a name but in 1780 the one nearest to Duke Street was called Lydia Ann Street. The street had on one side the Phoenix Foundry and on the other side a similar complex of factories. A walk down Lydia Ann Street today reveals on one side a housing complex where the Phoenix Foundry once stood and on the other side is a handsome building where steel and glass are interspersed with old brickwork which has been re-pointed and cleaned. On the corner of Henry Street is a Georgian house which could easily be mistaken for the house where William Fawcett lived for 60 years and the old and the new have been skillfully blended to retain the best of the past with the freshness of today. The whole complex is called The Foundry and there is nothing more explicitly condemnatory of 1960s architecture than those pristine walls looking down in silent disdain for the mediocrity and council vandalism of the past.

As for the original Quaker factory of Coalbrookdale in Shropshire where Abraham Darby first used coke in his smelting process over 300 years ago it is still in existence and has been classified as a World Heritage Site. Part of the site is still in use making Aga cookers while the greater part has been lovingly preserved as one of the foremost examples of work and life in a bygone era and an example of the Industrial Revolution frozen in time. Abraham Darby's original Forge can still be seen and the offices are now a museum as are the families' homes up the hill a few hundred yards away. The Quakers were always steadfast in their refusal to manufacture anything that had anything to do with violence but they still prospered and Abraham Darby the third had a great deal to do with the Ironbridge which gives the village its name and crosses the river Severn in such an elegant manner.

The family took many of their exhibits to the Great Exhibition in 1851 where Queen Victoria took in such oddities as jardinières made with iron cogs and gears and statues made from cast iron looking every bit as good as the traditional bronze.

A steamroller on the streets of Liverpool 1867

The Magnificent Map

George Perry, the first manager of the Phoenix Foundry, was a man of many parts and his talents extended far beyond the confines of the engineering factory. In any history of the foundry itself, his achievements are eclipsed by those of William Fawcett, but Perry's wide-ranging interests outside the workplace indicate a well-rounded individual whose interests extended to the Liverpool Library in Duke Street, the history of Liverpool and even to writing poetry. But his true talent lay in surveying, and in 1769, assisted by William Yates, George Perry produced his masterpiece - "The New and Accurate Plan of The Town and Port of Leverpool", an invaluable record of a Liverpool fast fading into history.

The street layouts on the map are virtually the same as they appear today and in that respect Perry's Leverpool is immediately recognisable but due to the periodic kaleidoscopic upheavals that beset the city centre, what is contained in those streets is not recognisable at all. Duke Street is a tree-lined boulevard, the top of Church Street is a vast timber yard, the city boundaries end abruptly at Wolstenholme Square and a short walk from Hanover Street is a rural haven of fields and property owned by numerous worthies of the town who will soon be commemorated in street names, as their fields are engulfed in a tide of urban sprawl. From our perspective, Leverpool could almost be an alternative version of the city, as envisioned and drawn by some ancient town-planner with leanings toward minimalism. From an even more distant vantage point, to paraphrase a popular cliché: *"It's Liverpool, George, but not as we know it."*

Plaque in Toxteth Chapel.

Apart from its historic value, Perry's map has a hypnotic quality and people have been observed studying it for hours, mesmerised by its twin qualities of familiarity and strangeness, occasionally tracing a street or building with an outstretched finger. On display in the Walker Art Gallery in 2008, the map was a centre of attention for a curious public. A feature of the map is the Dock which extended right up to Paradise Street and has recently been excavated, a portion of which can be seen from a viewing point in Liverpool 1.

George Perry was a remarkable man and his magnificent map stands as his monument. Sadly just 6 years after his marriage to Lydia Ann and 2 years after publication of his map, he passed away in February, 1771, aged 52 years and was buried in the Ancient Chapel of Toxteth Park.

SOURCES

Memoirs of Service Afloat.	Raphael Semmes.
The Secret Service of the Confederate States in Europe Volumes 1 and 2	James Dunwoody Bulloch.
Two Years on the Alabama	Arthur Sinclair.
Four Years in the Confederate Navy	William Stanley Hoole.
Recollections of a Rebel Reefer	James Morris Morgan.
The Last Shot	Lynn Schooler.
High Seas Confederate	Royce Shingleton.
The Rebel Raiders	James Tertius de Kay.
The Roosevelt Women	Betty Boyd Caroli.
Lelia	Chris Michael.
Fossets	Horace White CBE.
Ghost Ships of the Mersey	K.J. Williams.
The Company That Went to War	Ethel Nepveux.
The Pool of Life	Maggi Morris/John Ashton.
A History of the English Speaking Peoples	Winston Churchill.
The Confederate Ironclads	Maurice Melton
The Victorians	A.N.Wilson
Dumfries Library archives	

Government Parliamentary Papers on-line.

Blackwoods Magazine

The New York Times

The Liverpool Mercury

The Liverpool Echo

The Illustrated London News

Century Magazine

The Internet, which is fast becoming the largest library in the world.

Ars Gratia Artis

The pictures which are such an integral part of this publication would merit a publication of their own if they were analysed in detail. Some of them are my own photographs but these are small in proportion to the number of contemporary pictures included, and despite modern technology, they don't bear comparison with the fine drawings and sketches of artists who must have spent hour after hour on freezing cold quaysides to produce their painstakingly crafted gems.

For artists such as William Woods, besides being a labour of love, it was also a way to make a living and Woods sold his sketches to the Illustrated London News, where they were used to embellish stories of the Liverpool waterfront. Some of Woods's original sketches can be found in a massive volume, the size and weight of an average headstone, mouldering away within Liverpool Record Office. There's little information available about William Woods apart from the fact that he lived in Everton, but his drawings stand comparison with any of his peers and he deserves to be far better known.

We owe a great debt to others like Woods who plied their trade in Century Magazine, Harpers, The London Illustrated News and many other publications of the Victorian era, which took the trouble to illustrate their articles and neglected to name the artists.

The crystal-clear reproductions of Captain Wilson and his crew of two are courtesy of Bob Jones.

The photograph of the bell of the Lelia was generously donated by Chris Michael whose book called simply "Lelia" relates the tragedy in detail. His dives on the wreck of the Lelia are related, as is his serendipitous discovery of the bell,which cost him the small price of a lobster.

It seems that Victorian photographers had yet to discover how to make their subjects smile, and a stern-looking W.C. Miller and his wife are typical of pictures of the era. What is not typical is the amount of time and money that Richard Harris spent in restoring the photograph after it was almost lost in an accident and his generosity in allowing its use within these pages.

The paintings by Samuel Walters are also courtesy of Liverpool Record Office and such are their quality that it is almost obligatory to include at least one in any sea story.

The photographs of the blockade-runners on Lake Ontario are courtesy of the Canadian historians of the Great Lakes who are as passionate about their maritime history as we are about ours.

The Isle of Man Steam Packet Company supplied the Manx postcards.

The metal plaques are original art works for which I have to thank Fred O'Brien.

Frost Prioleau is to thank for the pictures of his ancestors.

INDEX

Abercromby, General Sir Ralph 132
Abercromby Square 125, 126, 127, 129, 132, 133, 136 -139
Aberdeen 102
Abolition of Slavery Act 7
Abolition of the Slave Trade Act 7
Adams, John Quincy 24
Adams,Charles Francis 24, 26, 28, 29, 30, 31, 44, 70, 78, 79, 113, 170
Adelphi Hotel 100, 112, 113, 118, 142
Adkins, Captain Simpson 175
Albert Dock 26, 57
Alcott, Henry William 107
Aleutian Islands 84
Allerton Hall 96, 113, 124 -126, 133, 139
America 7, 8, 10, 27, 57, 95, 122, 141
Anderson E.M 85, 109
Anderson, Major Edward C 20, 123
Anfield Cemetery 108, 116
Annapolis 55
Arctic Sea 83, 108
Armstrong Lt 109
Averett, Lt 67
Azores 32, 33, 37, 38, 39, 47
Aztec 5, 8

Balkail House 125
Barbados 67
Barney, Lt Joseph N 65, 69
Bartelli, steward 40, 53
Bath,Marchioness 120
Beardslee Lt 74
Bedford St North 111
Beecher, Henry Ward 115
Belvidere school 99
Benjamin, Judah P 14
Bering Sea 86
Bermuda 21, 137, 147, 149, 152, 164, 170, 171, 177
Berry St 116
Birkenhead 11, 18, 24, 27, 28, 32, 80, 84, 88, 114, 115, 118, 134, 166, 180, 208
Blackburn 120
Blake, Captain 43
Blakely cannon 18, 20, 38, 57, 123, 134, 198
Bold St 116
Bootle 116
Bowdler, Chaffer shipyard 150, 166, 180, 182
Bravay, messrs 79, 80
Brazil 44, 72, 73, 74, 75
Brest 67, 68, 69, 71, 78
Brodie, Andrew 156, 157, 158
Brosman, James 107
Bulloch, Anna 91
Bulloch Hall 91
Bulloch, Harriot 31, 92, 93, 95-100, 118
Bulloch, Henry 93, 97
Bulloch, Irvine 37, 53, 83, 91, 96, 97, 99, 100, 109
Bulloch, James (1) 90
Bulloch, James (2) 99
Bulloch, James Dunwoody 14-34, 37, 44, 61, 66, 68, 69, 70, 72, 77-85, 87, 88, 89, 91, 92, 93, 95, 96-103, 105, 106, 111, 112, 123, 124, 135, 137, 142, 147, 151, 170, 171, 177, 179, 182, 206
Bulloch, James Stephen 90, 91
Bulloch, Jessie Hart 92, 99, 100
Bulloch, Martha (Mittie) 91, 92, 97, 99
Bulloch, Martha Louise 95, 100
Bulloch, Stuart Elliot 87, 95, 97, 99
Butcher, Captain Matthew J 31, 32, 33, 37

Canada 13, 14, 110, 112, 115
Canning Dock 17, 26
Canning St 31, 99, 100
Cape of Good Hope 44,191
Capetown 45, 47, 49
Caren, John 108
Caribbean 7, 109, 135, 194

Caskie, Elizabeth Euphemia 92
Charleston 15, 20, 84, 88, 89, 90, 110, 111, 112, 115, 123, 128, 134, 135, 173, 175, 178, 186, 190
Chavasse, Christopher 138
Chavasse, Noel 138
Chavasse, Rev. Francis James 138
Cherbourg 47, 49, 50, 56, 57, 195
Chicora, house in North Drive 111
China 8, 67
Clarkson,Thomas 7
Clifton 96
Clyde, river 77, 81, 85, 88, 127, 173, 193
Coalbrookdale Iron Works 196 - 198, 210
Collins, Captain Napoleon 72-75
Copenhagen 81
Cork 47
Costa, John de 26
Cotton Famine 10, 11
Craven, Captain Thomas T 30, 32
Crimean War 29, 59, 96, 204
Cross, Harriot 92, 112
Crosby 94, 130
Crosby, Seabank Hotel 94
Cuba 63, 81, 110
Cunard building 17
Cunard line 31, 127, 132, 154, 193
Curry, Michael 156, 161
Custom House 17, 42, 194

Dahlgren cannon 54, 59
Darby Abraham 196, 210
Davis,Jefferson 11-14, 33, 37, 84, 93, 97, 109, 167
Dawley, Lelia Imogen 146
Decatur,Stephen 41
Denmark 81
Derwent Square 111
Devereux,Peter 128
Dickens, Charles 105
Dixon, Lt George 88
Dudley, Thomas Haines 23, 24, 26, 28, 32, 70, 78, 128, 134, 135, 137, 170
Duguid, James Alexander 24, 62, 102, 106, 151, 160, 172
Dumbarton 114
Duncan Dr 116

Edinburgh 89
Elizabeth St 105
Elliot, Esther 90, 91
Elliot, John 90, 91
Elmes, Harvey Lonsdale 117
England 7, 8, 11, 12, 19, 33, 69, 89, 93, 95, 104, 111, 113
English Channel 47, 49, 54-58
Erlanger Loan 80
Esmond St 108
Evans, James 39
Everton Terrace 191
Exchange Flags 25

Falkner Terrace 116
Fane, Lady Georgiana 119, 120
Farragut, David G 51, 92, 147
Fawcett Preston and Co 18, 26, 170, 171, 172, 174, 175, 176, 195, 196, 197, 199 – 204, 206 - 209
Fawcett William 198 – 206, 208 - 211
Fez 131
Foreign Enlistment Act 16, 24, 170, 171
Formby 94, 95 ,96, 111
Fort Fisher 165, 167, 169, 171, 174, 178, 179, 194
Fort Sumter 134
France 11, 12, 57, 109
Fraser, Trenholm and Co 15-17, 20, 23, 24, 31, 58, 95, 96, 109, 111, 112, 118, 120, 123, 124, 128, 129, 134, 135, 136, 148, 170, 171, 172, 174 – 178, 180, 181, 182, 184, 186, 189, 190, 191, 193

Galt, surgeon Francis L 37, 40, 46, 109
Garrett, George 88
Geneva 35, 42
Geneva Claims 106, 111, 128
George Forrester and Co 134, 202
Gibraltar 37
Gladstone, Sir John 13
Gladstone,William Ewart 12, 13, 121, 133
Glasgow 77, 127, 191
Golborne 105, 106
Gomez, President da Silva 73
Gossypium 8, 9
Grand Southern Bazaar 117, 121, 122, 128
Gray, Catherine Willis 119
Great Exhibition 15, 189, 210
Great Lakes 145
Great Orme 153
Greenock 21, 102
Greville, Charles 119

Hamilton, Elizabeth Lynch 128
Hamilton, Hannah Motte 128
Hampton Roads 74, 162
Hanckel, Allan Stuart 109-111, 174
Hartley, Jesse 18, 116
Havana 66, 81, 82, 110, 164, 170, 181
Herculaneum Dock 26
Herdman, William Gawin 116, 117
Hobbs, Robert 58
Hobbs, Russell Baker 58, 59
Hobson, Charles L 96
Holyhead 21, 102, 151, 153
Hope, Lady Beresford 120
Hora, Captain A 177
Hull, Frederick S 16-19, 24, 118, 171
Hunley, Horace Lawson 88
Huse, Major Caleb 20, 123
Huskisson, William 116
Huxley, Thomas H 29

Illustrated London News 59
India 8, 47
Industrial Revolution 9, 41, 94, 196, 199
Ireland 32, 35, 85
Irish Potato Famine 7
Irish Sea 25, 32, 162

Jamaica 43, 44
Japan 146, 162
Johns, Frederick Matthew 108
Jones, Quiggin and Co 42, 148, 150, 166, 167, 172, 174 – 178, 180, 182, 195, 206

Kell, Lt John Mcintosh 37, 38, 46, 47, 50, 52-56, 109
Khedive of Egypt 79, 80
Kipling, Rudyard 39
Klingender Mrs 120

Laird, John 18, 118
Laird, Macgregor 19, 20
Laird Rams 70, 77, 78, 80, 81, 87
Laird's Shipyard 18-20, 27, 28, 31, 42, 49, 78, 98, 150, 166, 170, 172, 177, 181, 202
Lake Ontario 173
Lake Huron 145
Lake Superior 173
Lamb, Colonel William 165, 167
Lancashire 9, 115
Lancaster, John 51, 53, 55
Laverty, Peter 151, 161
Lawrence, Edward 166, 172
Leigh 105, 106
Lhuys, Drouyn de 80
Lime St 15, 106
Lincoln, President Abraham 7, 10, 11, 12, 55, 79, 85, 110, 179
Lisbon 8, 115
Littledale, George and Henry 199, 200

Liver Buildings 18
Liver Hotel 26, 33, 94, 96
Liverpool Bay 30, 32
Liverpool Tower 21, 23
Llewellyn, Surgeon David Herbert 53, 56
Lockwood, Anna 178, 179
Lockwood, Captain Robert 193
Lockwood, Captain Thomas J 178 - 180, 193
London 24, 28, 44 56, 82, 109, 110, 113, 116, 122, 124, 128, 129, 176, 196, 197, 200, 202
Low, Lt John 21, 22, 29, 31, 44, 62, 101-106, 147
Low, Mary Elizabeth 104, 105
Lydia Anne St 197, 205, 210

Mackay gun 96
Madeira 82, 83
Maffitt, Captain John Newland 62-72, 78, 79, 85, 101, 103, 177, 181, 182
Maguire, Matthew 23, 26, 28, 96
Mallory, Stephen R 14, 15, 22, 33, 34, 62, 65, 66, 77-82, 87, 102, 123, 177, 182
Manchester 8-11, 88, 170
Manet, Edouard 57, 59
Manifest Destiny 42
Marine Terrace 94, 95
Maryland 36, 71
Maury Commander Matthew Fontaine 68, 112, 113, 142
Maxwell, Hyslop Maxwell 99, 100
May Blitz 42
McQueen, Captain Alexander 28, 32
Mersey, river 10, 17, 22, 23, 29, 59, 66, 79, 80, 85, 88, 107, 148, 150, 154, 155, 157, 158, 165, 166, 169, 171, 179, 180, 181, 189, 200, 202, 204, 208
Mexico 8, 9, 36, 43, 50
Miller, Thomas Lodwick 151, 155 – 158, 160, 162
Miller William C 17, 18, 24, 26, 42, 62, 85, 98, 113, 127, 147, 150, 151, 166, 170, 171, 172, 176, 195, 196, 206
Mitchell Margaret 91, 149
Mobile 64-66, 88, 172
Moelfre Bay 32
Montgomery, Matthew 187 - 189
Montreal 14, 15
Morris, Captain Charles Manigault 69-75

Napoleon the Third 49, 80, 119
Nassau 25, 62, 63, 66, 103, 149, 151, 164, 166, 167, 170, 171, 172, 178 – 181, 191, 193
Naval Medal of Honour 54
Newcastle 12
Newfoundland 39
Newsham Park 106
Newton, John 7
Newton-le-Willows 106
New York 14, 33, 34, 40, 44, 58, 67, 68, 84, 91, 92, 93, 96, 109, 110, 117, 122, 154, 173, 182, 200, 203
Norfolk Naval base 36, 37
North Drive 111
North, Lt James H 77
Nova Scotia 112
New Theatre Royal 114

Obey, Tynan Danford 156 - 158
O'Brien, Matthew 83
Our Lady and St Nicholas Church 17, 20

Pakenham, Kitty 119
Palmerston, Lord 12, 119
Paradise St 15, 211, 142, 143
Paris 51, 57 ,68, 109, 113, 119, 121, 122, 125
Parliament St 98, 151
Passmore Affidavit 28, 31
Passmore, William 28, 29, 31

Paynter, Captain 84, 134
Perry, George 196, 197, 198, 205, 211
Phoenix Foundry 196, 197, 204, 205, 209, 210, 211
Pierhead 23, 160
Pleasant St 116
Porter, Admiral David Dixon 85, 92
Porter, Lt T.K 74
Port of Liverpool Authority Building 18
Potter's (W.H) shipyard 42, 150, 166, 180
Preble, Commander 65
Prince of Wales 113, 122
Princes Landing Stage 82, 159
Princess Alexandra 113
Prioleau, Charles Arthur 136, 140
Prioleau, Charles Kuhn 15, 16, 19, 22, 96, 112, 113, 118, 123-129, 133 – 143, 170
Prioleau, Diane 142, 143
Prioleau, Elizabeth Lynch 128, 129
Prioleau, Frost Horry 142, 143
Prioleau, George Trenholm 137, 140
Prioleau, Grace Antoinette 140, 141
Prioleau, John 137, 140, 143
Prioleau, Judge Samuel 128
Prioleau, Judith Violet 140
Prioleau, Louis St Julien 129, 137, 140
Prioleau, Lynch Hamilton 129, 136, 140
Prioleau, Margaret 137, 140
Prioleau, Mary Elizabeth 118, 126, 128, 129, 133 – 136, 139, 140, 141, 143, 144
Prioleau, Reginald Anthony 140
Prioleau, Richard 136
Prussia 81

Quakers 23, 197, 198, 209, 210
Queen's Proclamation of Neutrality 30

Rathbone, Joseph 197, 198
Read, Laurens 63
Read, Lt C.W. 68
Rhyl 88, 170
Riviere, Henri de 81
Robertson, Moses. P 96
Rochdale 34
Rock Ferry 85, 152, 153
Roosevelt, Anna (Bamie) 91, 92
Roosevelt, Corinne 91
Roosevelt, Eleanor 91
Roosevelt, Theodore Snr 91
Roosevelt, Theodore (Teddy) 91, 92 ,97
Roscoe, William 7, 12, 121, 131, 132, 139
Rumford Place 21, 87, 96, 112, 123, 124, 134, 135, 136, 142
Ruskin, John 29
Russell, Lord John 24, 26, 28, 29, 70, 78-80
Ryle, Bishop John Charles 137, 138

Sailor's Home 28, 29, 42, 58, 82
Salthouse Dock 26
Sassoon, Siegfried 96
Savannah 21, 90, 102, 104, 147
Schelvin, Louis 187 - 189
Seacombe 31
Seaforth 26
Sefton Park 98
Semmes, Captain Raphael 30, 32, 33, 34, 36-41, 43-47, 49-56, 58, 62, 63, 71, 96, 101, 103, 104, 109, 110
Seward, William Henry 110, 148
Sheil Rd 105, 106
Sherman, General William T 85, 91, 173
Sinclair, Arthur 145
Sinclair, Captain Arthur 145, 146
Sinclair, Commander Arthur 85, 146 – 149, 151, 155, 162, 176
Sinclair, George. T, Midshipman 44
Sinclair, Lelia Imogene 152, 162
Sinclair, Lt Arthur 38, 40, 103, 107, 109, 146, 162
Sinclair, Terry 162

Sinclair, Upton 146
Sinclair, William B 72
Sinclair,William H 104
Singapore 45, 58, 110
Skinner, Captain Thomas 152 – 156, 161
Slidell, John 80, 109, 110, 118, 120
Southampton 30, 53, 58
Spence, James 118
Spencer, Anne Elizabeth 36
Stanhope St 116
Stanley Dock 26
Steele, Captain Joseph W 166, 167
Stewart, Martha 90, 91
Stobo, Archibald 89
Stobo, Jean 90
Stockton, Captain Robert 203
St George's Channel 32, 114
St George's Church 7
St George's Hall 117, 120, 128
St James Cemetery 98, 108
St John's Market 42
Strand, the 23, 194
Stribling, Lt J.M 63, 64
Sydenham Avenue 98

Taylor, Thomas E 163, 164, 166, 167
Terceira 21, 32, 33, 37, 44
Tessier, Captain 26
Thames, river 28, 82, 88, 124
Tower Buildings 23
Trenholm, George A 112
Trent Affair 109, 111, 112, 120

United States Consulate 18, 23, 70
Upper Newington St 113

Verne, Jules 105
Videky, Mr L de 73, 75
Virginia 74, 99, 145, 146, 152

Waddell, Lt Commander James Iredell 82 – 84, 134
Wall, Mary Elizabeth 102
Walters, Miles 116
Walters Samuel 35, 116, 130, 164
Washington, George 119
Waterloo, battle of 94, 119, 199
Waterloo Rd 97
Waterloo, the suburb 33, 94, 96-98, 120, 177
Water St 18
Wavertree 111, 174
Welles, Gideon 75
Wellington, Duke of 94, 119, 199
Wellington St 33, 95, 96
White, David 40, 41, 53
Wilberforce, William 7, 19
Wilkes, Captain Charles 109, 110
Williamson Art Gallery 18
Wilmington 147, 149, 164 – 167, 171, 174, 177, 182, 190
Wilson, Captain William 185 – 191, 193
Wilson, Thomas F 73-75
Winslow, Captain John Ancrum 50, 51, 54, 55, 58, 71
Wolseley, Sir Garnet 173
Woods, William 59, 155, 156, 157, 159
World War One 41, 127, 208
World War Two 88, 209

Yellowfever 63, 68, 177, 182
Yonge, Clarence Randolph 31, 33, 44, 78, 101

Zastro, Madame de Micheline 97

INDEX OF SHIPS

Abigail 136
Achilles 13
Agrippina 28, 33, 37
Ajax 105
Alabama 19, 20, 21 ,27, 30, 32-62, 66, 71, 72, 74, 77, 78, 79, 81, 82, 83, 87, 96, 101, 103, 104, 107, 108, 109, 110, 115, 118, 122, 135, 136, 148, 150, 151, 161, 162, 171, 177
Aldebaran 67
Alert 39
Alexandra 26, 113, 170, 171
Altamaha 39
Amanda 45
American Diver 88
Anglo Saxon 68
Annie Childs 22, 102
Antelope 204
Arabella 66
Arabia 112
Archer 68
Ariel 34
Atlanta (ironclad) 74
Atlanta 22, 147
Avon 71

Badger 174
Bahama 25, 33, 37, 62, 63
Banshee 150, 164, 166 - 170
Barcelona 33
Baron de Castine 43
Barracouta 84
Bat 85, 177
Benjamin F.Hoxie 67
Bentinck 202
Betsy Ames 135, 136
Bienville 92, 93
Blazer 159, 160, 161
Bouboulina 85, 179, 180, 182, 183
Brilliant 43

Caleb Cushing 68
Ceres 126,127
Charlotte 148, 180
Cheops 80
Chicora 150, 172, 173, 174
Circe (French) 56
Clarence 67, 68
Colonel Lamb 83, 148, 149, 176, 178, 179, 180, 182
Confederate States 84
Congress 162
Connecticut 171
Conrad 44, 104
Contest 45
Coquette 85
Corris Ann 66
Couronne 51
Crenshaw 43
Crown Point 67
Cuba 154
Cumberland 162
Curlew 73, 148, 182

Decatur 92
Deer 180
Deerhound 51 53, 55, 56, 107
Denbigh 170
Donegal 84, 134
Douglas 190 - 194
Dunkirk 39, 40

Electric Spark 71, 72
Elisha Dunbar 39
Elizabeth 190
Elizabeth and Emma 162
El Munassir 79
El Tousson 79
Emily Farnum 43

Emily St Pierre 185 - 190
Enrica 31, 32, 33, 37
Eolus 176
Estelle 66
Etna 200

Fingal 21, 22, 23, 32, 77, 93, 102, 147, 170
Florida 25, 29, 61-79, 83, 87,
102, 135, 136, 148, 150, 151, 170, 172, 177,
182, 196, 206
Foam 177
Foudroyant 132
Fox 175
Fulton 167

General Barry 71
General Pike 145
George Griswold 9, 11, 13, 115
George Latimer 71
Georgia 92, 114, 115
Gettysburg 193, 194
Gibraltar 20
Giraffe 172
Glad Tiding 10
Glasgow 191
Golconda 71
Golden Rocket 37, 109
Governor Buckingham 174
Grand Gulf 167
Greenland 71

Habana 37, 109
Hatteras 34, 43, 44
Herald 112
Hercules 29, 32
Hindostan 198, 202
Hope 13, 176, 178, 179, 180
Hornet 54
Housatonic 88
Howard 71
Howquah 174
Hunley 88

Irene 167

Jacob Bell 67
James Adger 166, 186
Japan 114
J.L.Smallwood 167
Juno 172

Kate 178
Kearsage 49-58, 71, 107, 108, 151, 161, 177
Knight Errant 105
Kursk 88

Lady Mary Wood 201, 202
Lafayette 43
Lamplighter 43
Lapwing 67
Lark 170, 181
Laurel 82, 84
Lauretta 43
Leeds 204
Lelia 85, 96, 145, 150 – 162, 168, 169, 174,
176, 180, 206
Let Her B 150, 172, 173, 174
Levi Starbuck 43
Lilla 135, 136
Lottie Sleigh 208
Lucy 150, 172
Lynx 174

Majestic 79, 80
Manchester 40
Marco Polo 142
Margaret and Jessie 190, 193
Margaret Y Davis 71
Martaban 47
Mary 171, 172

Mary Celestia 147, 150, 176
Mary Rose 56
Mary Wright 135, 136
Medina 204
Medusa 204
Merlin 204
Merrimac 162
Mersey 200
Minnesota 147
Mississippi 146, 147
Monticello 180
Montgomery 177
Morning Star 44

Nancy 146
Nansemond 193
Nashville 21, 91
Niagara 82, 115, 145
Niphon 174
Noor-el-Huda 148, 182
North America 14

Ocassa 80
Ocean Rover 39
Ocmulgee 39
Oneida 67
Oneida CSS 64, 65
Oreto 18, 22, 23, 25, 27, 28, 31, 62, 63, 102, 103, 106, 151
Oriental 202
Owl 85, 148, 177, 181

Penguin 182, 183
Petrel 43
Phantom 26, 85, 113, 150, 171
Plover 148, 182
Powerful 171
President 195, 200
Pride of Liverpool 157
Prince Alfred 63
Princeton 203

Quaker City 136

Ray 150
Redwing 203
Resurgam 88
Rhode Island 190
Rising Sun 89
Robert E.Lee 172
Rockingham 47
Royal Arch 160, 161
Royal Charter 199
Royal William 200
Ruby 181

Sacramento 82
San Jacinto 109, 110, 120
Santiago de Cuba 66
Savannah 39
Saxon 104
Scorpion 146
Scotia 97
Sea Bride 45
Sea King 82, 124
Seaman 64
Shalimar 102
Shenandoah 82, 83, 84, 86, 87, 91, 107, 108, 124, 134
Siccardii 21, 102
Sinclair 146
Slasher 160
Somers 36
Sonoma 66
Southern Belle 173
Sovereign 154
Snipe 148, 182
Sphinx 80

Sprucebay 174
Squib 147
Stag 180
Star of Peace 67
Starlight 39
Stonewall 81
Sumter 37, 54, 64, 103, 109
Supply 146

Tacony 67, 68
Talisman 44
T.B.Wales 43, 104
Terrible 29,
Texan Star 47
Theodora 110
Tigress 146
Tonawanda 39, 40
Trent 109, 110
Tuscaloosa 44, 104
Tuscarora 30, 32
Tycoon 47

Vandalia 146
Vanderbilt 45, 66
Veloce 200
Virginia 39, 162
Vixen 43

Wachusett 72, 73, 74, 75
Warrenko 173
Wave Crest 39, 40
W.C.Clark 71
Weathergauge 39
Weehawken 22, 147
Widgeon 148, 182
Wild Dayrell 150, 172
Wilhelm 200
William Fawcett 202
Windward 66
Winged Racer 45
Winona 64
Winslow 146
Wren 181
Yeddo 80
Zelinda 71

290 (the) 19, 20, 27-31, 33